Kurt Dietrich – Duke's 'Bones
Ellington's Great Trombonists

Kurt Dietrich

DUKE'S 'BONES

Ellington's Great Trombonists

ADVANCE MUSIC

Cover photo (Joe "Tricky Sam" Nanton): Collection of
Duncan P. Schiedt
Musical Notation: Vern Graham
Printed by TC Druck, Tübingen
Production: Hans Gruber

Published by Advance Music
Rottenburg N., Germany

Table of Contents

This book would not have been possible without the help of many people. Very early in the project, John Miner introduced me to some valuable sources and supplied me with numerous bits of information, saving me much toil. He opened up his large collection of records and books to me. To the very end, he has tracked down details that have made the book more accurate. Another great gentleman who has supplied similar support has been Art Pilkington, whose letters always seemed to come just at the times at which I needed certain information.

Others who were generous with help in obtaining information and recordings include Bob Snyder, Randy Bay, Bill Spilka, the staff at The Institute for Jazz Studies – especially fellow Wisconsinite Don Luck, the staff at the Ellington Archive at the Smithsonian Institution, and in particular Annie Kuebler, David Ginsburg at Central Michigan University, Sjef Hoefsmit, Jack Towers and Andrew Homzy. At International Ellington Conferences, many other people kindly told me their stories about Ellington's trombonists.

Especially helpful to me while I was working on my doctoral dissertation on Tricky Sam Nanton, Juan Tizol and Lawrence Brown were my esteemed major professor Bill Richardson; Les Thimmig and the University of Wisconsin-Madison Jazz Ensemble and my dear friend, pianist John Harmon, who allowed me to play many of the solos in this book in real musical settings; and Tom Oyster and Mike Post at Ripon College's computer center who helped me get so many bugs out. I also owe my thanks for the support given to me by Ripon College throughout the project, and especially by Dean Douglas Northrop and my late colleague Donald Spies.

I am grateful for the time given me by many who have been close to the Ellington scene for many years, including Stanley Dance and Barry Ulanov. Greatest thanks go to the generosity of the Ellingtonians who were so open and enthusiastic: Clark Terry, Louie Bellson, and the trombonists – Art Baron, the late Chuck Connors, Buster Cooper, Vince Prudente, Father John Sanders, Malcolm Taylor and Britt Woodman.

Parts of this book originally appeared in *Jazz Research Papers 1988*, the *Annual Review of Jazz Studies*, and *Black Music Research Journal*. I appreciate their permission to use those segments.

Special thanks go to a few individuals: Rob Hudson, who at the last minute stepped in to make the transcriptions more accurate; my great pal Fred Sturm for help and encouragement along the way; Mark Tucker, who spent so much time with the first part of this manuscript and whose support and scholarship have

Acknowledgments

been an inspiration; and Hans Gruber of Advance Music for believing in this project.

My deepest thanks go to my family. Without the editorial and "spiritual" support of my parents, Richard and Frances Dietrich, and my wife Maria and sons Erik and Paul, the project would never have been completed.

Duke Ellington is one of the most celebrated musicians in the history of American music. Ellington became an important figure in jazz and popular music early in his career, certainly by the 1930s. Before his death in 1974 he had been recognized with hundreds of awards of various sorts – honorary degrees, keys to cities, and citations that included the Presidential Medal of Freedom, the highest civilian honor that the United States government grants. The Pulitzer Prize, the one major award that eluded him, ironically led to a flurry of publicity for Ellington, while it brought into stark relief the ambivalence of America's cultural establishment toward jazz and popular music. When the music jury unanimously recommended that Ellington be awarded a special Pulitzer in 1965, only to have the recommendation rejected by the advisory board, Ellington's widely publicized response was "Fate is being kind to me. Fate doesn't want me to be famous too young."

Twenty years after his death, Ellington's reputation is secure, and is, in fact, growing. Following the lead of several other countries, the United States issued a postage stamp commemorating him in 1986. Hundreds of hours of performances by the Ellington orchestra, both previously and newly issued, have been released by record companies worldwide during the last ten years. Indeed, more of Ellington's work is now available on recordings than ever before, including new recordings of his extended works for symphony orchestra as well as those for jazz orchestra. Scholars and fans meet annually at international Ellington conferences. Books continue to be published about Ellington and his music, including two major works released just in 1993. His compositions are carefully transcribed, analyzed and performed in repertory groups around the world. And his songs are sung and played innumerable times each year in big city concert halls and night clubs as well as in small town ballrooms and meeting halls.

Both in performance and creation, there is no question that the contribution of the members of Ellington's orchestra was crucial to much of his output. Of primary importance to Ellington the composer was the fact that he had an orchestra at his disposal to perform his works immediately upon their completion. Virtually all of Ellington's works were written initially to be performed by his own orchestra. This did not mean just an orchestra of the instrumentation of the Ellington band, but rather the specific players that occupied the positions in this unique orchestra. Many of his works were not completed until the band members had played their parts, made suggestions, added solos that became integral parts of the compositions, or inspired

Ellington to modify or completely redo details or even large sections of the works.

Despite the fact that Ellington's music is flourishing today, little formal study has been devoted to the individual members of his orchestra. Jazz musicians continue to praise the contributions and acknowledge the influence of such great Ellingtonians as Johnny Hodges, Cootie Williams, Ben Webster and Jimmie Blanton, but for the most part these and other outstanding members of the Ellington orchestra have not been treated in the depth they deserve.

The purpose of the study recorded in this book is to focus on the work of the members of the trombone section that was at the heart of Ellington's acclaimed orchestra from its beginnings until Ellington's death in 1974. John Anderson and Charlie Irvis, the first two trombonists in bands that developed into the Ellington orchestra in the 1920s are dealt with briefly. Much of the study focuses on the three giants who **were** the section in the 1930s and early 1940s: Joe Nanton, Juan Tizol and Lawrence Brown. Joe "Tricky Sam" Nanton joined Ellington in 1926 and remained until his untimely death in 1946. During those twenty years, Nanton developed a style of playing with the plunger mute – often referred to as "wa-wa" style – that by consensus has never been surpassed in versatility and depth of emotion. Any consideration of Nanton necessarily must deal with the whole topic of this style. Juan Tizol, a native of Puerto Rico, joined Ellington in 1929 and remained until he joined Harry James's band in 1944. He also rejoined Ellington for almost two years in the 1950s and for brief periods in the 1960s. Lawrence Brown joined the Ellington band in 1932, a milestone year that many consider to be the beginning of the "glory years" for the band. After becoming one of the true "star" instrumentalists of the orchestra, Brown left the band in 1951, but returned for another distinguished ten-year tenure that lasted from 1960 into 1970.

There was some unsettling turnover in the trombone section in the late 1940s and early 1950s, which did result, however, in the emergence of one eminent trombonist, Tyree Glenn. In the 1950s the section again solidified into the outstanding section of Britt Woodman, Quentin Jackson and John Sanders. Another series of changes in the late 1950s and early 1960s led to the last relatively longstanding trombone section of Ellington's career – Lawrence Brown, Buster Cooper and Chuck Connors. Discused last are the players who held the section together during the 1970s and the legacy left by fifty years of trombone playing in the Ellington tradition.

Each of the significant trombonists is dealt with in several different ways: Biographical information, in no way intended to be
exhaustive, is presented. Information that seems pertinent to the
careers of each as members of the Ellington band is the focus.
While some of this information is anecdotal, the ultimate aim is
to try to relate each man to the music he created. The place of
these men as members of the Ellington organization, which in
some cases (particularly that of Juan Tizol) may transcend their
value as performers, is also considered. At the heart of my study,
however, have been the solos that these men recorded with
Ellington. Solos are transcribed and analyzed from the standpoint of "traditional" analysis of jazz solos, as well as consideration of the solos from the standpoint of trombone playing. It
is hoped that these mixed analyses not only "work" from a
theoretical point of view but prove to be useful to the readers of
the book.

The first of three appendices deals briefly with Ellington's
writing for the trombonists as a section or in conjunction with
other players, as opposed to his writing for the individual players. Appendix II records discographical information about the
music discussed in the text. Appendix III lists all of the tromon-
ists who played with Ellington and the dates of their tenure.

It is encouraging to see that the work of the great Ellington
trombonists is being rethought and reinterpreted in the work of
some of today's outstanding jazz trombonists. The ultimate aims
of this study are to introduce the unique work of Nanton, Tizol,
Brown and the others to those who are not familiar with it and
to shed more light on this work to those already familiar with
it. This book will, I hope, open up the legacy to more contemporary musicians and jazz fans.

List of
Musical Examples

Example

Transcribing jazz solos is always problematic. Exact rhythmic notation is practically impossible. Inflections can only be indicated by symbols that may be generally understood in the jazz community, but still seem sadly inadequate, especially for indicating degrees of inflection. "Blue notes" and other variations from equally-tempered tuning can be indicated, but again, only imprecisely. Of course there is no way to indicate what kind of tone quality the player is producing.

I have elected in these transcriptions to write so that the solos are easy to read and to follow. In the process, I have certainly simplified some of the subtleties of rhythm and nuance to some degree. It was a great temptation to insert numerous phrase markings in the solos. I decided not to impose my perception of phrasing on the creations of these trombonists. Especially on the older recordings, it is often difficult to hear where slurring has occurred, particularly because of the nature of slurring on the trombone. For the most part, I have used slurs only to mark either connections that were almost certainly made with the slide without any articulation from the tongue, or obvious lip slurs. Scoops or slides into notes and falls off notes, important stylistic devices of many of the players, have been added. It would have been very easy to clutter up the transcriptions with articulation marks, but ultimately, each listener/player must determine these and the phrasing for him- or herself.

It did seem essential to me in the transcriptions of the plunger specialists to try to communicate some sense of the sounds produced with the aid of the plunger. There is explanation of these in the text, with keys to the sounds supplied in some cases.

Obviously, the recordings of the solos must be heard in order to gain the most meaningful benefit.

Notes
on the
Transcriptions

Much of the information in the biographical portions of this study has come from three sets of interviews. I have referred in the notes to Bill Spilka's interviews with Lawrence Brown, Juan Tizol and Booty Wood simply as "Spilka." I have transcribed large portions of these interviews, but they are only in rough form. Patricia Willard interviewed Brown and Tizol and Milt Hinton interviewed Quentin Jackson for the Jazz Oral History Project of the National Endowment for the Arts. The taped interviews and transcriptions are housed at the Institute of Jazz Studies in Newark, New Jersey. I have referred to Willard's interviews as "Willard" (to distinguish them from Spilka's interviews of the same subjects) and Hinton's interview as "Jackson interview." Finally, I had the pleasure of interviewing Clark Terry, Louie Bellson, Art Baron, Chuck Connors, Buster Cooper, Vince Prudente, Father John Sanders, Malcolm Taylor and Britt Woodman. These interviews, which I have on tape, I have referred to as "interview with the author."

I have shortened the titles of books and articles that are referred to repeatedly. The following is a list of the abbreviated references used:

Bigard. Bigard, Barney. *With Louis and the Duke: the Autobiography of a Jazz Clarinetist.* Edited by Barry Martyn. (Reprint, New York, 1988)

Chilton. Chilton, John. *Who's Who of Jazz: Storyville to Swing Street.* 4th ed. (New York, 1985)

Collier. Collier, James Lincoln. *Duke Ellington.* (N.Y., 1987)

Feather. Feather, Leonard. *The New Edition of the Encyclopedia of Jazz.* (New York, 1960)

Gammond. Gammond, Peter, ed. *Duke Ellington: His Life and Music.* (Reprint, New York, 1977)

Stewart. Stewart, Rex. "Tribute to Tricky Sam (Joe Nanton)." In *Jazz Masters of the 30s.* (Reprint, New York, 1982)

Stratemann. Stratemann, Klaus. *Duke Ellington: Day by Day and Film by Film.* (Copenhagen, 1992)

Timner. Timner, W. E., comp. *Ellingtonia: The Recorded Music of Duke Ellington and His Sidemen.* (Metuchen, N.J.,1988)

Tucker. Tucker, Mark. *Ellington: The Early Years.* (Urbana and Chicago, 1991)

Ulanov. Ulanov, Barry. *Duke Ellington.* (reprint. N.Y., 1975)

For clarity, I have referred to Duke Ellington's autobiography *Music is My Mistress* and Mercer Ellington's memoir *Duke Ellington in Person* by title only in the notes. Gunther Schuller's two works and Stanley Dance's two works are also identified by title only. See the bibliography for complete bibliographic information.

Ellington's
Early Trombonists

Edward Kennedy "Duke" Ellington's initial foray into the New York music scene in the early part of 1923 proved to be brief, and ultimately unsustainable. But after a few months back in Washington, D. C., his hometown, he returned to New York in June with his cronies – drummer Sonny Greer, saxophonist Otto Hardwick, trumpeter Arthur Whetsol, and banjoist Elmer Snowden – and it didn't take long for this group to procure steady work, most often under the name "The Washingtonians." Snowden was the group's leader until he left the band sometime in January or February 1924, apparently after taking a little larger cut of the band's income than he was entitled to.[1]

The Washingtonians did not originally include a trombonist. The first trombonist to work regularly with the group was John Anderson, who joined the band in the fall of 1923. Little is known about Anderson. He was previously a member of a well-known vaudeville group, Wilbur Sweatman's "Acme Syncopators," and Mark Tucker postulates that Anderson, who also doubled on trumpet, "may have shone in vaudeville and novelty numbers (from his previous tenure with Sweatman)."[2] In any case, Anderson was not to become a distinctive voice with the Washingtonians as was his successor Charlie Irvis.

Irvis, born in New York City in 1899, was already well-known around Harlem before he joined the Washingtonians early in 1924. He had worked and recorded with various groups led by Clarence Williams, including the celebrated "Blue Five" groups that included Louis Armstrong and Sidney Bechet. Along with his boyhood friend, trumpeter Bubber Miley, he had played with blues singers and sat in with Willie "the Lion" Smith. Indeed, he was to continue these associations throughout his tenure with the Washingtonians.

Most observers consider Miley and Joe "Tricky Sam" Nanton as the originators of the plunger mute style that became such a vital part of the Ellington sound. However, while acknowledging that most subsequent plunger players derived their styles from Miley and Nanton, Ellington himself claimed that "Charlie Irvis was first." But, he continues, "Nobody ever really picked

1 There are several versions of Snowden's departure from the Washingtonians. Tucker, 109.

2 Ibid., 100, 107.

up on Charlie Irvis."[3] It is difficult to believe that Irvis's work in this vein actually preceded that of Miley. It seems more likely that they developed the style in conjunction with one another. Rex Stewart relates that the two were one of the working brass "pairs" that roamed the Harlem nightspots during this era.[4]

There is considerable disagreement among Irvis's contemporaries about exactly how he produced the sounds that so distinguished him. Willie "the Lion" Smith related that when Irvis was in his band "[he] carried a regular gut bucket around for a mute, and when I'd tell him to play soft he'd come on real low down with that bucket on the end of his slide trombone."[5] Ellington remembered it this way:

. . . Charlie Irvis, who was known as Charlie Plug. . . was called Plug because of the device he used on his horn. In those days they manufactured a kind of mute designed to make the trombone sound like a saxophone. The sax was still regarded as new then. Charlie had dropped this device and broken it, so he used what was left of it, rolling it around the bell of his trombone. He couldn't use it the way it was intended, because of the part broken off, but he'd get this entirely different lecherous low tone, and no one has ever done it since.[6]

Elsewhere, Ellington refers to this mute as "his [Irvis's] device and greater than the original thing." He goes on, "He got a great, big, fat sound at the bottom of the trombone – melodic, masculine, full of tremendous authority."[7]

Sonny Greer, drummer with the Washingtonians at that time (and with Ellington until 1951) states that Irvis "had an old tomato can, smashed in at the bottom like a cone, to get the same effect [the plunger effect] – those low notes and the growl."[8]

Ellington's first biographer, Barry Ulanov, claims that Irvis used "the cap of a bottle," a bottle by itself, and sometimes "a bucket over the trombone's bell." He colorfully describes Irvis's playing from this period.

[Irvis] played all around the bottom of his horn, growling elfishly, oafishly, suggestively, jungle-istically at the Kentucky [Club] customers. He tried to make the trombone sound like a saxophone, and rolled off long cadences of clear notes, broken by those exquisite shivers of sound, a bleat, a brump, a yawp, which European visitors would call 'echt Afrikanisch', 'vraiment Africaine', and in which the wealthy cultist could indulge his wildest fantasies about "the primitive Negro arts."[9]

Unfortunately, there is no recorded example of the exotic sounds that Irvis is reputed to have been making with the Washingtonians. There are only a handful of recordings of

3 *The World of Duke Ellington, 7.*
4 Stewart, 105-106.
5 Smith, *Music on My Mind,* 144.
6 *Music is My Mistress,* 108.
7 *The World of Duke Ellington, 7.*
8 Sonny Greer, "In Those Days," liner notes for record set *The Ellington Era, 1927-1940,* Volume II, Columbia C3L39-CL2364.
9 Ulanov, 45.

Irvis's playing with the band, none of which are particularly revolutionary. The longest example of Irvis's solo playing on these dates is on the cut *Rainy Nights,* from November 1924. Irvis plays a 32-bar chorus on this tune, essentially a paraphrase of the melody. His tone is big and round, quite different from the hard brassy sound of many of his contemporaries. This is the sound that Ellington called "melodic, masculine – full of authority." The solo is played mostly in the middle register of the horn and is smoothly articulated throughout, with much characteristic sliding from note to note. On *Trombone Blues* (recorded September 1925) Irvis has the lead in the first chorus, but again, there is nothing particularly noteworthy about his playing on this cut.

Washingtonians with Charlie Irvis (Collection of Mark Tucker)

Two cuts recorded on 1 April 1926 show Irvis in a considerably more conversational style. While the outstanding swing trombonist Jimmy Harrison is vocalist on these two tracks, and it is conceivable that he played the trombone solos as well, the style of the trombone playing strongly suggests that Irvis is the soloist. *(I've Got Those) 'Wanna Go Back Again' Blues* features what Gunther Schuller has described as "some rather good-natured Irvis trombone."[10] Some of the inflections in his solo on this tune are very close to the "wa" that became standard later

10 *Early Jazz,* 322.

on, but Irvis does most of the inflecting with his slide, rather than a mute. On *If You Can't Hold the Man You Love*, there is expressive speech-like inflection, with growling, and much less of Irvis's usual sliding from note to note than on most of his recordings. While it is a large step from this modest amount of "talking" to the remarkable "jungle" effects that Bubber Miley played on recordings only months later, this recording gives a hint of what kind of playing Irvis may have been capable of in this style.

One may speculate about why Irvis did not do any of the "lecherous," "suggestive," "jungle-istic" playing that he was known for on any of the recordings with the Washingtonians (nor did he on any of the "Blue Five" recordings). It may be that the style was not considered appropriate for the tunes that the group ended up recording. It may be that it was felt that more exotic playing would hurt sales of the records. It must be noted, however, that Miley, on trumpet, does a considerable amount of growling, note bending and plunger manipulation on some of these very same cuts. We can only regret that we have no recorded evidence of Irvis demonstrating the style which he helped pioneer.

We must believe, however, that Irvis did have a profound impact on Miley, Ellington, and on his successor Nanton as well as the direction that Ellington's music was to take. Dance claims that Ellington found this new "jungle sound" irresistible.[11] Ulanov describes Irvis as having "ruffled the placid surface of Ellington's 'conversation music' with a series of doo-wa's and rrr-ump's which were like injections of a nasty word, a saucy phrase, wonderful touches of musical innuendo. They added a fillip to the Washingtonians' music which made an already out-of-the-way band unique."[12]

If, as Ellington claims, Irvis was indeed "the first" with the new sounds, it would be hard to overestimate his importance to the first Ellington classics of 1926 and 1927, *East St. Louis Toodle-Oo* and *Black and Tan Fantasy*. Miley's growling on these tunes established a sound for the Ellington band that was associated with it for the rest of Ellington's long career.

When Joe Nanton replaced his friend Irvis in the summer of 1926, he was quick to pick up the role that Irvis had created, becoming an intimate partner with Miley in the "jungle" world of brass playing that became a trademark of the Ellington sound. Nanton had to step in and "reproduce the lowings of Irvis' 'bone, its ululations in definite pitch, its wit and wisdom, comedy and high tragedy of sound."[13] It was a task that Nanton was to accomplish in spectacular fashion.

11 "Duke Ellington," 13.
12 Ulanov, 45.
13 Ibid., 50.

Joe "Tricky Sam" Nanton: Master of the Plunger and Growl

Joe Nanton was born in New York City 1 February 1904.[1] His parents were from the West Indies, and Nanton grew up in the San Juan Hill section of the city. Cornetist Rex Stewart, Nanton's colleague in the Ellington band throughout much of the 1930s and '40s, has supplied more insight than any other source into Nanton's life and character in a heartfelt "Tribute to Tricky Sam (Joe Nanton)."[2] According to Stewart, Nanton "felt fortunate in having been born in New York City, where the educational advantages for Negroes far surpassed those of most other cities, particularly those below the Mason-Dixon line." Nanton also was "proud of being West Indian," as he "was convinced that the West Indians particularly appreciated and took advantage of the opportunities that the North offered them."

Little is known of Nanton's youth. It is clear, though, that he loved to read. Stewart claims that Nanton "owned hundreds of books on the most erudite subjects, ranging from psychology to philosophy, from history to astronomy." Nanton knew such diverse skills as "how to make home brew and how to use a slide rule. He could recite poetry by ancient poets that most of us never knew existed, and he knew Shakespeare." Duke Ellington's first biographer, Barry Ulanov, remembered Nanton as a very bright man who was very much interested in current events.[3] Nanton had a serious interest in the fate of African-Americans, including Marcus Garvey's movement to have American blacks return to Africa, during an era when Stewart says "political awareness was unheard of from a musician." Ellington, in discussing Nanton's background and interest in Garvey, claimed "[a] whole strain of West Indian musicians came up who made contributions to the so-called jazz scene, and they were all virtually descended from the true African scene."[4]

Stewart described Nanton physically as "a gingerbread-colored man, kind of on the squatty side. His facial contours reminded me of a benevolent basset hound, with those big brown eyes that regarded the world so dolefully, framed in a long face with just a hint of dewlaps." Nanton was known for his high squeaky voice, which seemed at odds with his trombone sound.

1 Noted jazz historian John Chilton lists Nanton's name as Joseph N. Irish (*Who's Who of Jazz,* 241). Chilton got this name from the British Public Records Office which had Nanton listed as Joseph N. Irish on the passenger list of the liner SS *Olympic* that took the Ellington band to Europe in 1933 (personal correspondence, 3 August 1989). I can find no record of the circumstances of his changing his name. Rex Stewart says that Nanton was "the middle of three sons of the West Indian Nanton family." Rex Stewart, "Tribute to Tricky Sam (Joe Nanton)," 110. All other citations of Stewart in this chapter are from this same work.
2 Stewart, 103-113.
3 Barry Ulanov, phone conversation with the author, 13 June 1989.
4 *Music Is My Mistress,* 109.

Before joining Ellington, Nanton worked with Cliff Jackson, Earl Frazier's "Harmony Five" and Elmer Snowden. He had worked at a number of Harlem "night-spots and after-hours joints," such colorful establishments as Edmond's Cellar, the Nest Club, and the Bucket of Blood. Ellington described Nanton in the time before he joined the Washingtonians (as Ellington's band was still known) as a musician who "had really never had his coming-out party, and he had never found a place to fit on a full-time basis. Nor had he a true running mate. He'd carry his horn around from one joint to another, and get to play a chorus here and a chorus there."[5] Stewart, however, reported that Nanton, like almost of all of the well-known Harlem brass players, was one of a "traveling" twosome, a trumpeter and a trombonist. Nanton teamed with Louis Metcalf, who was also to join Ellington.

Nanton apparently joined the Washingtonians sometime during their two-week engagement at the Plantation Club in late June, 1926.[6] Nanton, however, did not want the job. He later described the situation.

*"When Duke came and asked me to play in the band I didn't want to go because he was offering me my friend's [Charlie Irvis's] job. 'He'll be back next week,' I said. Duke insisted. I promised to join him, but I didn't show up. The following night Duke came by and asked why I didn't come in. This time he waited until I got dressed and he **took** me with him."*[7]

Stewart described Nanton's early days with Ellington.

When Joe Nanton replaced his old buddy, Charlie Irvis, in the Ellington band, he played his parts capably and eagerly waited, night after night, for Duke to let him take his "Boston," what the cats called soloing in those days. This went on for weeks as the newcomer literally sat on the edge of his seat waiting to show what he could do, but Duke never gave him the nod, doubtless because the arrangements were mostly built around Bubber Miley and Toby [Hardwick] at that time. Duke seemingly remained oblivious until Otto Hardwick, Duke's hometown crony and first sax man, yelled, "For Christ's sake, Dumpy, how long are you gonna let this man sit here without taking a Boston?"

Duke, with that famous sheepish grin, said, "Oh, yes. I've been saving him for the big punch. Sure, take it, Tricky."[8]

While the literal truth of this story may be questionable, Nanton was sufficiently worked into the band's routine to record his first solo with Ellington on 21 June 1926, on a popular tune of the day, *Li'l Farina.*

In the first few years of his tenure with the Ellington band

5   Ibid., 106.

6   The preceding information on Nanton's early career comes from a variety of sources, including Chilton, 241, Stewart, 106, Tucker, 188-189, and Tucker dissertation, 353.

7   Inez Cavanaugh, "Reminiscing in Tempo," 17.

8   Stewart, 108. Barney Bigard told slightly different versions of this story to Stanley Dance and in his autobiography. *The World of Duke Ellington,* 86. Bigard, 47.

Nanton was the only regular trombonist in the band. He was featured on the open horn and, increasingly, with the plunger mute, with its attendant growls and "wa-wa's." Charlie Irvis and Bubber Miley may have initiated the important brass component of Ellington's "jungle sound," but after replacing Irvis, and outliving the unfortunate Miley, it was Nanton who was destined to bring this art to its peak. Miley left the Ellington band in 1929, worked in New York, went to France with Noble Sissle, and returned to New York to work with several other bands. In 1931, Irving Mills, Ellington's manager, financed the establishment of a band led by Miley, but Miley died of tuberculosis on 20 May 1932.

Convention has it that Nanton got his nickname for the tricks that he did with the plunger while playing his horn. Otto "Toby" Hardwick, Ellington's old friend from Washington and a member of the band's reed section for much of the twenties, thirties and forties, had a different story. Hardwick gave a number of the Ellingtonians their nicknames and claimed, "I nicknamed Tricky Sam, too. He could always do with one hand what someone else did with two. Anything to save himself trouble – he was tricky that way."[9]

Nanton was a vital voice in the Ellington band for two decades. Chilton reports Nanton's absence from the band in October 1937, when he had pneumonia, but otherwise, Nanton continued through thick and thin. Stewart reported on how times during the first few years of the band's history were often lean. During the toughest of times, though, Nanton's loyalty to Ellington never wavered, and Stewart referred to his "extreme devotion . . . so rare that it is worthy of mention." Nanton was "a tower of strength, whether times were good or bad. Duke could always count on him to make the job, and not only that – Joe was so loyal that he refused to work for anyone else, not even a casual club date or a recording session."[10]

Nanton suffered a stroke in late 1945 and was temporarily forced to quit playing. He rejoined the band in May of 1946, but died in his hotel room in the Scaggs Hotel in San Francisco late in July 1946.[11]

While Nanton's style as a trombone soloist on the open horn will be discussed briefly, his role as soloist on the open horn diminished over time, until eventually he was heard exclusively with the plunger when soloing. His historical importance rests on his unequalled output as a plunger soloist. While a definitive history of the development of the plunger tradition is not attempted here, it is necessary to give some background of this tradition – the tradition of which Nanton became "the master,"

9 *The World of Duke Ellington,* 61.
10 Stewart, 108-109.
11 Art Pilkington has documented the numerous conflicting sources that list either 20 or 21 July as the date of Nanton's death.

in the words of Ray Nance, superb cornet plunger soloist and keeper of the flame in the '40s, '50s and '60s.[12]

In early jazz groups (during the late 1910s and the 1920s), straight mutes were often used with brass, particularly in recording, as the mute effected a bright cutting sound from the instrument. The great cornetist King Oliver is usually credited with being the first brass player to popularize the use of the plunger, also known as the plumber's helper, as a mute with brass instruments.

Keith Nichols wrote an extended article on muted brass in which he credited Oliver with being the "supremo [sic] of muted technique using bottles, beer glasses, and plungers to good effect," with the plunger being Oliver's "stock-in-trade." Johnny Dunn, popular trumpeter in New York during this same period, "claimed that he was the first cornet player to use a plunger . . . well, maybe in New York."[13] Garvin Bushell, who played with Dunn in 1921, credits Dunn with introducing wa-wa effects with the plunger. Dunn was replaced later in 1921 by Bubber Miley in the band that backed up blues singer Mamie Smith. In Chicago, Bushell and Miley went to hear King Oliver every night. According to Bushell,

That's where Bubber got his growling, from Joe Oliver. Before hearing Oliver, Bubber was trying to play like Johnny Dunn. (That's why Mamie had hired him to replace Johnny.) He had picked up the plunger mute thing from Johnny, but he never growled or used the half-cocked silver mute. It was in Chicago, after hearing Oliver, that Bubber changed his style and began using his hand over the tin mute that used to come with all cornets.[14]

Miley is usually credited with passing along these techniques to Charlie Irvis and Nanton. Gunther Schuller claims further that Irvis and Nanton were "also influenced by a now forgotten St. Louis trombonist, Jonas Walker, reputed to be the first to apply New Orleans 'freak' sounds to his instrument."[15] It is unclear where Schuller got this information. Stewart claimed that Nanton credited Irvis and Jake Green of Charleston, South Carolina ("whom we called 'Gutbucket'") as helping to form his style.[16] Nanton himself discussed the beginnings of his plunger work.

"A lot of people have asked me how I acquired and formulated my style. Well, around 1921 I heard Johnny Dunn playing a trumpet with a plunger, so I decided the plunger should be good on trombone."[17]

It was also in 1921, just after Miley had left Mamie Smith's group, that Nanton became friends with both Miley and Irvis.

12 *The World of Duke Ellington,* 132.
13 Keith Nichols, "Muted Brass," 204-206.
14 Bushell, as told to Mark Tucker, *Jazz From The Beginning,* 22, 25.
15 *Early Jazz,* 326.
16 Stewart, 104.
17 "Reminiscing in Tempo," 26.

They spent many hours together in Harlem night spots, so it is difficult to say with any amount of certainty who influenced whom, in what specific ways and to what degree.

There are two physical aspects to the plunger style that are superimposed on standard playing on a brass instrument: the mute combination and its manipulation, and the growl. Most of the exponents of the plunger style that developed in the Ellington band used a small metal straight mute in the bell in addition to the plunger. (Ray Nance, the great trumpeter of the 1950s and '60s, was a notable exception.) Art Baron, who played trombone in the band in the 1970s and became a serious student of the plunger tradition, claims that the type of mute used by the trombonists was the old Magosy & Buscher Non-pareil trumpet straight mute.[18] Nanton's long-time section mate Lawrence Brown said that Nanton built up the corks of this trumpet mute until he got just the effect he wanted.[19]

The use of the mute as well as the plunger presents two significant problems: tuning, and what brass players refer to as resistance. A number of players who used the mute adjusted the tuning slide when doing plunger work in order to compensate for the change in tuning. Evidently Nanton did not adjust the tuning slide, instead adjusting the tuning with the regular slide or "lipping" – making the adjustment in the embouchure.[20]

When a small mute is stuck into the bell of the instrument, a considerable amount of the flow of air is impeded, causing the buildup of back pressure. To project sound through this obstruction, particularly without any help from a microphone, tremendous effort must be exerted. (Nanton, of course, played his solos without a microphone for much of his career.) Barney Bigard described a memorable occasion that resulted from this condition.

Then there was the time Tricky Sam Nanton blew the back out of his trombone . . . He came to the front [of the stage] to take his solo and he blew so damned hard that the tuning slide at the back of the horn flew clean across the stage. He ran back and bent down to pick it up and that broke up the house. They just figured it was a comedy routine. What the devil. As long as they were satisfied.[21]

Manipulation of the plunger is a delicate affair, with an infinite number of variations possible. The basic "wa" sound is produced by going from a closed position with the plunger very close to the bell, thus stopping much of the sound, to an open position with the plunger pulled away from the bell, which stops virtually none of the sound. If this motion is slowed down, the

18 Art Baron, telephone interview, 19 May 1989. Mute manufacturer Tom Crown has recently started producing a copy of this mute.
19 Lawrence Brown, interview with Bill Spilka, 22 February 1978.
20 Nichols, "Muted Brass," 206, and *Duke Ellington in Person*, 25.
21 Bigard, 67.

sound goes from roughly an "oo" to an "ah." Sped up, "wa" is a good approximation for the effect. Nanton often played long passages with the plunger very tight against the bell, producing various sorts of stopped effects. Small deviations in the distance that the plunger is held from the bell can make considerable differences in the sound, and Nanton exploited a wide range of these possibilities. He also transformed the basic "wa" into what sounds unmistakably like "ya." If the process of forming this sound is slowed down, the sound can be broken into "ee" (rather than the "oo" of the "wa") followed by "ah." Nanton's "ya" sound, which he did not use extensively on record until the 1940s, has never been accurately replicated, although Tyree Glenn came very close on recordings that he made in the 1950s. It would seem that Nanton's sound was produced by some combination of jaw and tongue movements, although there is speculation that it may have been produced by the squeezing of the plunger itself.[22]

The growl, too, is a technique that is subject to considerable personal variation. Mercer Ellington described the growl in some depth.

There are three basic elements in the growl: the sound of the horn, a guttural gargling in the throat, and the actual note that is hummed. The mouth has to be shaped to make the different vowel sounds, and above the singing from the throat, manipulation of the plunger adds the wa-wa accents that give the horn a language.[23]

Clark Terry has described three ways that plunger soloists in the Ellington tradition effected the growl: the flutter tongue – a fast slapping of the tongue up and down in the mouth; a growl in the throat – vibration of the vocal cords; and what he described as a "buzz" in the vocal cords – in effect, singing while playing. Baron, who spent many hours talking with and listening to Cootie Williams when they were in the Ellington band together in the 1970s, describes the techniques in terms similar to those of Terry. He feels that the great exponents of the style on trombone – Nanton, Tyree Glenn and Quentin "Butter" Jackson – used some combination of the three. He suspects that Tricky Sam produced virtually all of his growling with some combination of the throat and voice, while Glenn and Jackson used more of a flutter tongue-throat combination.[24]

Nanton varied the intensity of his growl according to musical circumstances, having a seemingly limitless repertoire of growl effects at his disposal. His growls might sound rough, harsh, poignant, or humorous, depending on the desired effect. Nanton also occasionally used the growl when soloing on the open horn

22 Nichols, "Muted Brass," 206. Lawrence Brown told Bill Spilka that Nanton changed tones by squeezing the plunger, but he did not describe how those changed tones sounded. Ellington, too, makes reference to the squeezing of the mute (*Music is My Mistress*, 108).

23 *Duke Ellington in Person*, 25.

24 From interviews with Terry, 15 February 1989, and Baron (telephone), 19 May 1989.

in his early days with Ellington. Combined with his variable use of the plunger, he created a remarkably flexible, unique language. Bubber Miley was certainly vital to the creation of this language and Cootie Williams added to the vocabulary, but no one could match Nanton's fluency or command of the style.

Miley, Irvis and Nanton had been working on the plunger-growl style for a number of years before the Ellington band opened at the Cotton Club on December 4, 1927. It was at this fabled Harlem club that the connection between these expressive sounds and the jungle was indelibly imprinted on the consciousness of New York. The scene at the Cotton Club was a fascinating one, and what the public saw there may have been the strongest influence on their perception of the music they heard. Marshall Stearns's memories of those days at the club are informative.

The floor shows at the Cotton Club, which admitted only gangsters, whites, and Negro celebrities, were an incredible mishmash of talent and nonsense which might well fascinate both sociologists and psychiatrists. I recall one where a light-skinned and magnificently muscled Negro burst through a papier-mache jungle onto the dance floor, clad in an aviator's helmet, goggles, and shorts. He had obviously been 'forced down in darkest Africa,' and in the center of the floor he came upon a 'white' goddess clad in long golden tresses and being worshipped by a circle of cringing 'blacks.' Producing a bull whip from heaven knows where, [t]he aviator rescued the blonde and they did an erotic dance. In the background, Bubber Miley, Tricky Sam Nanton, and other members of the Ellington band growled, wheezed, and snorted obscenely.[25]

Ulanov also colorfully described the Cotton Club scene.

In a time when at least the sophisticated Ellington audiences were convinced that Africa strode almost unhampered beneath the tan skins of his musicians, those sturdy Primitive Rhythms conjured up true jungles, warriors on the forest march, lions and tigers and panthers and their tribal enemies among the humans.

When these audiences went up to the Cotton Club and found "shake" dancers performing incredible gyrations and undulations of their naked bellies, Snake-hips Tucker twisting his thigh joints and haunches as his name suggested, like a boa constrictor or rattler, they were certain they were looking at the direct descendants of the jungle tribes. Ellington's music lent further credence to this picture; Africa spoke in Harlem in the late twenties.[26]

Miley's importance to the Ellington group went beyond his

25 Stearns, The Story of Jazz, 183-184.
26 Ulanov, 73-74.

role as an innovator of plunger and growl technique. He is generally conceded to have been the band's most consistently rewarding soloist in the early years, as well as being co-composer of much of the band's early repertoire, including its best known pieces, *East St. Louis Toodle-Oo*, *Black and Tan Fantasy*, and *Creole Love Call*. Schuller compared Miley and Nanton and made a penetrating assessment of Nanton's work during this period.

If Miley was the prime musical inspiration of the early band, Tricky Sam Nanton was its unique voice. Like Miley, he was a master in the use of the growl, the plunger, and wah-wah mutes, and his style had a similar classic simplicity. But where Miley tended to be dapper and smooth, Nanton had a rough-hewn quality that actually encompassed a wider range of expression. Whether plaintive or humorous, his wah-wah muting often took on a distinctly human quality. His open-horn work also extended from the dark and sober to the jaunty or bucolic. But whatever he was expressing, his distinctive vibrato and big tone gave his playing a kind of bursting-at-the-seams intensity and inner beauty that made every Nanton solo a haunting experience. Melodically or harmonically (it comes to the same thing) Nanton was not as advanced as Miley. But this did not prevent him from creating, over a period of twenty years with Ellington, an endless number of beautiful solos, many of them marked by completely original melodic turns, all the more unforgettable because of their simplicity. In fact, Nanton's solo work, in its totality, is unique and perplexing. Here is a player whose solos rarely go much beyond a range of one octave; who has some real limitations instrumentally; and who, in a sense, plays the same basic idea over and over again – but who, by some magic alchemy, manages to make each solo a new and wondrous experience.[27]

The style that Miley and Nanton created became an essential part of the Ellington band sound. The "jungle sounds" that they were creating for the exotic shows of the Cotton Club have, in fact, become what some people feel is the single most distinguishing feature of the Ellington sound. Stanley Dance discussed this development.

Between them, Miley and Nanton made a fine art out of plunger playing. As his band grew in size over the years, Ellington created music that required the whole brass section to use plunger mutes, thus producing a new orchestral effect capable of much more than animalistic jungle imagery. It might be used rhythmically in the background or the foreground, or it might be used for hushed sounds that are evocative of mysterious, nocturnal chanting. It was [Ellington's] first major coloristic device, and it

27 *Early Jazz*, 332.

was to remain the most immediately identifiable characteristic of his music.[28]

Perhaps it is the early identification of the so-called "jungle style" with the primitive themes of the Cotton Club shows, or the seeming simplicity of Nanton's style, that has caused him to be thought of as a "natural" player for whom the style developed without serious effort or study. Ulanov, however, claims that Nanton was a very serious student of the plunger, who spent much of his time working with it. Nanton was apparently able to do a good imitation of his predecessor, Charlie Irvis, and he extended plunger technique by trying to find equivalent sounds for the whole range of human feeling.[29] Writers have used a wide variety of images to try to describe the effects of Nanton's playing. Vic Bellerby described the team of Miley and Nanton in action "cajoling forth cries of hoarse sadness, bitter derision and oafish delight from their instruments." He tried further to pin down the moods they created.

[The] growl specialists have sounded a variety of moods – rich humour, fierce satire and effervescent joy, but their most significant contribution has been to one form of Ellington's expression which may be described as a perception of the sinister and the occult, a sounding of the dark and instinctive.[30]

Richard Boyer tried his hand at describing Nanton's playing. (Unfortunately, he does not say what tune he or Nanton was talking about.)

[It] sometimes sounds like an infant crying, sometimes like a bubbly, inane laugh of an idiot, and sometimes like someone calling for help. Sam [Nanton] says, "It's a sad tale with a little mirth. When I play it, I think of a man in a dungeon calling out a cell window."[31]

Each listener brings his own background to these performances and leaves with his own impression. Reactions and descriptions vary, but Nanton's unique and colorful sounds never fail to move serious listeners.

While Nanton's first credited solo on record with Ellington is usually considered to be the previously mentioned *Li'l Farina*, there has been some disagreement about whether Nanton or Irvis plays on this cut. To me, both historical and aural evidence suggest that Nanton is the soloist. Named for the character from the *Our Gang* comedy series, *L'il Farina* was recorded at a brisk tempo. The trombone solo, on the open horn, bounces happily along. The tone quality and the manner of articulation of the soloist indicate that Irvis had been replaced. While the solo is not precisely in the style that Nanton was to exhibit on the

28 Stanley Dance, "Duke Ellington," in booklet to record set *Duke Ellington,* 14.

29 Ulanov, telephone interview, 13 June 1989.

30 Vic Bellerby, "Analysis of Genius," in Gammond, 161, 162.

31 Richard Boyer, "The Hot Bach," in Gammond, 33, and The *Duke Ellington Reader,* 223.

recordings from his next few sessions with the band, it must be noted that it was five months before Nanton was recorded again with Ellington. What is consistent from this solo to Nanton's later recorded work is good-natured, happy swing. This was characteristic of much of Nanton's work in the next few years. There is a growl on one note in the *Li'l Farina* solo, a technique that Nanton often used in the plunger, but also employed occasionally when playing the open horn. The style of the trombone solo is remarkably close to Miley's style of this same period.

When the band returned to the studio on 29 November 1926, it recorded the first of many versions of an Ellington-Miley classic, *East St. Louis Toodle-Oo*. Nanton's open solo was again rather jaunty, in stark contrast to the atmosphere of gloom that pervades much of the piece.

Perhaps the outstanding open horn solo that Nanton played in this period was from another often recorded piece, *Jubilee Stomp*. One can hear this solo develop over the course of a number of recordings from early 1928. On the 19 January date, Nanton played much of the musical material that would become part of the "finished" solo, but he seems decidedly tentative, and there are some noticeable "holes" in the solo. The recording of 21 March is spirited and convincing, although there is some sloppiness in Nanton's playing. Only five days later, Nanton played virtually the same solo, but cleaner, despite the slightly faster tempo. This 26 March recording (Example 2-1) shows a boisterous style that has been compared to that of Nanton's illustrious contemporary, J. C. Higginbotham. At an ambitious tempo, Nanton easily works his way through some technically difficult figures, notably those of measures 17-18 and measures 21-22. His tone is strong and brash, with no thinness in the higher register.

The agility displayed in this solo was characteristic of much of Nanton's work on the open horn, an agility heard less and less as the plunger took over his solo work with Ellington. Mercer Ellington noted this dichotomy in Nanton's playing.

Tricky Sam could move around on his horn when he wanted to, and he was not handicapped in execution, but his was a solo style based on only a few notes. It was very effective, too, and he was, of course, encouraged in it by Ellington.[32]

At least one critic, Barry McRae, however, has bemoaned what he called Ellington's "typing" of some of his sidemen in this manner. He called the effect of limiting Nanton to the role of plunger specialist "calamitous, because not only did it give him a set voice in his solo work, but it also robbed his admirers

32 *Duke Ellington in Person,* 51.

EXAMPLE 2-1

of the chance to hear his magnificent open tone."[33] This "set voice" was, however, developed to the fullest.

Different recordings point up different aspects of the development of Nanton's plunger style. On many recordings he revealed only one of the variety of tricks he had at his disposal. As his career progressed, the arsensal of tricks grew. But even on some of the earlier records, Nanton exploited a wide range of techniques that could combine to produce a striking statement. Another of the outstanding Ellington-Miley collaborations of the late 1920s was *Black and Tan Fantasy*. Like *East St. Louis*

33 McRae, Barry. "Joe 'Tricky Sam' Nanton," 14.

Toodle-Oo and other staples of the band's repertory during these years, *Black and Tan* was recorded several times. On the recording of 3 November 1927, Bubber Miley was on one of his temporary leaves from the Ellington band. Jabbo Smith filled in, but one of the sections originally played by Miley was covered on this date by Nanton. The blues spot that Nanton normally filled was played with particular distinction on this session (Example 2-2).

EXAMPLE 2-2

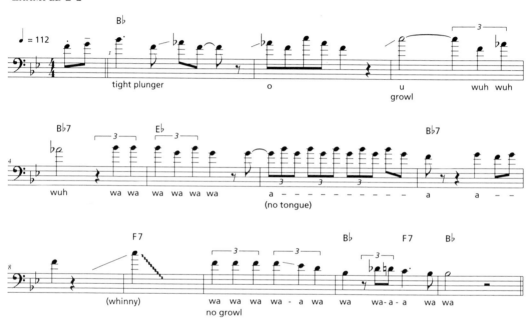

Nanton's first two measures are played into "tight plunger," that is, the plunger was held very close to the bell of the instrument. On the first note of measure two, however, the plunger is opened considerably more than on the other notes of this phrase. A heavy growl starts in measure three, and the plunger opens just slightly to produce an "u" sound, followed by three muffled sounding "wuh's." These turn into more characteristic "wa's" in measure four as Nanton opens and closes on each note through the end of measure five. The repeated triplet figure of measure six is played with the plunger held somewhat open throughout. It also seems that no tongue was used in measures six through eight.

In measures eight and nine, Nanton performed one of his most distinctive plunger effects ever. No established musical term precisely defines the effect. It amounts to an upward glissando, or slow rip, followed by a cascading descending glissando. The effect approximates a horse's whinny more closely than any other sound in common experience. In fact, this noted effect is usually referred to as a whinny. This was not a new effect in jazz. Cornetist Nick La Rocca had played a whinny on one of the first jazz records ever made, *Livery Stable Blues*, recorded by the Original Dixieland Jazz Band 26 February 1917.[34] Nanton's whinny, however, has a completely different effect from the humorous barnyard imitation of LaRocca. Except in other recordings of this work, Nanton did not use the effect in the recording studio again.[35]

In the last three measures of the chorus, Nanton again used a "wa" on virtually every note (the third and fourth notes of measure 11 being the exceptions), but without growl, creating yet another type of sound for this virtuoso performance. While dealing with this variety of sounds, a listener does not get the feeling that the solo is at all "gimmicky;" the deep feeling and integrity of the blues is maintained through the whole solo, indeed, through the whole tune.

In October of 1930, Nanton's plunger-muted trombone sound became part of one of Ellington's most celebrated creations, the classic *Mood Indigo*. The melody is presented by what might be called the *Mood Indigo* trio – Arthur Whetsol's muted trumpet, Barney Bigard's clarinet and Nanton's trombone. Part of the magic of this combination was simply the three sounds involved. Another large part of it was the way Ellington scored the instruments – trumpet on top in its middle register, trombone in the middle of the voicing in its high register, and clarinet at the bottom in its low, or chalumeau, register. The mutes on the two brass were a critical component of the sound. It was this simple, but enormously effective combination that years later led André Previn, jazz pianist turned world-renowned classical conductor, to make the widely publicized remarks,

Stan Kenton can stand in front of a thousand fiddles and a thousand brass, give the down beat and every studio arranger can nod his head and say "Oh yes, that's done like this." But Duke merely lifts his finger, three horns make a sound, and I don't know what it is.[36]

While *Mood Indigo* was the piece that made this combination famous, Ellington would continue to use it and to modify it, on "Mood Indigo" and other tunes. Recordings of *Mood Indigo* from the 1950s and '60s invariably start with a trio of horns, but there are a variety of combinations.[37]

34 An example of the whinny known by most music lovers is at the end of Leroy Anderson's popular classic *Sleigh Ride*.

35 However, on the 1943 Carnegie Hall concert (which was recorded), Nanton used whinny not only on *Black and Tan Fantasy*, but also on *Goin' Up*. I suspect that there must have been some discussion of the technique, or at least some playing around with it, in the band about this time, because Lawrence Brown used a "whinny-like" sound on *Goin' Up*, as did the whole trumpet section together.

36 As quoted in Gleason, *Celebrating the Duke*, 203.

37 There is further discussion of the *Mood Indigo* scoring in Appendix 1.

Time and time again in the late '20s and early '30s Ellington called upon Nanton to expose the theme or melody of pieces in the first chorus of an arrangement. Nanton carried out this assignment on tunes that ran the gamut from slow to fast, happy to sad, bright to dark. Most often, he exposed the theme of tunes that were medium to fast. While he employed a number of his plunger tricks, Tricky Sam usually played these melodies fairly close to the original written themes. On a number of occasions Nanton's straightforward rendering of a theme was accompanied by the filigree clarinet work of Barney Bigard. In the AABA format of most of these tunes, Nanton would often employ tight plunger for the first sixteen measures, perhaps with an occasional note or two opened to some degree. On the bridge, the plunger would be loosened, often with wa-wa and growl effects added (alternatively, Ellington might assign another soloist to play this contrasting material). The last eight bars might return to the style of the first sixteen or continue in the style established on the bridge. Two examples point up some of Nanton's stylistic traits in this role.

One of Ellington's most famous pieces, *It Don't Mean A Thing (If It Ain't Got That Swing)*, was first recorded 2 February 1932. This title, which has been a motto for jazzmen through the years, featured Ellington's new singer, Ivie Anderson. Before the vocal, Nanton takes the first chorus, as he had done on so many tunes before (Example 2-3). He swings easily over the brisk two-beat feel. The plunger remains tight for most of the solo. A notable exception is the "wa" played by the whole band in measure eight. The melody of this tune is distinguished by its repeated notes. After the melodic line of the vocal in the first four measures of each A section (it is a 32-measure AABA tune), the band answers with four measures on a single pitch. The rhythm of these measures is a catchy syncopated 3/4 figure over the 2/2 meter of the tune. Nanton, who played many solos that were built on only a few pitches, does the same here. He uses more than the single tonic of the written melody in the bars noted, but he stays for the most part with only three pitches – A-flat, G, and the tonic F. Nanton's only references to the written melody are in measures 9-10 and measures 25-26, where he plays four of the initial notes of the tune. But the melodic and rhythmic simplicity and the strength of Nanton's variation are such that with repeated listenings, one could be persuaded to hear it as the theme, rather than Ellington's melody.

EXAMPLE 2-3

Joe "Tricky Sam" Nanton, ca, 1930s (Collection of Duncan P. Schiedt)

Jazz scholar Dan Morgenstern has written at length about the Ellington band's recording of *In the Shade of the Old Apple Tree*, saying it was "the first popular song Ellington remembered hearing as a child." The recording of the song on 15 August 1933 was a popular and best-selling record. Morgenstern described the recording as "gentle, simple, affectionate, and full of humor," but Nanton's role in it as "Tricky Sam, at his most outrageous."[38] The first chorus is played by the saxophone section in a decidedly "sweet" style, with no jazz overtones. Humorous commentary is added by trumpeter Freddie Jenkins, including a quote from the *William Tell Overture*. When Tricky Sam takes the first 16 measures of the second chorus, the feeling of the tune changes abruptly (Example 2-4).

EXAMPLE 2-4

38 Dan Morgenstern, "Notes on the Music" in booklet for Time-Life record set *Duke Ellington,* 40-41.

Nanton stays very close to the original melody in the first
eight measures, but the effect that his "wa's" and growls on each
note have on the melody is indescribable. The listener may not
be sure at this point whether or not to laugh, but the next eight
bars of Nanton's unique telling of this story leads to an unam-
biguous end. Starting in the ninth bar, Nanton livens up the
rhythm slightly, while closing off the bell with the tight plunger
until the last two measures of the solo. The intensity of the
sound builds as Nanton ascends to the high D of measure 13.
Measures 15 and 16, played without rhythm section, amount to
a "raspberry," as Nanton uses the "wa" with heavy growling on
each note and then sits on the flat third of the closing dominant
chord.

The "wa's" in the first eight measures have some of the character of the "ya" that Nanton employed so effectively later in his
career. The last two measures might more accurately be described by "ya" than "wa," although the line between the two
is very fine at this point. One rarely heard this sound from
Nanton again on recordings until the 1940s.

Another recording from 1933 demonstrates the variety of
plunger sounds that Nanton then had at his disposal in a different context. *Harlem Speaks* was initially recorded 13 July in
London while the band was on its first European tour. Nanton
played a chorus earlier in the tune, but the last chorus is a brilliant display of his expressive powers (Example 2-5). Following
a powerful solo by Lawrence Brown, the band blazes away, but
Nanton's voice stands out. This was, incidentally, not the only
time that Ellington juxtaposed Nanton's solo muted voice
against the rest of the ensemble. The cutting quality of his muted
trombone (which Mercer Ellington likened to "tearing paper")
managed to balance the weight of the rest of the band.

In the whole thirty-two measure chorus, Nanton employs
only three distinct pitches. The true nature of blue notes is
explored in this solo, because all of the notes that are not either
F, E-flat or C in this solo sound somewhere in that hazy region
between G (the third of the tonic E-flat chord) and G-flat (the
flatted third [or in today's terminology, the sharp ninth] of the
tonic chord and the seventh of the subdominant A-flat chord).
These have been notated as G-flats, but a case could be made for
their being G-naturals, especially those from measure 25 to the
end. The solo, if one can refer to it as such, considering its lack
of melodic material, is vocal from the beginning to end. The
voice that it reminds one of is human in feeling, though not precisely in sound. For ease of reading, single vowels have been

EXAMPLE 2-5

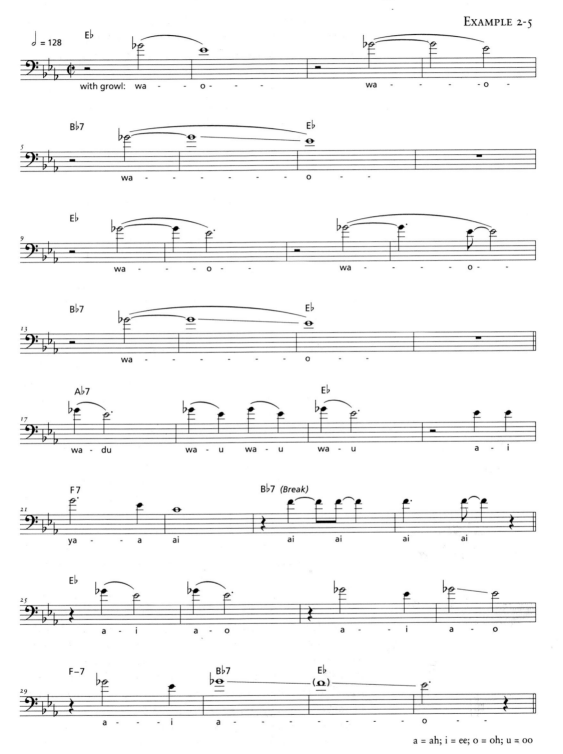

a = ah; i = ee; o = oh; u = oo

used in the transcription to approximate the sounds that come from the horn and plunger. In the example, a = ah, i = ee, o = oh and u = oo. The combination of "a" and "i" heard in this example is extremely rare in the Nanton canon. Besides the four distinct vowel sounds that can be heard, one also gets the sense of three different consonant-like sounds. The "wa" and "ya" have been described previously. (Although the "w" and the "y" are in essence a combination of vowel sounds, our perception of them in written English is that of consonants.) The "d" in measure 17 indicates an attack that is slightly harder than the others in the example. It is safe to say that no other jazz artist has created anything quite like this amazing thirty-two bars.

This extended discussion of sounds points to the conclusion that Nanton, aided and abetted by his colleagues, in particular trumpeters Bubber Miley and Cootie Williams, had created a unique plunger "language." Technical analysis can describe aspects of how the language is created, but it cannot really get to the heart of the matter – how the language communicates. Obviously, this language is non-specific enough that it communicates to each listener in a different way. And it is a language of sounds, rather than a language of pitch – the language with which composers from the Baroque era of Western music history used to communicate specific emotions. So while we cannot know just what Nanton was trying to get across, the deep expressiveness of the almost eerily vocal quality of this language cannot be ignored, even by casual listeners. The connection between voice and instrument that Albert Murray has called "vocal instrumentation" – a reciprocal stylistic exchange between singers and instrumentalists – has been at the heart of jazz since its inception.[39]

Ellington, however, eventually called for his plunger specialists to directly imitate the spoken word. Intonation of actual speech is found at the beginning of Ellington's celebrated *Harlem*, where Ray Nance clearly enunciates the two syllables of the title through his instrument. In the piece *Up and Down, Up and Down (I Will Lead Them Up and Down)* from the outstanding 1957 Ellington work *Such Sweet Thunder*, Clark Terry was asked to in effect speak the Shakespeare quotation, "Lord, what fools these mortals be," on his plunger-muted trumpet.

Terry has described how some of the men in the Ellington band of the 1950s would "talk" through their horns for a variety of occasions: when an attractive woman would walk by, or when making fun of "squares," or just passing the time.[40] This language was clear enough to communicate yet unclear

39 See Murray, *Stomping the Blues,* Chapter 7. The instrumental-vocal connection is also explored by LeRoi Jones (Imamu Amiri Baraka) in *Blues People,* especially 78-79.

40 Terry interviews.

enough to be open to individual interpretation. And while those who took part in it may have known more precisely what was being "said," even the uninitiated could very likely get the gist of the message. It was only a small step to Terry's celebrated "Mumbles," a sung vocal language that integrates a few clear words with many unclear syllables in a humorous and bluesy concoction that became his ticket to fame in the 1960s.

Nanton was considered an outstanding blues player from early in his career. One might note that in terms of note selection, and even in rhythmic complexity, Nanton was one of the simplest blues players in the history of jazz. Hughes Panassié, one of the pioneers in jazz criticism, declared,

Tricky Sam is one of the greatest blues players jazz has ever known. He needs only to play two or three notes with his inimitable expression and repeat them during the whole chorus to move the listener deeply. He tells more with a couple of notes than most trombonists do with many and complex phrases.[41]

Barry McRae wrote about Nanton's ability to "evoke an atmosphere of incredible melancholy while at the same time suggesting a feeling of almost light-heartedness, in much the same way as the great blues singers."[42]

A look at two of Nanton's blues solos on starkly contrasting tunes offers some insight into his blues playing. *Ko-Ko*, recorded 6 March 1940, is the definitive recording of one of Ellington's most celebrated works. It was reported that *Ko-Ko* was from an uncompleted work by Ellington, evidently about or inspired by Africa, entitled *Boola*. References to *Boola* appeared by the early 1930s, and the work was reported as a five-movement suite, then as an opera. Its theme was referred to early on as African, but later by Ellington himself as "the story of the Negro in America." Both the subject matter and the musical material of *Black, Brown and Beige* seem to be derived in part from this never-completed work.[43]

Ellington introduced *Ko-Ko* at the 1943 Carnegie Hall concert as

. . . a little descriptive scene of the days that inspired jazz . . . [I]t was in New Orleans, and a place called Congo Square, where the slaves used to gather and do native and sensuous dances — religious dances.[44]

Ko-Ko is a dark, fierce sounding piece, full of dissonance. Its basic form is that of a twelve-bar blues in minor, with extra introductory and closing material. For this brilliant piece, Ellington selected only two members of the band to play solos of more than a few measures – himself and Tricky Sam. (Jimmie

41 Panassié, Hughes, *The Real Jazz*, 106.

42 McRae, "Tricky Sam Nanton," 14.

43 The most comprehensive investigation into *Boola* appears in Tucker, "The Genesis of Black, Brown and Beige."

44 From the recording of the Carnegie Hall concert of 23 January 1943, Prestige Records P-34004.

Blanton played six measures of solo on bass, two measures at a time, on the next to last full chorus.) Nanton's two choruses come after the statement of a theme by Juan Tizol's valve trombone accompanied by the saxophone and rhythm sections (Example 2-6). It is difficult to imagine a prominent jazz player playing a simpler solo. The whole solo encompasses a range of only an octave. In the twenty-four bars, there are only three measures that have notes that go beyond the range of a fifth (from the tonic E-flat to the B-flat above it). In the first chorus, only two measures use notes other than A-flat and B-flat. Rhythmically, the whole solo is based on a figure of an eighth note on beat one followed by a longer note on the "and" of the beat. This figure appears in some form thirteen times in the twenty-four bars (measures 18 and 19 contain essentially the same figure, started on tied notes and inflected). What makes the solo work is the sound that Nanton produces. In the first chorus and the last phrase of the second chorus, one hears the now perfected "ya" sound that was uniquely Nanton's. The tight plunger sound provides contrast in the first eight measures of the second chorus. With this minimum of musical material, Nanton produced a highly-charged, emotional statement.

Given the heavily arranged nature of *Ko-Ko,* it would be interesting to know how much input Ellington had into Nanton's two-chorus statement. Was the solo strictly Nanton's creation, or was he directed (and to what degree) by Ellington? This becomes even more fascinating now that the score to *Black, Brown and Beige* has been discovered. In it, one finds that all of Tricky Sam's solo in the *Work Song* section is written out in the score.

Main Stem, another superb reworking of the blues by Ellington (only portions of it are blues), was recorded 26 June 1942. Although hard-driving, this blues is decidedly upbeat and bright. It practically bubbles with good spirits. Nanton's solo, one chorus, was again simplicity itself (Example 2-7). This solo was in the style that Nanton had been using for years, with a basic sound that he returned to often – the tight plunger sound. (Although there are slight variations in the sound, especially in measures one, nine and ten, the fundamental sound remains fairly constant.) The range of this solo is only a fifth. Each of the three phrases starts with a repeated A. The first five notes of the D scale outline the range of the solo. Nanton uses mostly the major mode to maintain the celebratory spirit of the piece, but adds blue notes in measures five, ten, eleven and twelve to intensify the blues feeling. The strength of this solo, like so many others, seems to come from its simplicity.

Example 2-6

During the first few years of the 1940s, Nanton seemed to refine his already distinctive plunger style and technique. The "ya" sound that had been heard occasionally became more prominent. The use of "wa" and "ya" was modified by the use of growls of varying intensities to produce a startling array of sounds. On slower tunes, the plunger was used perhaps to greatest advantage, because at a slow tempo the diverse techniques could be employed with greatest control. One of the most poignant of Nanton's plunger statements appeared on the February 1941 recording of the lovely tune attributed to Mercer Ellington, *Blue Serge*.[45] A transcription cannot begin to do justice to the effect that this solo (Example 2-8), combined with the moody reed and rhythm scoring, has on a sympathetic listener. Nanton alternates between "wa" and "ya", with two fairly closed notes (marked "+") also prominent. In the last measure, neither "wa" nor "ya" is used, but a "da" results when Nanton crosses over one of the overtone "breaks" on the instrument. Simplicity is again a key, but there is sophistication as well. Effective use is made of the ninth of the C minor chord at the very beginning of the solo, followed by the eleventh of the C minor chord in the next measure. The G that is used against the B diminished chord in measure four and as the eleventh of the D half-diminished chord in measure seven is striking in both measures. The flatted thirteenth of that same D chord in measure five is equally effective.

Analysis offers some insight into the construction of these solos, but it does little to relate their true strength and communicative power. The exact rhythms and inflections, too, cannot be precisely notated. One must listen to the recorded solos to hear their essence, which is contained as much in the sound of the notes and the manner of their execution as in the selection of notes.

The Ellington Orchestra made considerably fewer recordings in 1941 than it had in the previous three years, and in the first half of 1942 there were only a handful of recordings made before the American Federation of Musicians recording ban stopped recording activity completely. No more commercial recordings were made by the band until December of 1944. The lack of studio recordings from this period would have been regrettable under any circumstances, but it is particularly so because we know from live recordings that the band was performing at an especially high level during these years.

Although key members of the band had left – Cootie Williams in 1940, Jimmie Blanton in 1941, and Barney Bigard

45 Schuller speculates about the relative contributions of Mercer and Duke on this and other compositions from this period. *Swing Era,* 137.

EXAMPLE 2-7

tight plunger

EXAMPLE 2-8

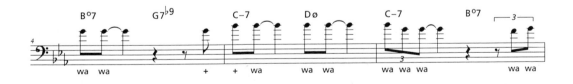

wa   wa wa wa   +   +   wa   ya ya ya

wa   wa   +   +   wa   wa wa   wa wa wa   wa wa

wa   wa   ya   ya - a   a - a - da - a

in 1942 – the performance at Carnegie Hall in 1943 shows
Ellington's orchestra in excellent form. This was the first of a
series of concerts that the band would play at the famed New
York concert hall. For this major occasion, a symbol of the
seriousness with which his music was being taken, Ellington
composed his magnum opus *Black, Brown and Beige*. Described
as "a tone parallel to the history of the American Negro," this
was not only by far the longest work that Ellington had written,
but it was a work about which he felt very strongly. This premiere appeared on a program that also featured some of
Ellington's finer works from the recent and more distant past.

Nanton was in brilliant form at the concert, soloing on over
a half dozen pieces on the concert, including an extended spot
in *Black*. On the section of *Black* that has become known as
Work Song, Nanton's plunger work may never have been heard
in a more vocal and affecting style. He played a variety of melodic passages in several different tempos. The different sections of
the solo are transcribed as Examples 2-9, 2-9A, and 2-9B. This
extended exposure again allowed Nanton to display his whole
arsenal of plunger sounds. The first three measures of Example
2-9 are tightly closed, almost choked (but as usual, there are
some slight variations in the sounds of individual notes).
Starting in measure 5 each note features a "wa," combined with
growl for three measures and then without growl. By measure
10, the wa's have changed to "ya," which remains the primary
syllable for the rest of the solo. It is worthy of note that Nanton
plays this whole first section of the solo as it is notated in
Ellington's score with the exception of measures 3 and 15.

Nanton's solo is interrupted by an eleven-measure passage
featuring the trumpet section. When Nanton reenters it is with
a repeated figure in a new key (Example 2-9A). The first two
beats of this figure are difficult to notate accurately, or even
clearly decipher aurally. The notated figure in the example is the
one that appears in the score; Gunther Schuller, however, transcribed this as a triplet figure, leaving off the first A-flat of the
sixteenth-note groups.[46] The confusion results not so much from
poor fidelity of the recording, but rather from the way Nanton
combines the glissandos between notes with the movement of
the plunger, with all of the notes having a choked quality but
each of varying degrees. The quarter notes in measures two and
four are either "wa's," "ya's," or something between the two. In
measure six, Nanton closes the plunger very slightly at the end
of each quarter with resulting effect being "wau, yau" ("wow,
yow").

46 Ibid., 144.

EXAMPLE 2-9

tight

wa with growl

no growl   wa   ya   ya   ya ya ya ya ya   ya ya

oo - wa

EXAMPLE 2-9A

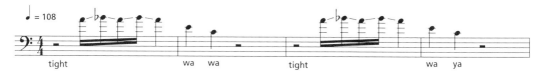

tight   wa   wa   tight   wa   ya

tight   wau   yau   ya's

fluff? closed

ya   ya

etc.   (band)   add growl   (band)

no growl

EXAMPLE 2-9B

growl   "ya's" throughout

no growl

growl   *louder*

growl fades out

The call and response device of a work song is most convincingly portrayed by Nanton and the band starting in meaure 16 and continuing over the next eight measures. As Ellington states in his spoken introduction to this movement (included on the Prestige recording), in a work song "there's a place for the song and then there's a place where you grunt [from] the impact of your work." Nanton's questioning calls in measures 16-17 and 18-19 are answered by emphatic chords from the band. Nanton heightens the emotional sense by adding growl in measures 18-21, but then removes it for a poignant close to the section in measures 22 and 23.

Nanton's final statement of the solo (Example 2-9B) follows another few measures of ensemble playing. Here, in the space of only twenty measures, Ellington goes through three key changes, with tempo changes roughly paralleling the changes of key. The vocal quality of Nanton's sound is eerie, particularly in the short F major section (measures 6-9). In measures 13-16, he repeats the call figure from part two, now a half step higher (in D-flat). The band's response is slightly different, but Nanton shapes his statements much as before, winding down beautifully to his final held note.

Nanton's entire solo lasts approximately three minutes – roughly the length of the 78-rpm record. This was the only time Nanton was ever featured on a recorded performance of this length. Later revisions of *Black, Brown and Beige* cut portions of *Work Song*, including some of the trombone solo. It is only on this January 1943 performance that listeners have the pleasure of hearing Nanton's masterful interpretation in its entirety. Neither words nor musical notation can describe the emotional impact that this deeply expressive playing effects. As with all great instrumentalists and vocalists, it is as if there is no instrument involved. The listener is aware only of the music, rather than how it is being produced.

When the band returned to the studio in December of 1944, it was without veteran trombonist Juan Tizol and one of its strongest soloists, Ben Webster. The band's personnel, however, remained formidable and its performance level high. The first works that were recorded were excerpts from *Black, Brown and Beige*. *Work Song* was shortened considerably from the original score, and Nanton's playing, while excellent, did not project the emotion that the live performance had almost two years earlier. A week later (19 December 1944) the excerpts were played again at Carnegie Hall. They were expanded from the studio versions and were more musically satisfying. Nonetheless,

Nanton's *Work Song* solos still did not seem to reach the heights of the premiere performance. He was again in brilliant form, however, and his solo on *It Don't Mean a Thing* is one of the few renditions of this tune recorded since its initial appearance in 1932 (see Example 2-3). On the concert's encore, *Frankie and Johnny*, Nanton was able in two outstanding blues choruses to display all of his tricks: tight plunger, growls, wa's, ya's, and various combinations of these. It was almost his last hurrah.

There are hardly any Nanton solos from 1945-1946. Another remake of *Black and Tan Fantasy* (11 May 1945) and a bubbling opening chorus on a broadcast transcription of *In a Jam* (17 July 1946, originally 1936) are among the few musical highlights that came out of the studio from Nanton during these years. When Nanton's inimitable voice was finally silenced in July 1946, it was the end of an era in Ellingtonia.

In 1971, twenty-five years after Tricky Sam's death, trombone great Dicky Wells included Nanton in his "ideal trombone section" from "the early days." "There would always have to be a place for Tricky." Wells claimed, "That man [Nanton] could say as much as a human voice on his horn."[47]

Nanton's friend Rex Stewart described Tricky Sam's playing in terms colorful enough to evoke some of the character of this remarkable body of music.

Only a few [musicians] have had that something, that rare gift of communication that Joseph Nanton had . . . Before the public he was at various times a clown, a tragedian, or merely the fellow on the corner, depending on the role Duke had assigned him . . .

What a variety of sounds he evoked from his instrument! From the wail of a new-born baby to the raucous hoot of an owl, from the bloodcurdling scream of an enraged tiger to the eerie cooing of a mourning dove, Tricky had them all in his bag of tricks, and he utilized them with discretion and good taste...

Nanton's playing differed from that of virtually all other trombonists in jazz. His sound was a voice unique to the instrument, and although many of his fellows played sweeter, faster, louder, and with considerably more technique, still Tricky possessed the gift of communication that is the essence of any music.[48]

47 *The Night People*, 138, 36.
48 Stewart, 103-104.

Ellington Rehearsal, ca. mid 1930s
Rear: Rex Stewart, Cootie Williams, Artie Whetsol; Trombones: Joe "Tricky Sam" Nanton, Juan Tizol, Lawrence Brown
Front: Harry Carney, Otto "Toby" Hardwick, Johnny Hodges, Freddie Jenkins, Barney Bigard
(Collection of Duncan Schiedt)

The Unique Juan Tizol

3

Juan Tizol Martinez was born to Juan Tizol and Manuela Martinez on 22 January 1900 in San Juan, Puerto Rico. Contrary to local custom at that time, he took his father's last name rather than his mother's.[1] He came from a musical family. He was taught music by his uncle, Manuel Tizol, of whom Juan said, "I shouldn't say [he was] the best, but one of the best musicians in Puerto Rico."[2] Uncle Manolo, as he was known, played cello, trombone and bassoon, and directed the municipal band and the symphony in San Juan. Juan's first instrument was violin, but he was given a valve trombone in school while still a youngster. In Puerto Rico at that time, slide trombones were used only in the army band. Tizol continued to play valve trombone throughout his career.

Because his uncle directed the band, young Juan was around musicians often and apparently learned much from them. He claimed to be only about eight years old when he started playing in the band that his uncle conducted.[3] He also played the euphonium. His experience as a young player in San Juan was rich and varied. In addition to playing with the band, he played for the local opera, for ballets and in dance bands. When he was about twenty years old he wrote a dance piece for his girlfriend, entitled *Julita*. His uncle arranged the piece for performance by the full forty-five piece municipal band.

Around 1920 a band was organized in Puerto Rico for the purpose of coming to the United States to work in Washington D.C. A ship's crew was paid off for their cooperation, and the band members came to New York as stowaways, only to arrive before they were needed for the engagement in Washington. Tizol had lost money gambling on the boat, and when he arrived in New York, he had neither money nor an instrument. His cousin Antonio, who had been in the United States for some time, arranged living accomodations, and Tizol worked several factory jobs before the band was finally called to Washington. In the meantime, he had bought an instrument at Carl Fischer's music store for fifty dollars, money that may have been sent from home. When the band made it to Washington, it took up

1 The bulk of the biographical information in this chapter is pieced together from the interviews conducted by Bill Spilka and Patricia Willard, with some corroboration from *The World of Duke Ellington*. Information on Tizol's career also comes from Chilton, Feather and Tucker.
2 Spilka.
3 Willard, reel one. In his interview with Spilka, Tizol said that he didn't start until he was about sixteen years old.

residence at the Howard Theater. Marie Lucas was the piano player and conductor of the all-Puerto Rican group, which played for the touring shows that appeared at the Howard. In addition, the band supplied the music for the silent movies, as well as overtures prior to the shows. In addition to Lucas's orchestra, the theater employed small dance or jazz groups (the term "jazz" did not yet have a completely established meaning). Duke Ellington was one of the piano players who played with these small groups "in the box" at the Howard.

The Howard, however, could not support the orchestra full-time, so Tizol went on to work at the Republic Theater with a group led by Russell Wooding. Wooding had a five or six piece group that played his arrangements as well as "stocks" (published arrangements) for the pictures. Tizol also spent some time with the White Brothers' band, where one of his bandmates was Arthur Whetsol, who was also a member of Ellington's band during long periods of time in the twenties and early thirties. Tizol also worked for Bobby Lee's Cottonpickers and in Gertie Wells's band during the 1920s, and he spent time in New Jersey with Cliff Jackson, possibly immediately before he joined Ellington.[4]

Tizol met his future wife Rosebud early in his stay in Washington, and the two of them opened a delicatessen in Washington sometime in the twenties. Rose recalled Tizol playing both a recording session and a radio broadcast with Ellington before he actually joined the band. Apparently Arthur Whetsol reminded Duke of the excellent valve trombonist whom he had heard play years before at the Howard Theater in Washington. In any case, Tizol got "the call" from Ellington to join the band in the summer of 1929.

At that time, Ellington was still in residence at the Cotton Club, but the band also took on *Show Girl* with the Ziegfeld Follies in July. According to Tizol, during this time the band would play a show at the Cotton Club, go over to Ziegfeld's theater to play *Show Girl*, and then head back to the Cotton Club for another show, which ended at three in the morning. Chances are that Ellington hired Tizol to have a good "reader" to play the new arrangements that the band faced for the Ziegfeld show. Tizol joined Joe Nanton in what was now a trombone section – even though it had only two members, and his addition expanded the number of brass in Ellington's band to five.[5]

Ellington was certainly aware of the implications of having a fifth brass voice available. Mercer Ellington wrote:

Although I couldn't yet talk to Pop on a musical basis [in

4   *The World of Duke Ellington,* 114, and the recollections of Tizol's wife on the Willard interview, reel 5.

5   Trombonist Harry White is in a band photo from 1928 and is usually listed as having been on a recording session from October of 1928. It is not known if he was in any way a "regular" member of the band for any length of time.

1929], *I remember being around when he was speaking about how different it was writing for five [brass] instead of four. He began to think of the brass as two sections now, where before the trombone's part had been written with the trumpets. When you wrote for four instruments, he explained to me, you did not have to decide which note to leave out. In writing three-part harmony, you had to decide which note of four you could leave out and still have a good sound. This was a new challenge, and it began to affect the way he had to write.*[6]

While Tizol was rarely featured as a soloist in his first several years with the band, Ellington discovered new scoring possibilities as he found different roles that Tizol was able to fill. On the recording of *Creole Rhapsody* (20 January 1931), Ellington first displayed at length the trombone duo, in a passage that sounds very much like the trombone trios he began to write after Lawrence Brown joined the band in 1932 – but, of course, with only two voices instead of three.[7] This was, by the way, a groundbreaking recording in that it was Ellington's first "extended" composition – its two parts each occupying one side of a 78-rpm record.

In the early thirties, Tizol's voice was often scored with the saxophones, commonly with his valve trombone carrying the lead. His distinctive sound blended beautifully with the saxophone section, and Ellington seemed to be fond of this scoring. Prominent examples include the second recorded version of *Creole Rhapsody* (11 June 1931), *Swampy River* (17 May 1932), *Clouds in My Heart* (18 May 1932), and *Delta Bound* (21 December 1932). While this type of voicing was frequently used on slower numbers, Tizol's agility on the valve horn enabled him to keep up with faster passages when he was scored with saxophones or trumpets. The valve horn also allowed Tizol to negotiate passages in keys that were awkward for the slide trombones.[8] Ellington also gave Tizol short melodic passages which he performed beautifully in a more "legitimate" style than that of most of his bandmates.

Tizol was an excellent player who could be counted on for clean and accurate playing, and he was by all reports the finest sight-reader in the Ellington band. Barney Bigard described Tizol as

. . . no doubt the best musician in the band at that time [the late '20s and early '30's]. See, they all had a sound musical knowledge but Tizol could just transpose like mad. He could cover anybody's chair. All over the band, anywhere you put him in, he would go like mad. He was a terrific musician.[9]

Along this line, Britt Woodman reported that in the 1950s

6 *Duke Ellington in Person*, 50-51.
7 This duet passage does not appear on the version of *Creole Rhapsody* recorded just a few months later (11 June 1931). For more on this duet, see Appendix I.
8 A case in point is *Ko-Ko*. As Schuller has pointed out (*Swing Era*, 116), the opening melodic line that Tizol plays includes a quick shift from B-flat to C-flat that is extremely difficult on slide trombone. On later recordings of *Ko-Ko* the whole section is heard playing this line, but the execution of it is not as smooth as might be hoped.
9 Bigard, 57.

Tizol had devilishly difficult sight-reading exercises on which he liked to test the new members of the band.[10]

The respect that the other members of the Ellington band had for Tizol's abilities is reflected in the many small band dates that Tizol played in the thirties and forties led by Bigard and Cootie Williams. Ellington featured Tizol not only on the Latin-flavored tunes that Tizol wrote, but also on Ellington's own major works, notably *Reminiscing in Tempo* and *Black, Brown and Beige*.[11] Ellington referred to Tizol as "one of the finest musicians I've ever known."[12] Long-time section mate Lawrence Brown called him "the pivot, the solid rock of the [trombone] section."[13]

Tizol the composer was first represented in the Ellington book by *Admiration*, which was recorded 20 March 1930. More Tizol compositions were to follow, many of them in a Latin vein, which was fresh and exotic in the thirties and early forties: *Moonlight Fiesta, Jubilesta, Pyramid, Conga Brava, Bakiff,* and *Moon Over Cuba*. Of Tizol's most famous piece in this style, Dan Morgenstern has written: "Even if Juan Tizol had composed nothing else, he would doubtless remain immortal for having written *Caravan* . . ."[14] Like some of Tizol's other pieces, *Caravan* was first recorded by a small group, in this case, Barney Bigard and "His Jazzopaters," 19 December 1936. The famous recording of this tune made by the full Ellington band is discussed in greater length later in this chapter.

Unquestionably, Tizol was instrumental in bringing the Latin influence to the Ellington band. On occasion he would play tambourine or maracas on these pieces.[15] Tizol also wrote pieces that were not Latin-influenced, including two lovely ballads, *Lost in Meditation* and *A Gypsy Without a Song*, as well as the perennial jam session favorite, *Perdido*.

There is little question that on a day to day basis, one of Tizol's greatest contributions to the Ellington organization was in his capacity as "extractor." Tizol took Ellington's working scores and extracted, that is, copied out, the individual parts from the score. As a well-trained musician, Tizol was evidently extremely facile at transposing the parts for each instrument in what Bigard called "such beautiful handwriting." Bigard described the process: "He [Tizol] would write all the individual parts out and give them back to Duke, who would in turn check them over then pass them out to the band."[16] With a composer who was as prolific as Ellington, countless hours must have been spent at this unenviable task, frequently under adverse condi-

10 Woodman interview with the author.
11 Schuller has incorrectly contended that Lawrence Brown played the extended trombone solo in the *Black* section of *Black, Brown and Beige* (*Swing Era*, 145).
12 *Music is My Mistress*, 56.
13 *The World of Duke Ellington*, 117.
14 "Notes on the Music," in booklet for Time-Life *Giants of Jazz* record set *Duke Ellington*, STL-J02 (Alexandria, Virginia, 1978), p. 42.
15 Willard, reel one.
16 Bigard, 63.

tions and ominously impending deadlines, as Ellington was notorious for bringing in new pieces, even major ones, at the last possible moment. Tizol recalled copying for "a couple of days and nights" with no sleep, with Ellington's personal physician, Dr. Arthur Logan, helping out with a "shot for the eyes."[17]

Tizol left Ellington in 1944. There is some speculation about why he decided to leave the band, but one of Tizol's principal concerns was that he was not spending enough time with his wife, who then lived in Los Angeles. Tizol signed a contract to join Woody Herman's band, but when he got a more attractive offer to join Harry James, Herman graciously let him out of the contract. James was based in California, and Tizol was able to spend more time at home. Last minute efforts by Ellington to keep him were to no avail.

After seven years with James, Tizol returned to Ellington at a critical juncture in the band's career. Ellington referred to this as "another one of those important intersections in my life."[18]

Juan Tizol (Collection of John Miner)

After numerous defections by crucial members of the band during the forties, Ellington was struck in 1951 by what some observers sensed would be the mortal blow to the organization. Two of the greatest soloists Ellington had, Johnny Hodges and Lawrence Brown, and the only drummer Ellington had ever had, Sonny Greer, left the band. Ellington managed to persuade Tizol to return to solidify the trombone section, and Tizol in turn talked two of his mates from James's band, veteran alto saxophonist Willie Smith and dynamic young drummer Louie Bellson, into coming with him. The damage caused by the loss of the Ellington veterans was minimized. This time around, Tizol stayed with Ellington for almost three years, although there were periodic absences when he went home to see Rose.

Tizol returned to James in 1953 and played with him on and off until 1960. Also during the fifties he worked long stretches with Nelson Riddle's orchestra, which included stints backing up Frank Sinatra and playing on Nat "King" Cole's television show. He returned very briefly to Ellington's band in 1960 and continued to work sporadically on the West Coast and in Las Vegas in the early sixties. Tizol retired to Los Angeles, where he died in 1984.

17 Willard, reel one.
18 *Music is My Mistress*, 57.

19 Designation of race in the
United States has long been a
delicate and often foolish affair.
"Whites" with a minute percen-
tage of black blood have been
considered black, yet "blacks"
with a minute amount of white
blood have never been considered white. I do not know Tizol's
family history and do not consider it important. Generally,
though, it is safe to say that
Tizol was considered white. See,
in particular, references in
Richard Boyer's article from
1944, reprinted in Gammond.

20 Personal interview with Clark
Terry, 17 February 1989.

21 Related at the International
Ellington Conference '91, Los
Angeles, California, June 1991.

22 The light-skinned Creole Barney
Bigard also was made up darker
than his normal complexion.

23 In particular, Tizol went into
almost uncontrollable laughter
in his interview with Spilka.

24 Mingus's version of the story is
on 233-234 of Beneath the
Underdog.

25 Mingus's preoccupation with
racial prejudice is well-known.
In his interview with Willard
(reel 3), Tizol, in addressing
Mingus's version of the story,
said flatly that "I don't believe I
ever used the word 'nigger' in
my whole life." On the basis of
his tenure of almost eighteen
years with the Ellington band, it
is difficult to believe that Tizol
harbored racist feelings.

There are several interesting footnotes to Tizol's career with Ellington. For many years the light-skinned Puerto Rican was considered the only white man in an otherwise all-black band.[19] Nothing in any record indicates that Tizol or the other members of the band were uncomfortable with this situation. Yet certainly there must have been some uncomfortable racial situations that arose from having this light-skinned member in a "black" band. Stories of problems with whites in black bands and blacks in mostly white bands are part and parcel of jazz history and the social realities of American life. Clark Terry has related a number of stories of unfortunate racial situations that the Ellington band had to deal with in the 1950s, when both Tizol and Louie Bellson were in the band – as well as at least one very light- skin-ned black, Willie Smith.[20] When Claire Gordon, a white woman, was band secretary in the mid-1940s, Ellington   suggested that there were times when she should not be seen on the street with "the men" of the band, at least not unless her "escort" Tizol was with her.[21]

One bit of documentary evidence that we have of the racial situation is footage from the 1930 Amos and Andy movie *Check and Double Check*, in which the Ellington band appeared. It is obvious from the film footage that Tizol had been made up to appear to have darker skin.[22] Whatever audience the movie studio considered most critical for the success of this movie, it was deemed inappropriate to have a racially mixed band appear on screen.

It may be something of a surprise to find that Tizol, the most "classically" trained of all the musicians in Ellington's band, was notorious in the band as its biggest practical joker. Stories abound of Tizol pulling jokes on various members of the band, as well as on Ellington himself. These incidents usually involved such standard items as itching powder, firecrackers, hot feet and worse. It is obvious from interviews that Tizol took great pleasure in pulling these tricks, as years later he laughed heartily at the memory of some of these incidents.[23]

A darker incident was related by Charles Mingus in his bizarre memoir *Beneath the Underdog*.[24] According to Mingus, a disagreement with Tizol, complete with physical threats, a knife and racial epithets, led to Mingus's dismissal from the Ellington band after only a short stay in 1953. Tizol's recollection of the event was much different from Mingus's, and Tizol vehemently denied the racial overtones that Mingus gave the story.[25]

Tizol joined Ellington as a very capable musician who had played in a variety of styles and settings. Tizol was not, however, an improvising jazz musician. Over and over he stated that he was not "a jazz man." In his profile of the Ellington band in 1944, Richard Boyer included a long "scene" about Tizol confronting his role as a player in the Ellington band. Some of it may have been fabricated, but its essence would seem to be basically accurate. When asked in 1978 whether or not this story was true, Tizol replied (somewhat unconvincingly), "I guess so . . . if he says so."[26]

Juan Tizol once asked gloomily, at one of the dressing-room sessions, "What do you see in my playing anyway, Duke? I don't call myself a hot man anyway." There was a hurt tone in his voice. "Not for me. I take all my solos straight. Sweet style."

"Well, Juan," Duke said gently, "there are times when a writer wants to hear something exactly as it's written. You want to hear it clean, not with smears and slides on it. Besides, your style is good contrast to the more physical style of Johnny Hodges."

"I play with a legit tone," Juan said, as though accusing himself of something rather unforgivable. "Duke, what is there about my trombone tone?"

"You get an entirely different quality," Duke said. "It's real accurate. So many look on the valve trombone as an auxiliary instrument, and it's your main instrument. That's a hell of an obligation. You got to live up to those valves and you do, Juan, you do. You know how many slide trombonists use a slide so they can fake, and when you object they say, 'Watta ya think this has got on it – valves?'"

"If there was any room in legit, I'd still go back to legit," Tizol said. He seemed inconsolable. "I like legit because I could feature myself better in legit than in a jazz band. I don't feel the pop tunes, but I feel La Gioconda and La Boheme. I like pure romantic flavor. I can feel that better."

Duke said to the room at large, "Juan's got inhibitions. He won't ad-lib. Once on the Twelfth Street [R]ag, he did some ad-libbing. Only time he ever did."

. . . "You're a hell of a good man, Tizol," Duke said, making a final effort to comfort his trombone. "We need a man who plays according to Hoyle. A guy who does only one thing but does it for sure, that's it."

"I'm only legit," Tizol said.[27]

The solo that Ellington referred to was recorded 14 January 1931 (Example 3-1). This was one of the relatively few "jazzy" solos that Tizol recorded with the Ellington band.[28] Whether the solo was "ad-libbed" – improvised – or not is open to question. Perhaps Tizol did some improvising when the tune was played on live engagements, but had the solo worked out by the time

26 Willard, reel 5.

27 Originally in *The New Yorker*, reprinted in Gammond, 41-42 and *The Duke Ellington Reader*, 231.

28 Another good example of his rare "jazzy" soloing is on *Moon Over Dixie*, recorded 2 February 1932.

the arrangement was recorded. The solo gives the listener a sense of its having been planned ahead of time. The first eight measures of the chorus proper use the 3/8 pattern of the melody of the tune. Tizol uses an ascending half-step pattern in contrast to the original melody's descending diatonic pattern which is given as Example 3-1A. The sequential pattern of measures 13 and 14 also suggests that the solo had been worked out, although of course many improvisers do create sequential patterns spontaneously. Assuming that the solo was worked out ahead of time, Tizol was not out of line with what was standard practice of the era. Not only were solos worked out ahead of time, but once solos were recorded, they were often performed like the recorded version for the life of the arrangement. (See further discussion of this subject in Chapter 4.) The most startling part of this solo is the two bar break at the beginning. This somewhat convoluted chromatic passage, which incidentally is extremely difficult to play at the tempo at which the piece was recorded, effects a modulation from the key of A-flat to C. Listening to this break, one is bound to feel unsettled until the new key is established at measure three.

On several occasions Tizol supplied Ellington arrangements with wild, improbable breaks. Another good example of one of these breaks can be heard on *Dinah*, recorded 9 January 1932.[29] Barney Bigard recalled the recording of one of Tizol's compositions.

I remember once we were making a record of Conga Brava and Tizol had a break. He break [sic] this break so it just sounded out of this world. It was great. A real gem, never-could-happen-twice sort of idea and it was so beautiful, but he stopped just short of the end and yelled, "Oh no. That's no good." Duke had a fit. "That was the best break you ever made in your life," said Duke. "Damn it. Why did you stop?"

"It wasn't perfect," said Tizol. He just wanted his music a certain way. Incidentally he never made the break again.[30]

As previously noted, Tizol most often appeared as a soloist with Ellington in the capacity of presenting a melody performed "straight." For the most part Tizol played these melodic solos very much in the manner of a "classical" player – with expression and feeling, but as the melodies were written, with little of the freedom of interpretation that so many jazz players employ in melodic statements.

An important feature of any solo melodic statement is tone quality. The unique Tizol tone has been described in a variety of

29 Schuller has notated this break (*Swing Era*, 52), and described it as "surely . . . the first bop 'lick' ever, long before Parker and Gillespie."

30 Bigard, 57-58. Tizol has no break on the recorded versions of *Conga Brava*, and one wonders if Bigard might have been thinking of some other tune.

EXAMPLE 3-1

EXAMPLE 3-1A

etc.

ways. Schuller describes it as "thin-ish [and] penetrating," and also "leathery." He attributes Tizol's "timbre and delivery" to his training in "the Italian concert/military band tradition which flourished in the nineteenth century in all of Latin America and survives to this day."[31] Alun Morgan simply calls the sound "warm."[32] Leonard Feather refers to Tizol's style as "mellifluous."[33] Tizol's sound resulted not only from his conception of sound, but also from his actual instrument. Most trombone players feel that valve trombone has a "stuffier" sound than slide trombone (although in popular Latin bands the sound of the valve trombone is often extremely bright). Tizol's horn was pitched in the key of C, unlike most valve trombones and virtually all slide trombones, which are pitched in B-flat. At least one horn that Tizol played, now in the possession of John Sanders (see Chapter 6) has a bore that is larger than that of most valve trombones rather than smaller, as would be expected from a higher-pitched instrument. Thus, Tizol was able to get a richer and "freer" sound than might be expected on valve trombone. Having listened to many recordings of diverse quality, I would describe his sound as rich and full, somewhat dark in timbre, with a characteristic vibrato that was fast and wide.

Caravan, one of Tizol's best-known compositions, was, as previously mentioned, originally recorded 19 December 1936 by Barney Bigard and His Jazzopaters. As on many of the other tunes that he wrote, Tizol has the first melodic statement in the big band recording of the tune recorded 14 May 1937. The long notes of this statement (Example 3-2) display Tizol's individual sound. At the beginning of the recording of *Caravan*, the rhythm section vamp immediately establishes the mood. The theme, especially in its novel setting by Ellington, reflects the exotic Near-Eastern atmosphere of its title, which was not supplied by Tizol. Tizol's "exotic" musical influences were of course from much closer – Latin America. A number of his pieces have elicited commentary that refers to the Mideast rather than their Western roots. Schuller describes the melody of *Caravan* as "[a] sinuous theme, one of those melodies which, once heard, cannot be gotten out of mind."[34] Tizol's statement of the melody is enhanced by Harry Carney's baritone saxophone countermelody and, at phrase endings, by the menacing plunger growls of Cootie Williams's trumpet. Tizol's delivery of the theme is freer rhythmically than might be expected from a musician who was so often classified as "legit." In the published edition of the piece,[35] all of the moving notes of the melody (measures 3-4, 7-8, 11-12, etc.) are written as quarter notes. The notated

31 *Swing Era*, 69, 88.
32 Alun Morgan, "Duke Ellington on Record: The Nineteen-fifties," in Gammond, 108.
33 Feather, 442.
34 *Swing Era*, 87-88.
35 The piano-vocal sheet music score of this piece referred to here was copyrighted in 1937 by American Academy of Music, Inc.

Example 3-2

example only approximates what Tizol actually played, but even in this approximation it is apparent that he did not play the moving notes as equal note values. The B section of the piece, measures 33-48, is of a completely different character than the A section. The switch from F minor to an F dominant harmony brightens the color of the composition, and while the rhythm section's vamp remains similar to what it had been for the first thirty-two measures, the impression is that it, too, has lightened.[36] Tizol's style also changes radically. The long lines of the opening section are replaced by swing eighth notes and triplets. This passage displays Tizol at his jazziest. Measures 33-40 not only swing, but sound very much up-to-date in the context of the jazz phrasing of 1937. The two beat triplet figures starting in measure 41 are not as modern sounding (they could have come out of the vocabulary of a soloist with a "sweeter" band), but they do help to make an effective transition back to the A theme, which is then stated by Barney Bigard.

Altogether this forty-eight measure passage is representative of the strength of Tizol's solo playing as both a persuasive interpreter of melody and as a technically accomplished jazz instrumentalist. Whether the B section of this solo was improvised or not cannot be answered. This section is virtually identical to what Tizol played on the original small band recording. This does not preclude, of course, his having improvised the solo at some point in its development. The important point, however, is that whether or not the solo was improvised, it is convincing musically in its setting – and, it swings.

Tizol's work in 1938 on *Battle of Swing* presents him in yet another context. This Ellington piece may not seem as distinctively "Ellington" as some of his other works, but it is an excellent example of swing music from this era. Schuller has discussed the piece at length, describing its look forward to Ellington's 1940 classic *Cottontail* and the language of bop, as well as its look back to the baroque concerto grosso concept.[37] Whether the baroque concerto grosso had any effect on the composition of this piece is open to question, but a prominent feature of this arrangement is the use of a four-piece "group within a group" that is contrasted throughout with the full ensemble.[38] (Later on this kind of group was referred to in Ellington's arrangements as the "pep section.") Tizol's contribution to the small group was his usual clean, accurate playing. He later plays a twelve-bar blues chorus on this cut (Example 3-3).[39] At this point, the piece has modulated to the key of G-flat, a key rarely encountered in jazz arrangements. The recently discovered score for this work,

36 The bass plays four to the bar for most of the A section and switches to a two-beat feel in the B section. Otherwise the vamp remains much the same.

37 *Swing Era*, 103. This section of Schuller's book first appeared in the essay "Ellington vs the Swing Era," the liner notes to the Smithsonian album *Duke Ellington 1938,* Smithsonian R003 P2-13367 (Washington, D.C., 1976).

38 For more on the use of the small group in *Battle of Swing,* see Appendix 1.

39 My thanks to Andrew Homzy for supplying me with the copy of this score.

with its original title *Le Jazz Hot*, reveals that Tizol's solo was completely written out. The setting, with its dissonant background figures in the trumpets, perhaps suggests something other than a conventional blues solo, and Ellington has constructed a chorus that gives Tizol a blues voice unlike any other member of the band.[40] Listening to the recorded solo shows that Tizol made some very definite interpretations of articulations, which are not notated in the original score. Something about the way he places brisk staccato articulations, particularly in the figure that appears in measures 3-4 and 7-8, gives the solo a slightly off-kilter feeling. The only change in notes that Tizol makes from what is written in the score is to raise the G-flats on beat four of measures 4 and 8 an octave into an easier range.[41] Uncharacteristically, Tizol slightly "muffs" the sixteenth notes in measures two and six, but they are notated as in the score, as it sounds as if he tried to play them as written.

Certainly Ellington conceived the solo with Tizol in mind, and it is fascinating that he gave Tizol this quirky and unique statement in the wonderful body of work that the Ellington band created in the late thirties and forties.

40 The reader may wish to compare it, for example, to Nanton's *Black and Tan Fantasy, Ko-Ko,* or *Main Stem* solos discussed in chapter 2, or Brown's *Bundle of Blues* or *Blue Light* solos in chapter 4.

41 Tizol also makes a slight rhythmic displacement in measure 2.

EXAMPLE 3-3

One of Tizol's most prominent solo roles was as one of the principal soloists on the acclaimed *Come Sunday*, from the first movement of *Black, Brown and Beige*. Tizol begins his solo with a few statements in the transition to the *Come Sunday* section. His is the only open brass voice, playing his lines first over the rest of the brass section, which is muted, then over the saxophone section. Tizol then offers the first solo statement of the *Come Sunday* theme (Example 3-4). The example is notated according to the score published by Tempo in 1946, with the eighth note as the unit of beat in the first four measures and the quarter note the unit of beat thereafter. It is played in Tizol's characteristic style: straightforward, with little inflection added to the line, but colored by his burnished tone and intense vibrato. The only accompaniment is sustained chords in saxophones and bass. The tempo is rather free at this point, with a noticeable accelerando in the third measure, followed immediately by a ritard. The next six measures (measures 5-10) are "filler," concluding with a quote from the spiritual *Swing Low, Sweet Chariot* in the final two measures. Eleven measures of saxophone section lead to the solo violin of Ray Nance, who states a new theme. After eight measures, Tizol reenters "underneath" Nance, with another statement of thematic material (Example 3-4A) – an ingenious variation on the main "Come Sunday" theme, in counterpoint to Nance's rhapsodic violin lines, and again backed by saxophones and bass. Tizol plays two virtually identical phrases (measures 1-8 and 9-16), while Nance plays two phrases that are quite different from one another. The rhythm Tizol plays in measure 3 is not what is written in the Tempo score, and is probably his own interpretive addition, yet he plays it the same way on both renditions of the eight bars. It is not clear from the recording if Tizol ascends to a high C at the end of the first eight-measure phrase or simply plays a middle C.[42] On the repetition of the phrase, however, he projects the high C beautifully. All of this activity precedes Johnny Hodges's sublime performance of the entire thirty-two measure theme.

In retrospect, it might be asked why Ellington had Tizol play this material. Why not Lawrence Brown, the superb lead player who was widely known for his brilliant ballad interpretations? Perhaps Ellington wanted the "classicism" of Tizol's approach to playing the melody, rather than the "romanticism" of Brown's usual style. With Tizol, Ellington knew that he would get a performance devoid of excessive ornamentation, rhapsodizing or sentimentality – criticisms that had been leveled at some of Brown's playing.

42 When Claude Jones played the solo on the December 1944 Carnegie Hall concert, he played a middle C the first time and a high C the second time.

EXAMPLE 3-4

EXAMPLE 3-4A

Juan Tizol was not primarily a jazz soloist. Yet his playing was an essential part of the Ellington palette for many years on the strength of his dependably accurate performance in a variety of ensemble roles and as a melodic soloist with a distinctive voice. His excellent command of the valve trombone can be heard to good advantage on many compositions in many styles. In addition to the four examples analyzed, I recommend in particular the Latin pieces *Pyramid* (7 June 1938), the previously-mentioned *Conga Brava* (15 March 1940), and *Bakiff* (5 June 1941). Fine ballad playing can be heard on *Lost in Meditation* (2 February 1938), *A Gypsy Without a Song* (20 June 1938) and Billy Strayhorn's outstanding composition *Chelsea Bridge* (17 September 1941). Tizol also wrote compositions that were critical to the development of a body of Latin American influenced music in the Ellington book. He was the copyist that brought most of Ellington's music to the band for the better part of two decades. Although Tizol left and returned to the Ellington orchestra on several occasions, his place in Ellingtonia was established by the time he first left in 1944.

Tizol's part for his own composition Bakiff, written in his own hand.
Duke Ellington Collection, Archives Center, National Museum of American History, Smithsonian Institution.
Music by Juan Tizol. Copyright © 1942 (Renewed) by Tempo Music, Inc. and Music Sales Corporation (ASCAP).
All rights administered by Music Sales Corporation. International Copyright Secured.
All Rights Reserved. Used by Permission.

Lawrence Brown (Photo by Duncan P. Schiedt)

Lawrence Brown, the Virtuoso

4

Lawrence Brown was born 3 August 1907 in Lawrence, Kansas. When he was six or seven years old, his family moved to Oakland, California. Brown's mother played piano and organ, and his father, an African Methodist Episcopal minister, did a lot of singing. Growing up in a relatively musical environment, young Lawrence first got excited about music when he "got crazy about a violin." One of his father's church members gave him a violin, but he "got sick of that pretty quickly."[1] Subsequently, he started playing instruments in the Oakland school music program. His first wind instrument was tuba. He studied this instrument long enough to get to the point where he played a solo – *Silent Night* – at age nine or ten. But the tuba is, of course, a heavy instrument, and he "got sick of carrying that." While Brown experimented with a number of other instruments, he was also learning keyboard, presumably from his mother.

While doing janitorial work in his father's church with his two brothers, Lawrence discovered a trombone in the church choir loft.

And I had never inspected the feel of trombone. And so after a while I said, "Well, here's one I've never tried." And I theorized that the trombone should be the violin of brass instruments. And the tone of the trombone was about the same as a cello. And I like the cello tone very much. So I said, "Now, why, if it's the string instrument of brass instruments – why can't I play the same thing on trombone that they play on cello?"[2]

Evidently, Brown saw the trombone as a melodic instrument from the very beginning. He wanted to play melodies on the instrument, rather than "the usual oompah or whatever, dixie-type playing that was done [on the trombone at that time]." He played cello parts and cello solos on the trombone. He joined the school orchestra in Oakland, but shortly thereafter moved to Pasadena in southern California.[3] In Pasadena, Brown "really started playing in the school orchestras in a big way and really became interested in the trombone as the instrument that I thought I would stick with."[4] It is unclear from the interviews exactly what the sequence of events was in Brown's school

1 Unless otherwise noted, biographical information comes from Brown's interviews with Bill Spilka and Patricia Willard, with corroboration from *The World of Duke Ellington*.

2 Spilka.

3 Willard, reel 1. At one point in the interview, Brown says that he was about twelve years old when the family moved to Pasadena, at another point he says that it was around 1923, when he would have been about sixteen. Dance says that Brown lived in San Francisco for a year before moving to Pasadena. (*The World of Duke Ellington*, 118.)

4 Spilka.

career, but he did talk about his practice habits from those days.

I would rehearse for hours and hours, playing melodies, listening to tone and trying to improve my conception of how I wanted the instrument to sound. I would sit up after school and way up in the night with no lights on and just listen to the tones come back from the walls, and phrase things as I would like to hear them, until I became quite adept at the playing of these melodies.[5]

The wife of Brown's teacher in Pasadena, Mr. Parker, would accompany Brown on piano, and Lawrence would perform solos at churches. One of the highlights of Brown's early performing career, and an experience that he was never to forget, took place on Mother's Day, evidently in 1927. Brown was selected to play for a crowd of some 6,000 people at a performance by evangelist Aimee Semple McPherson in her temple. The stage-fright that Brown felt at this performance stayed with him throughout his career.[6]

Against the wishes of his father, Lawrence also became interested in jazz and dance music. He would sneak out of the house at night to go hear dance bands. Because of the disagreement with his father about jazz and dance music, Lawrence moved out of his family's home when he was about eighteen and moved in with a cousin in another part of Pasadena.

Brown was attending junior college in Pasadena and studying in the pre-medicine program, but after leaving home he started performing professionally almost immediately. Brown remembers playing a date with a group led by Les Hite shortly after Hite came to California. Brown was still a student at Pasadena Junior College, but played the engagement with a group with which he was to spend a great deal of time in a few years.

His first regular job was with a band led by Charlie Echols at the 401 Ballroom in Los Angeles. He soon joined Paul Howard's Quality Serenaders, and also worked up and down the West Coast with a band led by Curtis Mosby. Brown recorded a number of titles with Howard in 1929-30. Paul Howard eventually ended up working at Sebastian's Cotton Club in Culver City. Several leaders led the band at the club the next few years, but Brown and Lionel Hampton, who had individual contracts with the club's ownership, stayed on. In 1930, Les Hite took over leadership of the band. Louis Armstrong had two extended stays at Sebastian's during 1930-32, and Brown, as a member of Hite's band, recorded four cuts with Armstrong in 1930. Throughout his time at Sebastian's, Brown and the other members of the band were working almost constantly at movie studios in Hollywood. They appeared regularly in movies that

5   Willard, reel 1.
6   Willard, reel 2. Commenting on this experience and his continued stage fright for the rest of his career, Brown said, "I can do anything I want when nobody's there. But the minute you see . . . those people out there, then something happens."

featured cabaret scenes or other scenes with live bands. This lucrative sideline to their regular engagement allowed Brown to indulge in one of his early passions, a sixteen-cylinder Cadillac.

One of Brown's specialities at Sebastian's Cotton Club was his working in the manner of a strolling violinist at the club, going from table to table playing requests for the patrons. It is even reported that he played right in the ear of those making the requests.[7] One can imagine that he must have played with a very soft and elegant sound to carry off this particular enterprise successfully. Brown likened the technique to the use of sub-tone on saxophone.[8]

As comfortable as Brown's life in California was, his stubbornness and sense of propriety, coupled with what turned out to be a happy coincidence, caused him to turn his back on it all. Armstrong's manager called a picture session for the afternoon of Easter Sunday, 1932. Brown refused to show up for the session and gave his notice. Apparently during the very same week, Ellington's manager, Irving Mills, had heard Brown in his feature at Sebastian's, *Trees*, and he was so impressed that he told Ellington that he should hire Brown. Mills was so insistent about Brown's ability that Ellington hired Brown without ever hearing him play. According to Brown, Ellington said, "I never knew you, I never met you, I never heard you. But Irving says get you, so that's that." On the Tuesday after Easter, 29 March 1932, Brown left Sebastian's and his life in California to join Ellington.[9]

Brown went back East with the Ellington band, but did not start playing with the group right away. Legend has it that Ellington's superstitious nature prevented him from adding a thirteenth member to his band, so Brown had to wait in the wings for Otto Hardwick to return from one of his periodic leaves from the band so the band would have fourteen members rather than the dreaded thirteen.[10] The pay in the Ellington band was much less than Brown had been earning in California, and he planned to be back in California (and with his beloved Cadillac) within a year. With the tight times of the Depression, however, he decided to stay with Ellington. He stayed for nineteen years.

The noted Ellington historian Stanley Dance has written about this critical juncture in the history of the Ellington band. "In 1932 trombonist Lawrence Brown came in, and the classic Ellington period may be said to have begun."[11] The date marks, of course, not just the year that an exceptional player was added to the band, but also a point where Ellington's creative genius

7 Correspondence from Art Pilkington, 29 December 1989.
8 For further information, see *The World of Ellington*, 121-122.
9 Willard, reel 3.
10 Mark Tucker, notes to interview with Lawrence Brown, 13 April 1985, Los Angeles, California. Tucker, however, also reports that Stanley Dance calls this nonsense, claiming that thirteen was Duke's lucky number.
11 "Duke Ellington," 21.

was coming into its full flower. Certainly, though, the addition of Brown gave the band not only a virtuosic new soloist, but also produced the first prominent trombone trio in a jazz band – a device Ellington was quick to exploit.

When the band went to the recording studio in May of 1932, Brown recorded his first solos with the band. A brilliant new soloist was revealed to the record buying public, and the Ellington band was never to be the same again. On May 16, *Sheik of Araby* was recorded, followed by *Best Wishes* on the 17th and *Slippery Horn* on the 18th. These three recordings tell much about what Brown was to mean to the band.

Sheik will be discussed at some length later on; let it suffice here to quote Stanley Dance. "[I]t was not his romantic way with a ballad that originally impressed musicians. It was his speed, as on *The Sheik of Araby* [sic]."[12] *Best Wishes* was a "sweet" ballad that featured Brown in a role that Ellington had him assume time and time again. *Slippery Horn* was the first feature for Ellington's new three-man trombone section, one of the first in jazz. The section's excellent opening chorus was topped off by Brown's high F on the last note, a note that was virtually unheard of for trombone in a section context.

While Ellington had the luxury of a trio of trombones for the first time, he did not revise the old tunes for his new man. Brown had to make up his own parts for arrangements that were already in the band's book.

In some ways Brown's personality did not seem to fit into the Ellington band. Throughout its history, but perhaps especially in the 1930s, the band was known to be made up of men who lived life to the fullest. Never would the band be accused of being a group of choirboys. Into this came Brown, whose ways led to him being called "The Deacon," and "Rev" (short for "Reverend"). Rex Stewart again gives insight into one of his bandmates.

Lawrence Olin Brown played a golden-toned horn which long ago catapulted him into the select hierarchy of creative innovators. Larry, in appearance, resembled the Baptist minister who has wandered into the wrong place seeking converts more than he looked like the popular conception of a jazz musician. He was a handsome man, always immaculately dressed. And his personal life bore no relation to the image his horn conveyed. He neither drank nor smoked, he used neither slang nor profanity; and he seldom bothered to smile except through his instrument, which expressed all of the emotions ranging from savagery to tender, sensuous love for humanity.[13]

12 *The World of Duke Ellington*, 117.
13 Stewart, *Boy Meets Horn*, 153.

Quentin Jackson, who was Brown's section mate in the Ellington band of the late 1940s colorfully described Brown's place in the band and some of his habits.

. . . He was very immaculate, very immaculate. A very clean guy. . . [A] very neat guy. . . Here was a guy that used to shave with two razors so his face would be really clean . . . he would shave with a safety razor and then he would finish it off with a straight razor. I think Lawrence used to let the cuffs down [on] his pants and dust them out at night even. . . Ben [Webster] nicknamed him Sweety Brown because of him being so nice and always so neat and everything. And he kept this sponge in his pocket, Lawrence did, to wipe his face off all the time, you know, so that there would be no shine on his face."

Brown apparently rarely went out and jammed with any of the other band members. And "he wasn't a guy that you could kid with or nothing, either." Bandmate Barney Bigard spoke about Brown's "grumpy" nature.[14] Yet Jackson adds that "he was so perfect and he soloed so perfect."[15]

It is no secret that Brown did not get along particularly well with Ellington. Collier talks about the "abrasive" relationship that existed between the two men.[16] Personal animosity between the two led to professional differences. Brown did talk about one fairly serious disagreement he had with Ellington about who should get credit for the composition of *Sophisticated Lady*. He spoke further about being fired by Ellington when he refused to take over the plunger parts after Tricky Sam Nanton's death in 1946. A conciliatory phone call, however, brought him back after only a few days away from the band.[17]

Through all of this, Brown remained one of the band's most important soloists, and he was called upon by Ellington to supply just the right musical touch in a variety of compositions throughout the glory days of the '30s and '40s.

Brown finally did leave the band in 1951 and spent most of the next decade in New York City. He first worked with the small group of Johnny Hodges, who had left Ellington at the same time as Brown after an even longer tenure with the Ellington band. Later, Brown joined the staff orchestra at CBS in New York. He recorded prolifically during the '50s, not only with Hodges and with the CBS orchestra, but on record dates with artists running the gamut from Jackie Gleason's romantic orchestra to the shouting of blues singer Joe Turner.

In 1960, Brown returned to Ellington. After "Butter" Jackson, Booty Wood and Lou Blackburn had left the band, Brown finally took over the plunger role that had been created by his longtime section mate Tricky Sam Nanton. Stanley Dance

14 Bigard, 70.
15 All quotes except Bigard's from Milt Hinton's interview with Quentin Jackson, June 1976.
16 Collier, 129-130.
17 Willard, reel 5.

described Brown's position in the 1960s:

[A]ll the traditional Ellington trombone roles are united in Brown. The melodic theme statements fall to him; the romantic variations and "that fast stuff" are delivered in the style he originated; and . . . he is also responsible for the plunger solos.[18]

In 1970, Brown left the Ellington band for good. He never played his horn again. He went to Detroit and got married and after about a year joined his cousin's consulting firm in Washington, D.C. While there he was on the advisory committee at the Kennedy Center for the Performing Arts. In 1972, he moved back to Los Angeles, where he worked for the musicians' union for several years. He died in Los Angeles, 5 September 1988, at the age of 81.

The impressive style and technique that many listeners were introduced to through the early recordings that Brown made with Ellington were already known to some jazz insiders, particularly those on the West Coast. Some of Brown's recordings with Paul Howard from 1929 and 1930 display a body of technique that was already fully developed. Brown never recorded anything with Ellington that surpassed the technical intricacy of his solos on *Charlie's Idea*, *Harlem*, and *Cuttin' Up* with Howard's band. Years later Quentin Jackson said,

Nobody ever heard a trombone player like that. Nobody knew who he was or anything because nobody ever went to California. I never heard nothing [sic] so fast. I never heard a trombone player like that, not like Lawrence was playing in those days.[19]

The recordings that Brown did with Louis Armstrong in 1930 show to good advantage his already well-developed ballad interpretation. On *If I Could Be With You* and *I'm Confessin'* Brown plays much in the style of the decorated ballad statements that he made famous with Ellington. *I'm In the Market For You* features an unabashedly "sweet" melodic statement from Brown of the sort that certain jazz critics decried when it would appear in Ellington charts. With Ellington, however, Brown brought to the broad jazz and dance band audience a style unlike that of any other trombonist of the time.

It is noteworthy that there was no problem in Ellington's trombone section of Brown taking over spots that had previously been held by the other trombonists. Each of the players was exhibited in a style that he (in conjunction with Ellington) had established as his own in the band. When Brown first joined, he was immediately featured on up tempo numbers that displayed his excellent and seemingly effortless facility. He also

18 *The World of Duke Ellington*, 118.
19 Jackson interview, reel 3.

became associated with slower "mood pieces" and ballads, as well as assuming the role of accompanist on a number of vocals in the Ellington book. Joe "Tricky Sam" Nanton maintained the role he had developed along with Bubber Miley in the '20s as a premier plunger soloist. Juan Tizol, as a soloist, was primarily entrusted with straightforward melodic statements, often on pieces of Latin American influence that he composed, and he continued his valuable role as a voice that could be scored with saxophones or trumpets. Together, the trombonists formed a section that could negotiate such challenges as *Slippery Horn* with their new man, Brown, playing the lead parts.

Sheik of Araby was recorded on Brown's first day in the studio with the Ellington orchestra. Besides the speed mentioned previously, there are a number of other things that must have impressed musicians about Brown's solo (Example 4-1). Brown was a trombonist who played easily, almost effortlessly, at both the top (measures 9, 28-32) and bottom (m. 8, 20) of the horn. He also negotiated the difficult passage of octave leaps (m. 21-22) and the almost equally difficult sixth and seventh leaps (m. 25-26) with ease. A beautifully controlled lip trill, started three beats after the principal note is reached, climaxes the solo in measures 29-30. Throughout, there is a swing feel that is decidedly relaxed for 1932. The shape and pacing of the solo are also impressive. To break up the predominantly eighth note flow of the solo that was established in the first half, quarter-note triplets are used to excellent effect, particularly in measures 17-19. There is a logical progression to the technical display of measures 21-22 and 25-26, and finally into the long glissando and the held and trilled note immediately before the end. While Ellington's arrangement of this Broadway show tune could have been eminently usable as a dance tune (and probably was), surely its main purpose was to show off the abilities of Brown.

It is reported in Ulanov's 1946 biography of Ellington, and subsequently elsewhere, that this solo was one of the two recorded solos that Brown had worked out ahead of time – that is, these solos were not improvised.[20] In a 1976 interview, Brown clarified how he planned out solos. He claimed that not only did he plan the *Sheik of Araby* solo ahead of time, but that he "did that almost every time."

In playing a tune I always kept the idea that there should always be some semblance of the melody, and never get too far away . . . [so] that the public couldn't tell what you were playing . . . [W]henever I would be given a solo . . . where the whole number sort of depended on me, I would plan the whole num-

20 Ulanov, 102.

ber. I had a system which I used to try to perfect these solos. I wouldn't get up and just play anything that came across my mind. I would first go into a study without the horn. I would mentally play the lead – I mean the theme, then with slight deviations, and then with more deviations, and then hear where the band would come in and make embellishments, and then I would come in with more.[21]

This careful planning and "practicing" resulted in polished performances and solos that were meaningful and well-organized. Quentin Jackson says that Brown "had everybody trying to play his solo on the *Sheik*."[22]

Slippery Horn featured Brown in a short solo spot and playing an astounding high F at the end of trombones' section chorus, but the tune was predominantly a showcase for the new three-man trombone section. Ellington has written that the title was inspired by his new man, and Brown's work in the studio on the three days that produced *Sheik of Araby*, *Best Wishes*, and *Slippery Horn* certainly makes it obvious that he had brought a new and facile voice to the section and band. In 1976, Brown claimed that he never knew that the composition was inspired by his playing – Ellington had never told him.

When the band went back into the recording studios in September of 1932, Brown was again featured on several solo spots. *Ducky Wucky* (Example 4-2) flirts with being a corny novelty number, but Brown's opening chorus is a stylish, beautifully played statement. Here, Brown is at what Schuller calls "his most dapper."[23] Once again, as on *Sheik of Araby*, the medium tempo allows Brown to play passages that are of considerable difficulty on the trombone with what seems to be the greatest of ease. The jerky long-short eighth note rhythm of the melody dominates the whole solo, but Brown manages to prevent it from becoming "ricky-ticky." It would be interesting to know how much of this melody was preconceived. The first four measures appear later in the tune in the saxophone section, but the remainder of this solo could be Brown's creation based on the chord progression. Especially striking, particularly from the standpoint of trombone playing, is the long descending glissando from the end of measure 12 through measure 13 and into the beginning of measure 14, where it briefly turns around. The solo builds to a peak in the last two measures of the bridge (measures 23-24), where the triplets, with the accents changing each beat, build tension to the high E-flat at the end of measure 24. Brown then "dirties up" the next few measures with short glissandos on the tonic, followed by the G-flat in measures 26 and

21 Willard, reel 4.
22 Jackson interview, reel 4.
23 *Swing Era*, 58.

Example 4-1

27, which becomes part of the chord in measure 28. The solo then winds down to a relaxed conclusion.

In the next several days, Brown recorded two more fine swing solos, on *Jazz Cocktail* and *Swing Low*.

In only a few brief months with Ellington, Brown had already established himself as Schuller characterized him –

three trombonists rolled into one: a superb original lyric stylist, a first-rate section leader and virtuoso technician, and on many occasions a highly original jazz trombonist . . . [24]

Late in his life, Ellington reserved his highest praise of Brown for his ability as an accompanist. In his autobiography *Music Is My Mistress*, Ellington stated,

As a soloist, his taste is impeccable, but his greatest role is that of an accompanist. The old-timers used to say, "Soloists are made, but accompanists are born." Lawrence Brown is the accompanist par excellence. [25]

On record, Brown first displayed his ability as an accompanist on *Baby!*, recorded in December of 1932 with Adelaide Hall as vocalist. Hall had established herself as a vocalist with the Ellington band on the famous 1927 recording of *Creole Love Call*. She was not the band's vocalist, per se, but she worked with the band at the Cotton Club in New York. Unlike her improvised wordless vocal on *Creole Love Call*, *Baby!* finds her in a more traditional role as a vocalist, singing this light tune in rather straightforward fashion. Like some of Brown's later vocal accompaniments, his work on *Baby!* is notable in that much of it could stand by itself as a fine jazz solo, yet it complements the vocal beautifully, without calling undue attention to itself. As might be expected, Brown saves much of his most active playing for the ends of phrases, where Hall is either holding notes or resting. He does nothing especially ambitious in this accompaniment, for the most part staying safely within the chord structure, and at two points playing close to the melody, even as Hall is singing it. He displays his outstanding technical ability with octave jumps and a beautiful lip trill, but again, never in a way that brings attention to the technique itself. The real strength of Brown's contribution is in the easy way that his relaxed commentary fits with the vocal. One of Brown's better known accompaniments will be discussed at greater length later in this chapter.

On 15 February 1933, Brown recorded another excellent swing solo on the standard *I've Got The World On A String*. But this recording date was more important for Brown and

24 Ibid., 681.
25 *Music is My Mistress*, 122.

EXAMPLE 4-2

Ellington for its introduction of what was to become an Ellington classic, *Sophisticated Lady*. There has been considerable speculation about the origin of the themes of this song. Brown discussed with Patricia Willard at some length how the tune evolved. He described it as "one of those [tunes where] everybody jumps in and helps out," but he went on to add that "mainly I had a theme which I played all the time which is the first eight bars." Otto Hardwick is often given credit for the theme of the bridge of the song. Brown expressed bitterness that he was never given co-composer credit for this song, his recompense for these eight bars (which, when repeated, become twenty-four of the tune's thirty-two bars) being a "terrific check of $15." With Ellington, evidently, "that check cancels you out. See, no one knew what was going to happen. You never know when you have a good coming number on your hands . . ." He even admitted that "in fact, we didn't care. We just was [sic] doing something we wanted to do." A theme or phrase like this "[was] not a solo – it was just a thing you played. There are always a lot of pieces or a lot of footage we'll say that was just played along. It had no particular meaning, or wasn't meant to be a piece. It was just like a – say an obbligato against something, or even an exercise study. But you pick up everything, you know." It was Ellington who was so good at "picking up everything." Brown claimed further that

> . . . this is one of the first times that we [he and Ellington] came near breaking up, because I told him that "I don't consider you a composer. You are a compiler." To which his ego boiled over.[26]

The fact that tunes were often sold in this manner in the '20s and '30s does not seem to have diminished Brown's ill feelings. And whatever the creative process, an evergreen was born.

On this February date (Example 4-3), Brown's reading of the first eight bars is close to how we have come to know the tune. On the last eight bars of the first chorus (essentially the same material) he repeats the material almost the same as previously, but with two chord members on each of the descending chromatic chords in the second and fourth bars of the phrase (only one note per chord is in the written melody) and slightly more rhythmic freedom. This chorus is capped off with a beautifully controlled high C. When the band re-recorded the tune in May (Example 4-3a), Brown has the first sixteen bars to state "his" theme. He seems somewhat more at ease with the melody, and his sound on this recording is beautifully creamy and lush. This is a good example of Brown's sound that Collier has described

26 All of the quotes about *Sophisticated Lady* are from Willard, reel 4.

After 16 measures out, Brown returns with the final eight measures of the chorus.

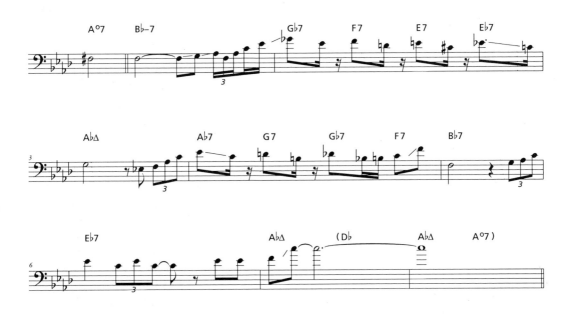

as "rich as chocolate and smooth as velvet."[27] The first eight measures again are about as straightforward as a jazz musician is likely to get with a theme. But in the next eight measures Brown allows his facility to surface briefly. The embellishments of measures 10, 11 and 12 are smooth enough to keep the flow of the theme going without interruption. The crisp virtuoso pickup at the end of measure 13, however, seems a bit out of place in this lyrical context. It almost seems as if in his youthful exuberance Brown could not hold down his remarkable technique for sixteen full measures.[28]

Brown first appeared on record as a blues soloist with Ellington on the excellent *Bundle of Blues*, recorded the same day as the second *Sophisticated Lady*, 16 May 1933 (Example 4-4). Ellington fashioned this rather simple arrangement as a slow blues that would feature several of his outstanding sidemen. Brown plays an impressive solo. As usual, he is in excellent command of the instrument, and his statement flows effortlessly. The recurrence of his opening figure in the ninth measure gives coherence to the solo. The wonderfully relaxed rhythmic feel to the solo is epitomized by measure five. It is impossible to notate the rhythm of this measure accurately: in the body of the solo, the notes have been written as three groups of four eighth notes. The notes Brown plays are grouped in this manner, but the groups of eighth notes speed up in the middle of the measure and then slow down slightly going into measure six. The way the notes fit the meter is approximated in Example 4-4A. Ellington's substitute blues chord changes give this tune a somewhat "major" cast. Brown uses the "blue" B-flat (the seventh of the C9 chord) extensively in measures five and six, and the high B-flat in measure ten is a true "blue" note, as it is almost a B-natural. Despite the use of the blue notes, and granting that the changes lend themselves to a more "major" sounding blues, Brown's solo is not as "bluesy" as that of several of his bandmates. The blues was to remain an area where Brown spoke with his own unique voice, but in a style which was never convincingly bluesy to some listeners. Most certainly his blues style, especially in the 1930s, did not feature the proliferation of "blue notes" or the "gutbucket" quality of some of his contemporaries. Granting that it is dangerous to describe music in nonmusical terms, one might describe the effect of Brown's blues playing as nostalgic, or reminiscent of a sense of malaise, rather than reflecting pain, deep suffering or sorrow. Many jazz fans, those who might have, for example, leaned strongly toward the style of blues of Brown's contemporaries, trombonists Big Charlie

27 Collier, 128.
28 On the recording of *Sophisticated Lady* from 14 February 1940, Brown plays full arpeggios on the chromatic seventh chords of the tenth and twelfth measures and ends his solo with a stunning high E-flat.

EXAMPLE 4-3A

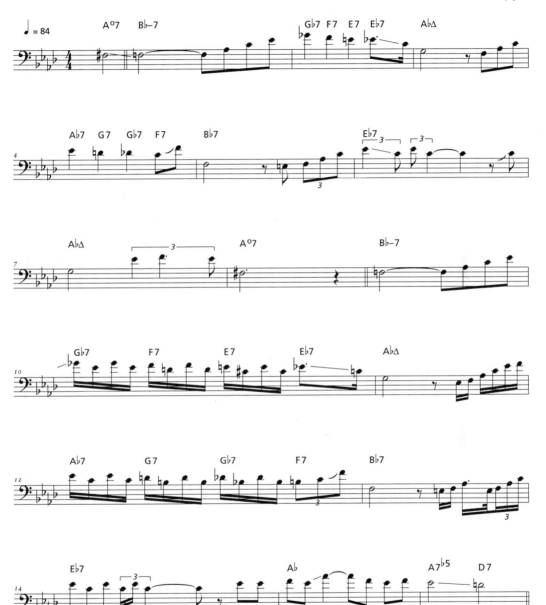

Green of Fletcher Henderson's band or the growling plunger work of Tricky Sam Nanton, did not care for the more understated, "cleaner" blues soloing of Lawrence Brown. Reaction to Brown's style is explored further later in the chapter.

Brown's place in the Ellington band was well established within a year of his joining. Unlike some of the other soloists in the band, Brown did not fill just one stylistic niche. He was the romantic balladeer, the outstanding section leader, the fabulous technician, the convincing swinger at medium tempos, the accomplished accompanist and the occasional blues player. A review of his solo work from the next several years shows him to have continued to function in all these contexts with a high degree of consistency and success. He continued his fine swing soloing on tunes like Fats Waller's *Ain't Misbehavin'* (13 July 1933), and Ellington originals like *Dallas Doings* (16 September 1933), *Chatterbox* (20 September 1937), and *Skrontch* (24 February 1938). He accompanied Ellington's regular band vocalist Ivie Anderson on tunes ranging from the infectious *Isn't Love the Strangest Thing* (27 February 1936) to the maudlin *My Old Flame* (9 May 1934).[29] His ballad interpretations were heard on both good and bad tunes, but they were an integral part of such Ellington classics as *Solitude* (10 January 1934) and *In a Sentimental Mood* (30 April 1935), as well as other fine standards, such as *There Is No Greater Love* (27 January 1936).

As he did for several of his great soloists, Ellington wrote a so-called "concerto" for Brown. *Yearning for Love (Lawrence's Concerto)*, recorded 17 July 1936, was not to be the great success that Ellington's concertos for Barney Bigard and Cootie Williams were, but it is a pleasant ballad that shows off Brown to good advantage. Schuller feels, however, that Brown "deserved at least a three-movement concerto to showcase his varied talents properly."[30]

As the Ellington band developed toward what many consider to be its peak years, the late 1930s through the early 1940s, Brown, too, continued to perform at a consistently high level. Three outstanding performances from 1938 highlight Brown's work from the beginning of this period.

Braggin' in Brass, recorded on 3 March 1938, caught the band at its virtuoso best. Based on the chord changes to the jazz chestnut *Tiger Rag*, the showy trumpet section work was based on a solo that trumpeter Freddie Jenkins perfected while with the band earlier in the '30s. The trombone section chorus from this flag waver chart is no less amazing today than it must have

29 This is the date of the recording with Ivie Anderson singing the tune. Only a few weeks earlier (23 April 1934), the band had recorded the tune with considerably different effect with guest vocalist Mae West.

30 *Swing Era*, 85.

EXAMPLE 4-4

EXAMPLE 4-4A

been when it was first performed. This passage is discussed in Appendix 1. Later in the piece Brown has a short solo spot (Example 4-5). The tempo (half note = about 152) is almost too much even for Brown's advanced technique. The first few bars of his solo are not quite as steady as they might be, but he recovers to deliver a convincing, yet musical statement – in a style that Schuller describes as "blistering." Few other trombonists in 1938 could have technically managed to deliver a solo based on eighth notes.

EXAMPLE 4-5

One of Brown's most famous and long-lived swing features at a moderate tempo was *Rose of the Rio Grande*, first recorded 7 June 1938 (Example 4-6). Brown's work on *Rose* was not as flashy or spectacular as on either the early *Sheik of Araby* or *Ducky Wucky*, but it was beautifully controlled and swinging throughout. After a short introduction, Brown takes the first chorus in this recording.[31] Example 4-6 is a transcription of Brown's second chorus, which followed Ivie Anderson's vocal chorus. The most notable feature of this third chorus is the unity attained through the extensive use of repeated figures in measures 1-2 and 5-6, and measures 17-18 and 21-22 (with a chromatic change to fit the chord changes). Measures 25-28 are virtually identical to the same measures in Brown's first chorus solo.

31 This first chorus has been transcribed by David Baker in *Jazz Styles and Analysis: Trombone*, 29.

EXAMPLE 4-6

This was the second of the two solos that were worked out completely ahead of time as reported by Ulanov in his book.[32] Brown did play the solo very close to its originally recorded version all the way into his second tenure with the band in the 1960s.[33] Schuller has discussed the whole issue of jazz players memorizing solos in connection with this very same 1938 solo and its subsequent performances.[34] Regardless of its origin and the process of its refinement, the solo stands up very well after many years and repeated hearings.

In December of 1938 Brown recorded another lovely blues solo, on an arrangement that recalled *Bundle of Blues* from more than five years earlier. *Blue Light* again featured a skeletal arrangement and a string of solos. The scored instrumentation for most of the arrangement features the *Mood Indigo* instrumentation – muted trumpet and trombone and clarinet in the low register with rhythm section.[35] There is no melody to *Blue Light*, rather there is just harmonic and instrumental color. Brown's solo (Example 4-7) follows the introduction, Barney Bigard's solo and an ensemble chorus. Technically, it is one of the simplest solo choruses that Brown ever recorded. There is nothing difficult to play in this chorus. The transcription only hints at the rhythm as Brown plays it, as he stretches and compresses the figures, placing them early and late in relation to the beat. It would be impossible to notate the rhythm completely accurately without writing something that would be almost indecipherable. It is very difficult to hear the harmony in both the horns and the rhythm section, but it is clear that there is some disagreement between Brown and the other players at some points. Some of the variations in the harmony are indicated in the chord changes in parentheses. Unlike some of his other solos, Brown claimed that this solo was completely "extemporaneous."[36] The solo's haunting melody was memorable enough that in 1946 Brown and Ellington fashioned a whole piece based on it – *Transblucency*. How bluesy is this solo? It is in the same style that was exhibited by Brown in *Bundle of Blues* – that is, it sounds like Lawrence Brown, but no one else, playing the blues. Schuller describes this solo as being "mysterious in the way the notes of [Brown's] theme and melody, worlds away from the blues, nevertheless merge with the basic blues frame."[37]

Through the triumphs of Ellington's great compositions and performances of the early forties, Brown carried on the roles assigned him with superlative professionalism. He can be heard at his usual level of excellence on recordings of small groups led

32 See note 20 in this chapter.
33 Listen to the version on the LP *Ella & Duke at the Cote D'Azur* (Verve v/v6-4072) or on Atlantic Jazz CD 304-2 The Great Paris Concert.
34 Notes to *Duke Ellington 1938*.
35 See Appendix I for the scoring of "Mood Indigo."
36 Willard, reel 4.
37 *Swing Era*, 110.

EXAMPLE 4-7

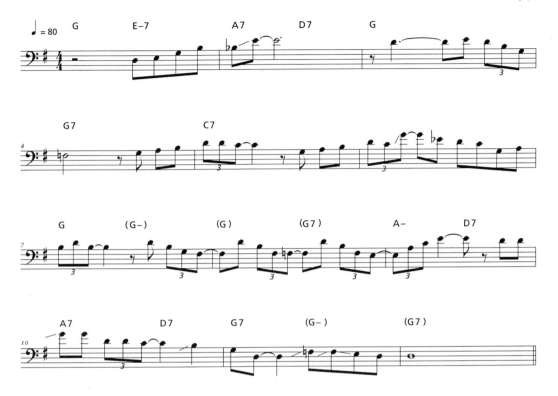

by Johnny Hodges and Rex Stewart as well as in the Ellington big band. One hears little really new in Brown's playing during this period, but he continued to play at an extremely high level. A review of the recordings of his ballad playing in the forties presents one with a body of almost flawless trombone playing. Claude Jones, who played alongside Brown in Ellington's trombone section from 1944 through 1948 once remarked in an interview that, "I sat next to [Brown] in the Ellington band for five years and never heard him make one mistake . . . and I can't say that for any other trombonist I know."[38] One can listen to recordings from just about any period in the 1940s and hear good examples of Brown's playing, but two short time periods offer especially fine examples. There are four cuts from the first half of 1942 that are particularly ravishing in sound and execution – *Moon Mist* (21 January), *I Don't Mind* and *Someone* (both from 26 February), and *My Little Brown Book* (26 June). The beauty of Brown's tone is apparent even though the first three of these solos are muted. The lovely sound of Brown's

38 Edwards, Sam. "An Evening With Claude Jones," in the column "Jazz Round-Up," *Brighton and Hove Gazette*, May (date obscured), 1961.

open horn can also be heard to good advantage on three out-standing ballad performances from 1947 – *Lady of the Lavender Mist* (14 August), *Golden Cress* (1 September), and *Maybe I Should Change My Ways* (6 October).

Quentin Jackson, who replaced Jones in the trombone section echoed Jones's sentiments and went further.

. . . I have never worked beside a man that played as consistently and as beautiful as this man played. He had so much soul — I have to say soul. He could play blues, he could play melody, and he could almost cry on the trombone. He made such beautiful records.[39]

Interestingly, Brown complained of his sound and the way it recorded. He thought it was "mooey" and had too much "oo" and not enough "ee." He compared it unfavorably with Tommy Dorsey's sound.[40] Duke, though, had obviously found a sound and a style that he thought was ideal for presenting a certain body of his work and he used it over and over.

Brown's swing playing did not change noticeably in general style or substance, but he continued to adapt to Ellington's experiments in style. Ellington's hard-driving *Main Stem*, recorded 26 June 1942, was almost in the style of rhythm and blues that was to emerge some years later. The chart elicited from Brown one of his most forceful and convincing solos (Example 4-8).

39 Jackson interview, reel 3.
40 *The World of Duke Ellington,* 120.

EXAMPLE 4-8

The bright tempo does not hinder him in the least. While obviously blowing hard and loud, he is able to easily negotiate the challenging arpeggio figure of measures 7-8, the triplets of measure 9, and the descending scalar passage of measures 13-14.

A good example of Brown the accompanist is on the well-known *I Let a Song Go Out of My Heart*, the recording under consideration from 15 May 1945 (Example 4-9). Brown's work on this selection is not continually changing in the way that some "modern" jazz accompanying is. His statements on all three of the A sections of this AABA song are virtually identical. The strength of the accompaniment is in its feeling of "rightness." Brown's part makes sense by itself, and more importantly, it fits neatly and comfortably with Joya Sherrill's vocal. In the A sections Brown tends to move when the vocal is static and remain inactive when the vocal is moving. The two parts are beautifully complementary. At the pickup into the bridge (measure 16) it becomes obvious that this particular rendition of the tune had either been performed a number of times, carefully rehearsed, or this particular section written out. The rhythm of measures 16-18 is considerably different from the way the tune is most often performed, but Brown and Sherrill execute this subtle rhythmic twist in almost exact synchronization. Also striking about the recording is the way the timbres of Sherrill's voice and Brown's trombone are so compatible, while operating in almost the same pitch range. It is hard to imagine another member of the Ellington band of this period who would have sounded as "right" in the same musical situation.

Despite the fact that Brown's blues playing was not bluesy in the sense that many other jazz players' was, Ellington assigned Brown yet another, "bluesy" role in the 1940s. The prototype of this role was unveiled in the 1943 film *Cabin In The Sky*. In the film, the band is playing for a group of energetic dancers. After concluding a hot dance number, Brown appears at the front of the stage and becomes a preacher preaching to his flock. The band punctuates Brown's long unaccompanied statements with short chords. Brown's playing in this performance was definitely of the "get down and dirty" school of blues playing – loud brash playing with a lot of blue notes. This cut was never recorded commercially, but a performance of it is preserved on the recording of the 1943 Carnegie Hall concert under the title of *Goin' Up*. Brown also became the "blues shouter" on one of the band's most famous blues, *Things Ain't What They Used To Be*,

EXAMPLE 4-9

and two other tunes that like *Goin' Up* were not blues in form, but certainly were in spirit – *I'm Just a Lucky So-and-So* and *Build That Railroad*. Most surprisingly, Brown "dirtied up" the extended performance of the classic Ellington ballad *Solitude* in the December 1950 recording. His solo chorus is complete with the stop time chords from the band that are strongly reminiscent of the preacher section of *Goin' Up*.

The now widely-disseminated recordings of the famous Fargo dance date of 1940 and the Ellington Carnegie Hall concerts of 1943, 1944, 1946 and 1947 give another perspective to Brown's playing. It is clear from these recordings, despite the sound limitations of "live" recording, that Brown in general did not play quite the same way in live performance as he did in the recording studio. Solos for which we may compare live recordings with studio recordings are usually very close to the same in most musical terms. Notes and rhythms may be virtually unchanged from performance to performance. What is noticeably different is that it is obvious that Brown was blowing harder and playing louder in the live performances than he normally did in the recording studio. Even in many ballad performances his tone quality was "harder" sounding – that is, it was brighter and had more edge. This increased hardness is particularly noticeable in the faster pieces in which the orchestra and/or the rhythm section is playing louder. During this era, Brown rarely had the help of a microphone to get his sound over the rest of the band, and it is apparent that he felt the need to play louder. While Brown's playing at this greater volume was for the most part still admirably clean and well-executed, it sounds on some occasions as if some flexibility was lost on fast passages, and also as if the lush romanticism of his tone quality on ballads was sometimes compromised. Neither of these results is surprising, and is in fact still common today in performances in a wide variety of musical circumstances. There are times, however, when Brown sounded every bit as refined in live performance as in the studio. His performance of *Melloditti* on the 1946 Carnegie Hall concert sounds as if it could have been recorded in the most ideal studio situation.

Ellington continued to create features for Brown. *Blue Cellophane*, recorded at the December 1944 Carnegie Hall concert and then in the studio 4 January 1945, featured Brown throughout at the medium tempo on which he thrived. *Transblucency (A Blue Fog You Can Almost See Through)* was performed on the 4 January 1946 Carnegie Hall concert and recorded in the studio seven months later. As previously noted, the melody for this tune was directly derived from Brown's solo from the previously described *Blue Light*. Ellington again set the melody in a modified *Mood Indigo* instrumentation. With clarinet and muted trombone (probably Claude Jones), the lovely voice of Kay Davis is substituted for the original muted trumpet. Brown supplies a moody improvised chorus on open trombone. *On a Turquoise Cloud*, from 1947, co-composed by Brown, featured the same group of three instruments with more solo commentary from Brown. The film *Symphony in Swing* shows Tyree Glenn playing the trombone part in the trio on this selection. *Golden Cress*, also co-composed by Brown, features him at his best, as it goes from a ballad at the beginning to a double-time swing section in the middle and then back to a ballad at the end.

As previously alluded to, certain jazz critics had unfavorable opinions about Brown's sound and his style. Other critics proclaimed their admiration for Brown's abilities but felt that he was wrong for the Ellington band. The amount of commentary that appeared in print about Brown's playing, his place in the Ellington band, and what he meant to Ellington's music, was extraordinary.

In 1933, already famous jazz impresario and writer John Hammond had some thoughts about Brown.

He is a virtuoso of the first rank, one who is ever conscious of his technical ability. Probably no other trombonist has his equipment.

But I'm afraid that this brilliant musician is out of place in Duke's band. He is a soloist who doesn't respect the rudiments of orchestral playing. Constantly he pushes himself to the foreground. In any other orchestra no objection would be raised; but Duke's group is very properly the voice of one man, and that gent is not Mr. Brown.[41]

In the very same issue of the British weekly *Melody Maker*, Hammond's British crony, Spike Hughes (who also wrote under the pseudonym "Mike"), who had just returned from a trip to the United States, continued the assault.

[Brown's] solo work is altogether too "smart" or "sophisticated" to be anything but out of place in Duke's essentially direct and simple music. Brown is as much use to that band as Kreisler would be playing first fiddle in the New York Philharmonic. It is not that his individuality is too strong, just misplaced.[42]

41 *Melody Maker,* May 1933, 351.
42 Ibid., 355.

In one of the first serious, large-scale treatments of jazz, *Le Jazz Hot* (1934), Frenchman Hughes Panassié wrote about Brown at some length. Some of what he had to say echoed the sentiments of Hammond and Hughes. He declared that some people ranked Brown at the top of the trombone world along with Jack Teagarden, while others considered him "distinctly inferior" not only to Teagarden, but to J.C. Higginbotham, Dicky Wells, Benny Morton, and others. Panassié attributed this to Brown's "unevenness and the special characteristics of his technique." Brown was supposedly "content to reproduce the Teagarden accent by using analagous phrases, without troubling to reproduce the robustiousness [sic] or the rough intonations."[43]

Panassié continued at some length about Brown's sound.

Some say that [the] ravishing tone of Lawrence Brown is too sweet for use in hot performances, that his intonations are too refined, too affected, and that he is good only when he plays straight. It is true that in certain cases his playing seems too sweet, a little insipid and too tame. But he is a musician whose temperament is well suited to mild, delicate interpretations. He is not built, as it were, for that hot playing in fast time which calls for a fiery, forceful performance. When he tries to play forcefully, his style becomes artificial. It is not that he lacks the necessary instrumental technique; on the contrary, he is one of the most astonishing trombone virtuosos. But he is not naturally congenial to this sort of performance.

Panassié went on about Brown's ability to succeed at slow and moderate tempos, and he had especially kind words for the "fantastic passages" of Brown's solo on *Ducky Wucky*. His final comments again echoed those of Hughes.

We must remember that Brown is principally judged by his work with the Ellington orchestra, with which he has played since 1932. Duke's band requires soloists who can adapt their inspiration to that of their leader, and Lawrence Brown has too much personality – or, if you prefer to say so, a personality too different from that of the Duke – to yield easily to these demands. He was not meant for the particular orchestra, and his playing often seems complicated and artificial because of the constraint he puts on himself or which is imposed upon him. Near Ellington, his personality cannot expand. Let us await more favorable circumstances before making up our minds.

In 1938, Hughes, who was by this time a decidedly influential commentator in the jazz press, renewed the attack and went on an extended crusade to convince readers (or perhaps he was

43 These and the following quotes are from Hughes Panassié, *Hot Jazz: The Guide to Swing Music*, 83-4.

trying to convince Ellington himself) that Ellington had made mistakes – both in hiring and keeping Lawrence Brown and in the general direction of the band. Hughes felt that Ellington had slid into "musical decadence," and that the "sophistication" that had taken over some of his music was destroying the basic strength of the music. Hughes exposed his arguments in consecutive installments of his weekly column in *Melody Maker* in October and November. In the 29 October column, entitled "The Exotic Mr. Brown," Hughes stated, "I am going to suggest that the musical decadence of Ellington dates from the time Lawrence Brown joined the band." Hughes again defended Brown's abilities as a trombonist; he claimed that his objection was "purely one of style." Hughes still liked much of what Ellington was writing and performing, but felt that Ellington was not being true to his real convictions. He diagnosed Ellington's problem in these terms:

Something got into Duke's system about five years ago: a poison for which nobody has yet bothered to find the antidote. The germ was Lawrence Brown – the exotic, undisciplined luxuriance of his trombone playing.

Supposedly, the arrival of Brown in the band ended the band's musical homogeneity. The very first ballad that Brown recorded with Ellington, *Best Wishes*, was "the turning point." Brown was described as "musically-speaking, a foreigner in Duke's band." Brown was not musically "clear-thinking" in the way that Ellington was. As for his trombone style, "[h]is tone is rich, his improvisations extravagant, his intonation not always above suspicion, his phrasing inclined to overwork the glissando and the grace-note."[44]

The following week's article was entitled "Why Did Duke Pick Lawrence Brown for His Band?" Hughes asked the pertinent question, "Perhaps you wonder why I should consider the presence of a single trombone player in Duke Ellington's Band to be of such importance." Hughes questioned why Ellington ever hired Brown in the first place. (Perhaps he would have felt vindicated had he known that Ellington hired Brown solely on the recommendation of Irving Mills, without ever hearing him.) Hughes finally got to the heart of his argument by further describing Brown's playing. "Brown's trombone playing, with its lack of clarity, its rich, schmaltzy phrases, stands as a model of what too many Americans imagine to be Sophistication [sic]."

The argument was continued with the theme that "Duke is not a sophisticated composer." Hughes felt that anything that smacked of sophistication in the Ellington book was the music of "a musical social climber." The hit *Sophisticated Lady* was

44 All quotes from *Melody Maker*, 29 October 1938; 8.

the "apotheosis of Brownerie." That Brown was the principal villain in this affair was shown by Hughes's declaration that "[e]ven after the arrival of this artist [Brown] Duke still managed to produce music in which the only un-Ellington passages were those played by Brown."[45]

The argument was summed up in the concluding article, "Decline and Falter."

I have called Lawrence Brown a symbol. He symbolizes the "smartness" and "nonchalong" [sic] sophistication of Sophisticated Lady and Rude Interlude, the flashiness and superficiality of a "moderne" Broadway revue.

Duke embraced this symbol whole-heartedly, and that was that so far as Duke's natural gifts, his sincerity and genuine self-expression were concerned.[46]

Even with Brown's contributions to Ellington's great works of the 1940s this sort of criticism did not die. It was notably revived in Great Britain in the late 1950s with the publication of the collection of essays *Duke Ellington: His Life and Music.* After praising one of Brown's ballad performances, Jeff Aldam stated that "at other times Brown shows an unfortunate tendency to excessive sentimentality in slow numbers." He also commented on Brown's "pompous and declamatory phrasing in stomps – played withal with somewhat wooly tone and careless pitching."[47] In another similar criticism, Vic Bellerby stated,

Lawrence Brown will always be a problem to the Ellington writer. His rich tone and prodigious technique played a great part in the formation of the brass section. Often, as in Under [sic] a turquoise cloud or Delta Serenade, he blends perfectly with Ellington's mood, but frequently he indulges in an excess of glissandi and over-ripe sentimentality of phrase which spoil the mood.[48]

Essentially these critics all take the same stance. Hughes's criticism, which was aimed at Ellington as well as Brown, points up the crux of the matter. The mood Ellington created, through Brown, on pieces like *Delta Serenade* and *On a Turquoise Cloud* may be pleasing to some listeners, whereas it may be too "sweet" or "sophisticated" to others. Yet some who might find *Delta Serenade* or *On a Turquoise Cloud* objectionable might find Brown's solos in *Blue Light* or *Prelude to a Kiss* in perfectly good taste. What to one listener is over-ripe sentimentality might be lush romanticism to another. What is patently obvious from today's perspective is that Ellington would not have allowed Brown to interpret his pieces in a way that he, Ellington,

45 *Melody Maker,* 5 November 1938; 5.
46 *Melody Maker,* 12 November 1938, 7.
47 Jeff Aldam, "The Ellington Sidemen," in Gammond, 199.
48 Vic Bellerby, "Analysis of Genius," in Gammond, 166.

felt spoiled the mood. He simply would have called upon a different soloist.

Speaking to the more specific issues, while it is one thing to dislike Ellington's (and Brown's) "sweet" side, it is impossible to accept the claim that Ellington's music was unsophisticated, even in the 1930s. The diversity and complexity of his output was already such that it could support such widely differing soloists as Brown, Tricky Sam Nanton, Johnny Hodges, Rex Stewart, Cootie Williams, Harry Carney, and later on many others. Were Hammond and Hughes implying that the "sophisticated" pieces were the "sweet" tunes? If so, they were ignoring the considerable sophistication of some of the hot numbers. If not, just how was one to tell which pieces were more or less sophisticated according to these critics' reckoning? Perhaps the term "sophisticated" was just a catchall term that stood for any of Ellington's music that Hammond and Hughes did not like. In any case, they turned what is usually a term of praise into one of derision.

As far as the criticism of Brown is concerned, what could Hammond have meant by the rudiments of orchestral playing that Brown does not respect? There is nothing in the recorded output that would indicate that Brown was anything but ideal as an "orchestral player" – that is, a section man. Despite the great differences in sound and musical personality among the three trombonists in the band, the trio rarely sounded anything but excellent on record. Further, there is nothing that indicates the section or anyone in it as being out of balance with the rest of the band. Brown's outstanding reliability in performance has been noted previously.

The larger issue is one which is enlightened throughout the fascinating *The Duke Ellington Reader*. Ever since the early 1930s, many critics, and probably a reasonably large number of jazz fans as well, loved Ellington's "hot" side, but did not care for his "sweet" side. In fact, one either accepts this side of Ellington's musical personality – and accepts Brown's role in it – or rejects it as one of Ellington's weak points. (It might be added that there probably has also been a a reasonably large number of music lovers who preferred the "sweet" side to the "hot" side.) Hughes and Hammond were big fans in the thirties of "hot jazz," and any bow that Ellington made in the direction of "sweetness" was a step in the wrong direction as far as these two critics were concerned. In the late 1930s Hammond started championing what he considered a "hotter" band – the Count Basie band.[49]

Even the "hot versus sweet" debate, as can be seen in the

49 Hughes, surprisingly perhaps, resigned from the staff of *Melody Maker,* quit his leadership of a jazz band, and concentrated on "classical music."

Reader, has not been the whole issue. With Ellington's extended works, from *Creole Rhapsody* through works like *Reminiscing in Tempo* and particularly *Black, Brown and Beige*, some critics and fans alike have not been able to figure out just what kind of music Ellington has produced. Convenient labels just don't seem to fit. Or perhaps a label fits some of the music but not all of it. Ellington always preferred to describe what he was doing in such terms as claiming that he was trying to "work out some of my ideas of Negro music." He very much disliked labels, he disliked attempts to pigeonhole his music, and he obviously wanted to write and perform music of tremendous variety and scope. Millions of fans have accepted and embraced all or parts of the legacy since the 1920s.

Brown displayed considerable bitterness in some of the interviews he underwent later in his life, but on the subject of all this criticism, he displayed equanimity.

Well, I . . . can see what they would mean because the era before me — well, colored bands didn't play sophisticated music. They were jazz bands. You know, the old tailgate type or raucous type of music. Very few of them played real sweet. And since that was my type of music, why that's all I knew. In fact that's all I was going to play . . . [50]

Schuller, a great champion of Brown's playing, makes the following assessment of Brown's place.

Certainly the major new voice [to join Ellington in 1932] was Lawrence Brown, an extraordinarily versatile trombonist who brought a number of unique musical qualities to the orchestra and to Duke's sonoric palette. I believe the impact that Brown had on the so-called Ellington effect . . . has never been fully appreciated. Not only did the Ellington band become the first to acquire a permanent trombone trio, but Brown was the first trombonist of any major black orchestra to develop a full-blown ballad and lyric style. This was some years before the emergence of players like Tommy Dorsey and Jack Jenney, still a time when the trombone was associated almost exclusively with "hot" jazz, and hadn't quite lost its New Orleans "tailgate" ancestry.

Brown, as leader of Ellington's trombone section, was not only a great lyric player, but his solo style was so unique that it was virtually inimitable. At the same time he was no less of a "hot" improviser, and as a result there was no role (other than the "growl and plunger" technique, handled by Joe "Tricky Sam" Nanton) to which Brown could not be assigned. Such ver-

satility was unprecedented in the 1930s and is still relatively uncommon today.[51]

Brown established his position with Ellington in the '30's as an outstanding, technically proficient improviser on fast and medium tempo tunes, a romantic interpreter of ballads, an occasional blues soloist and an exceptional accompanist. While continuing to work within these established roles in the 1940s, upon occasion he also became a "blues shouter." Until he left the band in 1951, the great value of Brown's versatility was continually used to advantage throughout his tenure with Ellington. If recordings can be accepted as a reasonable representation of live performance, Brown's standard of trombone playing maintained an exceptionally high degree of accuracy and consistency. His command of the instrument ranks him as one of the greatest trombonists in the history of jazz.

Shortly after his return to the band in 1960 he also found himself saddled with the additional role of his longtime section mate Tricky Sam Nanton as one of the band's principal plunger mute soloists (a role, incidentally, that he did not particularly care for). Brown had truly fulfilled what might be seen in retrospect as a prophecy rather than a completed act in what Ulanov had written years earlier. "The trombone was no longer just a barrelhouse horn – it was every kind of horn at once; and Lawrence Brown, indubitably the most versatile of trombonists, could play them all."[52]

51 *Swing Era,* 46-47.
52 Ulanov, 97.

Sonny Greer (drums), Fred Guy (guitar);
Trombone section: Wilbur De Paris, Claude Jones, Joe "Tricky Sam" Nanton, Lawrence Brown
Trumpet section includes Taft Jordan and Shorty Baker
(Collection of Duncan P. Schiedt)

A Time of Transition: 5
The Late 1940s

Despite the massive demand for manpower in the armed services, the Ellington band's personnel was relatively untouched during World War II. In May of 1943, however, Lawrence Brown went West to his home in California, apparently to wait for a call from his draft board for induction. One of the Swing Era's finest trombonists, Sandy Williams, substituted for Brown and remained with the band for much of its lengthy residency in the Hurricane Club in New York. But when Brown's call did not come, he returned to the band in about six weeks.[1]

When Juan Tizol left the band in 1944,[2] it was the first long-term change in the historic, long-standing section of Nanton, Tizol and Brown. It was, however, only the first of numerous changes that took place in the next few years.

Tizol was replaced by Claude Jones, who was one of the most technically accomplished and influential of Swing Era trombonists. Born in Oklahoma in 1901, Jones apparently was part Native American. Garvin Bushell, who "became like brothers" with Jones claims that "[w]hen I met Claude, he used to whoop and do his Indian dance."[3] Jones went to Wilberforce University in Ohio, where, according to his brother-in-law, future Ellington trombonist Quentin Jackson, he originally played drums. By the time the Synco Jazz Band, which soon became the famed McKinney's Cotton Pickers, emerged from Wilberforce, though, Jones was playing trombone.

During the '30s Jones had a significant role in the seminal band of Fletcher Henderson, which he joined and left several times. His work with the Cotton Pickers and Henderson established his reputation as one of the finest of jazz trombonists. He also played with Don Redman and Chick Webb before joining Cab Calloway in late 1934 for a stay of more than five years. After leaving Calloway in January of 1940, he played with Coleman Hawkins, Zutty Singleton, Joe Sullivan, Henderson yet again and Benny Carter, with return trips also to the bands of Redman and Calloway before joining Ellington.

Jones's superb playing on numerous recordings, particularly with McKinney's Cotton Pickers and with Henderson, reflects

1 Stratemann, 242.
2 According to Stratemann (253), Tizol had also been away from the band for about six weeks in August and September of 1943, when he was replaced by Bernard Archer.
3 Bushell, *Jazz From the Beginning*, 13.

the excellent technique he had developed. Like Lawrence Brown and others of his generation, Jones was very probably influenced by the early jazz trombonist Miff Mole.[4] Dicky Wells, who played with Jones in Henderson's band, said that Jones's cleanliness of execution was almost a burden to him.

"Yeah, that was a pretty solo you played," Claude would say, "but there wasn't enough fuzz. Everything was too exact. Don't try to play like I play. I play too clean and I'll never be nothing."[5]

Yet this very ability, along with a wealth of musical ideas, had made Jones one of the most respected trombonists in jazz.

Although he had continued to do considerable playing with bands in New York, Jones had not been working full-time in the music business for several years preceding his joining Ellington. And despite spending over three and a half years in the Ellington band, he never was to become a "true" Ellingtonian. He never got a chance to show himself off as he had in other bands, probably for several reasons. The main reason was that he was, in effect, a victim of the "chair" system in Ellington's trombone section. Unlike in many bands, where the chair designations imply a sort of hierarchy of importance in the section, in Ellington's band, the chairs designated function. The first chair, occupied for many years by Lawrence Brown, included most of the highest pitched or "lead" trombone parts, as well as the solos originally designed for Brown. Joe Nanton established what became known as the "third" chair, where the plunger specialist was to sit for years. Tizol had to this point been the only occupant of what became known as the "second" chair. The parts had all been written for Tizol, including the melody lines on many of his own tunes. Not being a jazz soloist, he did not have improvised solo spots written into his parts. His relatively few solo parts were completely notated. Therefore, the few solos that appeared in the parts that Jones played with Ellington were written-out melodic solos.[6] Recorded examples that feature Jones are the extended solo passages in *Come Sunday*, heard on the 1944 Carnegie Hall concert, and a chorus on Tizol's tune *Bakiff*, heard on the 1947 Carnegie Hall concert.

Another possible reason for Jones's lack of solo space was that he was playing an instrument that he may not have been completely familiar with. Jones had made his reputation as a slide trombonist, but played valve trombone during at least some, if not all, of his time with Ellington.[7] It is not clear what kind of facility Jones had on the valve instrument, but perhaps he did not feel comfortable improvising on valve trombone.[8]

In addition, there has been talk for years – which came out into the open in Mercer Ellington's book *Duke Ellington in*

4   Zieff, Bob, "Claude Jones," in *Grove's*, Vol. 1, 629.

5   Wells, *Night People*, 42.

6   For more information on Tizol's chair, see chapter 3, and also see chapter 7 for what happened to the second chair when Chuck Connors started playing bass trombone.

7   Although there are a number of photos of Jones playing valve trombone, Stanley Dance does not recall him playing the valve instrument. Despite Dance's recollection, a large variety of evidence supports Jones playing valve trombone – not the least of which is simply the fact that he had taken Tizol's place.

8   He had, however, played trumpet as a youth, so this might not have been a problem.

Person[9] – about the jealousy of the Ellington veterans of their solo space and their unwillingness to give up any of their space to newcomers. It may be that Ellington, in trying to mollify his other men, never gave Jones the chance to establish his solo voice in the band. Indeed, while virtually all of the replacements that came into the band in the '40s and '50s were tried veterans of other good bands, few of them were able to establish themselves as distinctly "Ellington" voices.

Another possibility is that Ellington just never decided how to use Jones as a new and different strand in the Ellington cloth. Finally, since Jones had been relatively inactive for several years before joining Ellington, perhaps he just did not feel ready to take on solo responsibilities.

How much this lack of solo space bothered Jones is difficult to know. It didn't bother him enough to cause him to quit until he had put in a fairly lengthy tenure with the band, but according to Quentin Jackson, Jones's brother-in-law, there was at least some dissatisfaction. It was Jackson who was called to take Jones's place with Ellington, which certainly must have been an awkward situation. But as Jackson later recalled,

Then I got to thinking and I said – Well, I knew Claude wasn't getting along over there. I knew that . . . [t]here was a little jealousy thing going on in there, you know, between him [Jones] and Lawrence. I found out later, because he didn't want to play on valve trombone and Duke wanted him to play valve trombone because Tizol played valve and that's what he [Ellington] wanted in that particular chair, you see. And so Claude didn't really get to play solos like he wanted to . . .[10]

Also, Jones may have been battling some problems with alcohol as well at this time. In any case, Jones left and Jackson came in, playing his first job with the Ellington band in October of 1948. Jackson's importance to Ellington did not become clear until the 1950s, so his story is dealt with in the next chapter.

Jones returned to the Ellington band briefly in 1951. But evidently he was again having alcohol problems, and shortly after Britt Woodman replaced Lawrence Brown, Tizol returned and Jones was out again. He then left the music business, never to return to it.

A notable guest trombonist appeared with the Ellington band on a recording session in May of 1945. Tommy Dorsey, like Ellington, contracted to Victor Records, was the guest soloist on Ellington's beautiful but rarely played *Tonight I Shall Sleep (With a Smile On My Face)*. Except for twelve measures by Johnny Hodges, Dorsey was the featured voice throughout the

9 See *Duke Ellington in Person*, 64.
10 Jackson interview, reel 5, 57. Nonetheless, whatever jealousy Jones may have felt towards Brown, he expressed admiration for Brown's playing. See Chapter 4.

tune, exhibiting his patented ballad sound and style – a ballad style, incidentally, not notably different from Lawrence Brown's. In return for Dorsey's appearance, Ellington recorded a selection with Dorsey's band.

In November of 1945, Tricky Sam Nanton reportedly had a stroke and did not play for several months. Ellington hired another excellent veteran trombonist, Wilbur De Paris, to fill in. Although Nanton rejoined the band sometime in the spring of 1946, his health remained a concern. As a consequence, Ellington kept four trombonists on the payroll until Nanton's death in July 1946.

De Paris was born in Crawfordsville, Indiana on 11 January 1900. His father, a bandmaster and teacher, initiated the musical training of Wilbur and his brother Sidney, who became one of jazz's finest trumpeters. Wilbur started on alto horn at the age of seven, and trumpeter Bill Coleman reports having seen De Paris playing baritone horn around 1910. His father had a carnival band with which Wilbur was soon playing. Later came tent shows and the fabled Theater Owners' Booking Association (TOBA) circuit. The TOBA, at its peak, booked black artists and acts, primarily revues made up of musical comedy and vaudeville acts, into theaters all over the South, Southwest and Midwest. While the heavy schedules and meager wages caused the TOBA to be referred to by many of its employees as "Tough on Black Asses," it provided valuable work for a large number of black artists and brought them to audiences who otherwise would not have had the opportunity to see or hear them.

According to Chilton, while a member of Mack's Merrymakers in the early twenties, De Paris, playing C melody saxophone, sat in with Louis Armstrong in New Orleans. Coleman also places De Paris in an orchestra in Cincinnati around 1919. Eventually he went to the East coast and started leading his own band in 1925. During the '30s he played with a host of name bands, including the Mills Blue Rhythm Band and the bands of Noble Sissle, Benny Carter, Teddy Hill and an almost three-year stint with Louis Armstrong. Besides working with those bands, he also recorded with Jelly Roll Morton. In the '40s he played briefly with Ella Fitzgerald and Roy Eldridge and recorded with Sidney Bechet. Prior to joining Ellington, he had again led his own band.[11]

With Ellington, De Paris seems to have been mostly a "part" player and was only rarely a soloist. While De Paris nominally replaced Nanton, I have found only one example of De Paris doing plunger work, a sixteen-bar spot on *Ring Dem Bells*, on

11 Most of the biographical information is from Chilton, with some reinforcement from the first two Feather *Encyclopedias* and the two claims from Coleman, *Trumpet Story*, 2, 10.

a 1946 Chicago concert. Quentin Jackson, however, claimed that De Paris did play other plunger parts, saying that "it had been all right, but not exactly the way Duke wanted it."[12] A perusal of the works that the band was playing during the period between Nanton's death and De Paris's leaving the band shows that the pieces that had originally featured Nanton were just not being played. De Paris was occasionally featured on the open horn, perhaps most notably on *Solid Old Man* on the Carnegie Hall concert recording from January 1946. Following a couple of solo interjections into the first chorus of the arrangement, De Paris is given a full sixteen measures of solo space later in the performance. His big brash sound and energetic but uncomplicated style fit well into this exuberant piece. While De Paris's solo voice was not to be heard often with Ellington, it later became a jazz fixture in New York during the 1950s, where De Paris led the house band at Jimmy Ryan's club.

Perhaps the most significant development in the trombone section in the second half of the 1940s was the emergence of Tyree Glenn. Before joining the Ellington band, Glenn had been in a number of bands, most notably Cab Calloway's band from 1940-46. His background includes some interesting and diverse sorts of experience. Born in Corsicana, Texas, in 1912, Glenn's first experience with a name band was Tommy Myles's group in Washington, D.C., during the mid-1930s. Prior to that, according to Quentin Jackson, "Tyree didn't like for anybody to say it, you know, but Tyree used to be with the minstrels." According to Jackson, Glenn played banjo with Jimmy Perkins's minstrels. From there he moved to Johnson's Happy Pals in Richmond, Virginia, and then went on to play with Eddie Barefield and Benny Carter before joining Calloway.

While with Calloway, Glenn prevailed upon his section mates Claude Jones and Quentin Jackson – both future Ellingtonians – to help him hone his skills. According to Jackson, ". . . he used to worry Claude and I [sic] to death to teach him different things." Apparently Jones taught him lip vibrato and Jackson would "map out" little solos for him to learn and play.[13]

After a European tour with Don Redman in 1946, Glenn joined Ellington in 1947, in effect, taking the place of Tricky Sam Nanton, who had died in July 1946. In fact, Glenn replaced Wilbur De Paris, but as mentioned previously, De Paris evidently was not doing much plunger work.[14] With Glenn's entry into the section, the trombone plunger tradition was revived.

Glenn's outstanding ability with the plunger was showcased early in his stay with the band on the 14 August 1947 recording

12 Dance, *The World of Swing*, 298.

13 Jackson interview, reel 3, 53.

14 Although James Lincoln Collier has suggested that De Paris left the band when Ellington asked the men to take a pay cut, there seems to be no documentation of this. The fact that De Paris formed a small group that opened early in July at Jimmy Ryan's, within weeks of his departure, suggests that he had previously been considering leaving Ellington.

of *H'ya Sue*. From the opening chorus, where Glenn's tightly muted high C explodes into two startling fast "wa's" every two measures, this new voice invigorates the whole performance. His two choruses (Example 5-1), filled with bluesy figures reminiscent of but not completely indebted to Nanton, establish him as Nanton's worthy successor. The first four measures, which are repeated almost exactly in measures 5-8, were probably worked out ahead of time, if not written out. Glenn's figures are answered by tenor saxophonist Al Sears throughout the first chorus. His second chorus (measures 13-24) was, on the other hand, probably improvised, at least to start with. The sequential construction of this chorus (note the similarities between measures 13-16 and 17-20) and the figure in measure 23, which is derived from measure 1, however, again suggest that this half of the solo, too, might have been played the same, or close to it, in live performance. Glenn's sounds are similar to many of those of Nanton. Yet it is Glenn's use of the various sounds that helps distinguish his plunger playing from that of Nanton and Quentin Jackson, who was to hold the plunger chair in the 1950s. (See Chapter 2 for key to vowel sounds used in plunger examples.) Peculiar to Glenn's plunger vocabulary is a distinctive fast vibrato on many of the longer notes. Good examples of this vibrato occur on the last notes of measures 3, 7, 15 and 19 in this solo.

Glenn was not, however, as Nanton had become in his latter days, exclusively a plunger specialist. In fact, he was one of the most versatile musicians ever to play with Ellington. In October of 1947, Glenn was featured on a recording of a tune for which he received co-composer credit along with Ellington. *Sultry Serenade*, as the tune became known, was simply titled *Tyree's No. [Number]* in the original sketches and parts.[15] It seems likely that the melody of the eight-measure A section of this AABA tune was Glenn's creation (see Example 5-2). A quirky but catchy figure is repeated with slight variation twice in each A section. The bridge (B section) consists of a simple sequence through a standard chord progression. Glenn's improvised chorus (Example 5-2A) is a most attractive combination of arpeggiated and scalar swing figures with a few bluesy and riff-like figures inserted (measures 5-6, 21-22) to effectively give variety and shape to the solo. Spice is added through some effortless lip trills (measures 5-6) and a concluding whole tone figure (measures 31-32). Throughout, one is impressed with the strong but pure open sound of Glenn's horn, his technical facility, and the ease with which he ascends to high D in the top part of the horn's range.

15 Some parts and sketches for sections of the original arrangement are in the Ellington Archive of the Smithsonian Institution.

Tyree Glenn (Photo by Duncan P. Schiedt)

EXAMPLE 5-1

EXAMPLE 5-2

A section

B section

Example 5-2a

Swing playing and plunger playing were not the only roles that Glenn could fill. Two films from 1949 and 1950 feature notable examples of his musical flexibility. In February of 1949, the band recorded four selections for the film *Symphony in Swing*. Glenn is prominent for his contributions on two of the pieces. *On a Turquoise Cloud*, a beautiful mood piece co-written by Ellington and Lawrence Brown, is the sort of "color" piece, and in a shade of blue, as were most of the color pieces, that Ellington reveled in. Making the most of the visual medium, much of this selection is heard while clouds float by on the film. While Brown is the featured trombonist on the piece, Glenn is a member of the trio that presents the first theme. Glenn is playing with the plunger in a modification of the trio that Ellington first brought to prominence on *Mood Indigo*. In this version of the trio, Jimmy Hamilton plays clarinet and Kay Davis's crystalline vocal substitutes for the original trumpet. Glenn's plunger sound is not at all that of the earthy Joe Nanton, but rather a floating, seamless, pure-toned instrumental voice. The lyrical style is such that Glenn has been mistaken for Lawrence Brown on this recording. Glenn and Ellington are the featured soloists on the concluding number of the film, *Frankie and Johnny*. Some years earlier, Ellington had concocted a piano fantasy on this old folk ballad that later in the arrangement featured blues choruses played by Tricky Sam Nanton. An outstanding version of the arrangement with Nanton as soloist was recorded on the Carnegie Hall concert of 19 December 1944, where it served as a crowd-pleasing encore. Undoubtedly limited by the length of the film, the 1949 version is shorter, yet it shows Glenn to excellent advantage. The camera does a closeup of the bell of his trombone, showing in detail his manipulation of the plunger. An idiosynchratic vibrato that he sometimes employed when using the plunger appears briefly. Glenn's blues chorus features just about every plunger trick in the book. While his style and sound in the plunger were certainly different from those of Nanton, in performances such as these Glenn suffers little, if at all, in any comparison to his distinguished predecessor.

In March of 1950 the band recorded the Ellington novelty *The History of Jazz in Three Minutes* for the film *Salute to Duke Ellington*. This whirlwind tour of historical jazz styles runs the gamut from dixieland to bebop. At one point the reed section intones a lovely ballad-like passage in the style of Glenn Miller, with clarinet playing lead. The band answers this episode with a humorous clapped and chanted cadence. The Miller-like passage returns, but with Glenn playing the lead line in a silky, lyrical ballad style that seems to be a bow to Tommy Dorsey, rather than Miller. Glenn can be seen employing a very fast, tight slide vibrato (quite unlike the vibrato he often used in the plunger), a trait of Dorsey's, but also characteristic of Glenn's playing in this style. He had also used it, for example, for *On a Turquoise Cloud.*

Glenn was also an accomplished vibraphonist, a capacity in which he occasionally appeared with Ellington, most significantly on the 1947 *Liberian Suite.*

In 1962, Ellington summed up Glenn's strength's.

Tyree, to me, is a very beautiful trombone player. He plays real good legit trombone, and when he applied the plunger to it his tone remained very precise and clean, so that you were tempted to like it better than Tricky's, because it was so clean. But then, Tricky's was so plaintive. Tyree is a very agile-minded musician and he always wants to do a lot of things. I'm sure he had enjoyed Tricky before. He must have, because he couldn't have done the plunger work so well if he hadn't enjoyed doing it. He still uses the plunger and he is one of the most effective plunger trombones I have ever heard.[16]

According to Quentin Jackson, however, Ellington said that Glenn played the plunger solos "a little bit too pretty." He said to Jackson, apparently suggesting that he not follow Glenn's example, "Let's not play this too pretty. . . you know, this is folklore."[17] A similar sentiment was expressed by British critic Jeff Aldam.

[Glenn] is unlikely to be mistaken for Nanton, however, for there is little of sadness in his make-up and his work in this vein [the plunger solos] is jaunty and humorous. Even on a blues he seems to be having fun.[18]

Yet Jackson, who had also spent years with Glenn in Calloway's band, remarked of him in the interview just mentioned, "Oh, what a beautiful trombone player."[19]

The beginning of the end of Glenn's tenure with Ellington came in 1950, when the band was to go to Europe. According to Raymond Horricks,

Talk of a European tour with the full band in early 1950 had hastened [Glenn's departure]. Tyree had visited Europe in 1946 with Don Redman, and in Paris there had been a friendship with a French girl. The trombonist's wife announced that there would be no more European trips for him.[20]

Ellington took trombonist Ted Kelly with him in Glenn's place. Kelly was in Europe for two weeks, returned to the States to marry, and never played with the Ellington band again.[21]

Upon the band's return from Europe, Glenn joined the band in December for the recording session that produced the marvel-

16 *The World of Ellington,* 7.
17 Jackson interview, reel 6, 7.
18 Aldam, "The Ellington Sidemen" in Gammond, 199.
19 Jackson interview, reel 3, 52.
20 Horricks, "Duke Ellington on Record: The Nineteen-Forties," in Gammond, 103.
21 Jackson interview, reel 5, 69. See Chapter 6 for how the missing parts were covered.

ous album that became known as *Masterpieces by Ellington*. It is on this collection that Glenn produced his most memorable recorded solo with Ellington, on the extended arrangement of *Mood Indigo*. In some ways reminiscent of his filmed solo on *Frankie and Johnny*, this solo goes beyond it both in virtuosity and musical effect. The variety of Glenn's effects can be seen in the transcription, Example 5-3. The plunger is used tight against the bell (note that the small "o's" in measures 9 and 11 are the standard notation for open plunger, rather than the "o" vowel sound), in "wa's" and even Nanton-like "ya's." Flutter-tonguing (recalling Nanton's growls), fast lip slurs resulting in what amount to trills (measure 19) and multiple tonguing (measures 25-28) are effortlessly woven into the solo's flow in a way that makes them seem an essential part of the musical fabric. It should be stated that the notation in measures 25-28 is only an approximation of an effect that cannot be accurately represented on paper. Glenn uses rapid multiple tonguing (it is not possible to determine whether it is double or triple tonguing) while quickly opening and closing the plunger in an unforgettable "talking" effect. This device, which has become common usage among many plunger specialists, can be traced back at least as far as 1927, when Bubber Miley employed the same sort of effect on *Black and Tan Fantasy*.

The chorus features Glenn alone with the rhythm section. It is hard to know how much this part of the arrangement had been rehearsed, if indeed it had been rehearsed at all. While it may have been improvised right on the session, it is so beautifully constructed that it sounds as if it could have been written out ahead of time. The internal relationships within the solo are astounding. Measures 1-2 are reflected in measures 5-6, with a related phrase – measures 13-14 – reappearing in the second half of the chorus in measures 21-22 and 29-30. In fact, measures 5-8 are repeated almost verbatim in the second half of the solo, in measures 21-24. Measures 3-4 are repeated in measures 15-16 and 31-32 to close each half chorus. In both halves of the solo the ninth through twelfth measures consist of a two-bar repeated figure (measures 9-12 and 25-28). The total statement is most memorable.

After the *Masterpieces* session, Glenn played a few more dates in the New York area with the Ellington band, but although he subbed with the band even into the 1970s, his regular employment with Ellington was over.

As the Ellington band entered the 1950s, Lawrence Brown was the only carryover from the great trombone section of the '30s and early '40s. Tyree Glenn, an important contributor to the band in the late '40s, was about to leave. And even though Brown, too, was soon to depart, it would not be long before the trombone section would find a new stability and strength.

Example 5-3

New Life: 6
The Section of the 1950s

The trombone "section of the '50s" had its own identity, considerably different from that of the classic trio of Nanton, Tizol and Brown. It did not, however, emerge all in one piece, and it always maintained some tie with past sections. One could even identify two definitive sections in the fifties, with two of the players remaining the same, but the "second" chair, Tizol's old chair, changing. The first of these sections took shape within a couple of months of Lawrence Brown's departure.

In early 1951, after his remarkable tenure of nineteen consecutive years in the section, Brown left along with drummer Sonny Greer and alto saxophonist Johnny Hodges, two other stalwart members of the Ellington orchestra, both of whom had been with Ellington even longer than Brown. Greer was with Ellington before he even left Washington in the early 1920s; the seemingly irreplaceable Hodges had joined Ellington in 1928 and his liquid alto sound, his earthy blues playing and his unmatched handling of ballads had become indispensable elements of the Ellington sound.

With these important defections, it was a critical time in the Ellington band's history. In fact, it was a critical time historically in the life of big bands in jazz. Count Basie had been forced to break up his band the previous year, Woody Herman's Herds were working only sporadically. There was serious question as to whether any artistically vital big band could survive on the road in the financial climate of the early 1950s.[1] Making the situation more serious, Ellington was not recording as often as he might have wished, and he certainly was not turning out hit records.

Hodges was Ellington's biggest star, and he felt that it was time to go out on his own. He was lured by the possibilities, both artistic and financial, of having his own group. Perhaps, too, he sensed the crisis that was overtaking big bands, including his long-time employer. He formed a small group, which included Brown and Greer, that was to have considerable commercial success for several years.

1 Some of the "sweet" dance bands from the swing era, or their ghost bands, managed to survive, but none of them was breaking any new musical ground.

With three of his star attractions gone, there was considerable speculation in the jazz press that Ellington's band could not survive.

The salvation of the Ellington band came in what became known as the "raid" of Harry James's band. Ellington contacted Juan Tizol, long-time veteran of his band who had left in 1944. Tizol talked the dynamic young drummer Louie Bellson and veteran alto saxophonist Willie Smith, who had played lead alto for many years with the great Jimmie Lunceford band, into joining him in his return to Ellington. James was apparently quite gracious about letting his men go, although it seems that it would have been difficult to hold them back in the light of the fact that they were only working a few days a week with James.[2]

Tizol, of course, came back to his old chair – the valve trombone chair. He played the parts that he had played for years: the solo melody statements on his own compositions and some of those of Ellington, the second (and usually middle) voice in the three-part trombone section, other parts that were often written voiced along with saxophones, and occasionally the lowest voice in the brass texture.

Yet a major problem remained. How could Lawrence Brown be replaced? Brown, who was the crucial element in the definition of Ellington's trombone writing; Brown, the great balladeer; Brown, the suave, facile and superb swing soloist.

While Brown's departure left a large musical gap to fill, during the latter half of the 1940s his solo space had declined from the high of the early '40s, when he seemed to be soloing on almost everything. Part of this was attributable to the fact that Tyree Glenn, from the "third" trombone chair, not only played the plunger-muted solos, but was also getting his share of ballad and swing solos, which cut into Brown's share of solo space. Furthermore, it seemed that the band's arrangements featured fewer trombone solos during this period than they had in the late '30s and early '40s. This trend was to continue into the '50s and '60s, as more and more solos were covered by saxophones and trumpets, rather than trombones. For the most part, historians have noted how little Ellington was affected by the rise of bop in the 1940s. However, in the reduction of the solo role of the trombone in favor of the more technically oriented saxophone and trumpet, Ellington, if not overtly affected by the development of bop, at least made changes that paralleled it. The increased technical demands of bop were much better suited to the "faster" instruments, and it was only the most facile of trombonists who were able to "keep up." For whatever reasons, it was during this time that Ellington started leaning toward the

2 This information is generally known, but was confirmed in conversation with Louie Bellson. He even related that James told the "defectors" to take him along with them.

reeds and trumpets in his selection of soloists.

The man who replaced Lawrence Brown showed some notable parallels to Brown. He came from Los Angeles, he had a somewhat light, smooth sound, and he was one of the great technicians the instrument had known.

Britt Woodman was born in Los Angeles in 1920. He grew up in that city, counting among his close boyhood friends future jazz great Charles Mingus.[3] Introduced to the trombone by his father, William, Woodman quickly developed into a formidable player. Woodman claims that his father was an extremely accomplished trombonist, "as great as Lawrence Brown." People often suggested that Britt sounded like Lawrence Brown, but he asserts that he actually sounded like his father. His father was a thorough teacher as well as a stern taskmaster, who not only taught Britt the rudiments of playing, but pushed his son to the point where he could play such technically challenging pieces as *Flight of the Bumblebee* and the virtuoso trombone solos of Arthur Pryor. There may well have been a future for Britt in symphonic and concert music, but his father felt that there was no chance for success in that field for a black player.

The elder Woodman was also something of an entrepenuer, and he organized his three oldest sons, William, Coney, and Britt and others into The Woodman Brothers Band, billed as "The Biggest Little Band In The World." Britt, like his brothers, had learned to play several instruments – in his case, tenor saxophone and clarinet in addition to trombone. In an early version of the band, one could hear "4 Musicians Who Play Like 8." The original fourth member of the group was drummer George Reed, who was soon to join Horace Henderson's band. When the fourth Woodman brother, Lawrence, grew old enough to join the act, he played drums and tap danced – and "got most of the tips." Later on, a young Ernie Royal played trumpet with the group.

While still in school, Britt often subbed for his father in the orchestra at Los Angeles's Follies Theater, and by the time he was in his late teens, he had worked with pianist Phil Moore and the great swing arranger and composer Jimmy Mundy. Finally, in 1940, he joined Les Hite's band – the band in which Lawrence Brown had made his name in the early '30s. Woodman was in military service from 1942-1946, where in service bands he not only played swing and dance music, but also continued his technical development by playing such selections as *Carnival of Venice* on the baritone horn.

Upon discharge from the service, Woodman returned to Los

3   Woodman appears in several of the episodes in Mingus's autobiographical work *Beneath the Underdog*. In our discussion, Woodman detailed a number of incidents in which he witnessed, and aided in, Mingus's early development. He also confirmed some of what Mingus related in his book.

Britt Woodman, 5/94
(Photo © by P. Brunner)

Angeles. During the next couple of years, he worked with Boyd
Raeburn's band, Eddie Heywood's small group, and a mid-'40s
edition of Lionel Hampton's big band. Woodman's solo on the
Raeburn band's barn-burning *Boyd Meets Stravinsky*[4] was an
indication of his technical prowess and one of the directions in
which his solo work would go. He entered Westlake College in
Los Angeles in 1948 and studied harmony, arranging and sol-
feggio for the next two years. During this time, he also spent
considerable time with a loosely organized group known as the
"Stars of Swing." Along with Woodman's old pal Mingus, this
group included another boyhood friend, saxophonist Buddy
Collette, and another saxophonist who was to become important in his own right, Lucky Thompson. Woodman has characterized this group as a sort of musical cooperative, with no
nominal leader. He felt that it may have served as a model for
some of Mingus's later groups (some of them known as Jazz
Workshops), although in those groups Mingus was clearly
leader. Woodman now rues the fact that he was not one of the
"jammers" in this outfit, rather sticking to his assigned parts,
while some of the others dominated the improvisation.

4   This cut recently appeared on
the Smithsonian Institution's
record set *Big Band Jazz*. See
discographical notes.

Woodman got the call to join the Ellington band from Las Vegas in February of 1951. Woodman believes that he was recommended for the band by the manager of Boyd Raeburn's band. When he joined the band, the other members of the trombone section were Quentin Jackson and Claude Jones, who was back for a short stay. Jones was gone in March, and with the return of Tizol the section became Woodman, Tizol and Jackson.

While Ellington's recording situation remained shakier than it had been in the late '30s and early '40s, the personnel of the whole band, not just the trombone section, was solidifying, and in some ways strengthening. Besides Tizol, Smith, Bellson and Woodman, other relative newcomers who were especially valuable additions to the band were trumpeters Clark Terry and Willie Cook, and the brilliant tenor saxophonist, Paul Gonsalves. One might argue that the personnel of the band was stronger than it had been since the early 1940s.[5]

With the final departure of Tyree Glenn in late 1950 and the return of Juan Tizol, Quentin Jackson soon became the new plunger man in the trombone section. It seems only natural that Jackson should have taken on this demanding role. Britt Woodman claims that Jackson knew virtually all of the trombone solos that were on Ellington's recordings. Jackson related that Ellington told him, "Tyree [Glenn] told me that you could play anything. So he told me that you could do this [take over the plunger role]."[6]

Indeed, Quentin "Butter" Jackson was a remarkable figure in the history of jazz trombone. Born in Springfield, Ohio in 1909, Jackson was something of a child prodigy. By age four, he had performed a piano solo in church. In addition to his interest in piano, he was also interested in singing at a very early age, and at age eleven or twelve, he took up violin and was soon soloing with his school orchestra. While still in his teens, he heard McKinney's Synco Septet (the forerunner of McKinney's Cotton Pickers) and was taken with the playing of the group's excellent trombonist, Claude Jones. Jones started seeing Jackson's sister (who he eventually married), so stopped often at the Jackson home. Aware of Jackson's musical background, and bemoaning the lack of good trombonists, Jones finally talked Jackson into taking up trombone.

Young Quentin was soon playing with area bands – the Buckeye Melodians (at one time led by Basie saxophone great Earle Warren's father) and from Cincinnati, Wesley Helvey's band. Trombonist Floyd Brady, then with Zack Whyte's band, a

5   Britt Woodman feels that the band of the early 1950s was the strongest, or at least tightest, group that Ellington ever had.
6   All quotes from Jackson interview for the Smithsonian Oral History Project (reel 1, 17).

more prominent territory band, took the inexperienced Jackson under his wing and introduced him to the famous Arban brass studies as well as the recordings of Miff Mole. In January of 1930 Jackson left Helvey and himself joined up with Whyte, for whom young Sy Oliver, who was later to become one of the great arrangers of the swing era, was writing arrangements.

In December of 1930, Jackson joined McKinney's Cotton Pickers, one of the finest bands in jazz. Part of the reason Jackson was picked up was his singing ability, as vocals were important in McKinney's book. In the trombone section, he joined Ed Cuffee, who had taken Claude Jones's place. It was here, for his young, tender and rotund appearance, that he acquired his lifelong nickname, "Butter." In 1932 Butter went to New York with the intention of joining Fletcher Henderson's band, to sing, play trombone, violin, and piano! But he was "intercepted" by McKinney's former musical director, Don Redman, and joined his band instead. In Redman's band he joined his old friend Claude Jones and Benny Morton in one of the first, and finest, trombone trios in jazz history.[7] At about that same time, he also played a week with Cab Calloway in the Cotton Club in New York and was asked to join Calloway's outfit.

Some years later, in 1940, Jackson left Redman and finally did join Calloway. At roughly the same time, Tyree Glenn also joined Calloway's band, taking the place of Claude Jones. Thus was established another of the excellent trombone sections of the Swing Era: Jackson, Glenn and Keg Johnson.[8] As well as playing trombone, Jackson continued his singing with Cab Calloway's band. Eight years later, when he quit Calloway, there was, as he described it, "a long lull." Ellington went to Europe without his band, but before leaving told Jackson not to take a regular job with anyone. Still, Jackson needed work, so he temporarily joined Lucky Millinder but remained only three weeks before he was fired. This was the only band from which Jackson was ever fired. Millinder told Jackson that he was a great trombone player and a gentleman, but just not what he was looking for at that time.[9] This seeming misfortune did, however, lead Jackson to the Ellington band.

To complete a tangled web of relationships with other trombonists, Jackson joined Ellington after the European trip, by stepping in for his brother-in-law Claude Jones and rejoining Tyree Glenn, his long-time section mate from Calloway's band. His first engagement was in late October at a place in Washington that was then called the Duke Ellington Club.[10]

Jackson had prepared himself for the move to the Ellington band back in 1943, when he would leave his job with Calloway

7 Along with Ellington's, this was the beginning of three-man trombone sections in jazz.

8 Jackson says in *The World of Swing* that there were four players in Calloway's trombone section when he joined – himself, Jones, Glenn and Johnson. If this is correct, it must have been a time of transition, as Jones was soon gone.

9 Jackson interview, reel 5, 54.

10 In his interview, Jackson claimed that his first date with the band was October 21, 1948 at the Ellington Club. Records show, though, that the band was at the Paradise Theater in Detroit from October 15-21 and did not start its engagement at the Washington club until October 22.

at the Strand Theater in New York and go and sit in with Ellington's band at the Hurricane Club, where it was "in residence" from April through September. He said that he sat in Tizol's chair, in effect, the one that he was to take over. Sandy Williams was filling in at this time for Lawrence Brown, who was on temporary leave. According to Jackson, Tricky Sam Nanton "used to tell me all the time . . . 'Gee whiz, when are you going to give me a break? When are you going to sit in my chair, man?' I told him . . . 'It'll never happen. I'll never try to play – I'll never be able to grab that plunger.'"[11] But circumstances were to prove different within a few years.

While Jackson did take over the "second" chair, Tizol's old position, there is some question as to how much he actually played valve trombone. There is, however, at least one photograph of him with a valve trombone in the Ellington band.[12] Because Tizol had not been a jazz soloist, the second chair in Ellington's trombone section had traditionally been the least visible. On the 1950 tour of Europe, this began to change. Glenn did not make the trip (see previous chapter), so Jackson had already started to do the plunger solos. Ted Kelly, who was hired to fill the open chair just for the tour, returned home after only two weeks to get married. Then, several weeks into the tour, in Italy, Lawrence Brown got sick. Butter took the opportunity to show his great versatility. As Jackson described it,

"that left me by myself. I was playing Lawrence's solos, playing Tricky Sam's chair, and I would take different parts and whatever part that I thought would fit in different spots, see? I would play that part whether it was first, second, or third, whatever I thought would fit. And I had to do that by myself until we got back."[13]

Also on this trip, Jackson's nickname went international, as Ellington began referring to him as "Monsieur du Beurre."

Back from the trip, Glenn rejoined the band to play the plunger solos on the *Masterpieces by Ellington* album in December. But in the first few months of 1951, when Glenn made his final break[14] and Tizol returned, Jackson vacated the second chair, which he had been playing for most of the period since 1948 and permanently moved to the third chair. This resulted in his picking up the plunger solos and also the lowest notes in the trombone sonority, a function in which he excelled. In 1953, however, after Tizol left the Ellington band for the second time, Jackson again played the solos that Tizol was responsible for on tunes that Tizol had written, such as *Caravan* and *Bakiff*.[15] He was also often called upon by Ellington to play old tunes and standards that were requested by audiences. According to John

11 Jackson interview, reel 6, 5-6.
12 This photograph is in the album booklet for *Duke Ellington and his orchestra: Carnegie Hall, November 13, 1948*. Vintage Jazz Classics VJC-1024/25-2.
13 Jackson interview, reel 5, 69.
14 Glenn did make some appearances with the band in the 1970s.
15 According to John Sanders, he only took over these solos from Jackson after he had been in the band for about two years and had finally taken up the valve trombone.

Quentin "Butter" Jackson
(Smithsonian Institution)

Sanders, "[Butter] played all the old songs."[16] He took over this role from his former section mate Lawrence Brown, who had been the previous "standard player."

Britt Woodman had the highest praise for Jackson, claiming "Butter was an institute. Something that you'd pay a million dollars for, he had it natural." He "did everything;" played "trombone, bass [Jackson filled in on bass a number of times in the Ellington band], piano, drove the bus," he even "ran a switchboard at a hotel." He had "a beautiful velvet voice." "He knew all the Lawrence Brown solos, he could play all Cootie Williams's solos." Once on a job he even played piano on the introduction to a tune that Ellington himself had forgotten.

16 This and subsequent quotes by Sanders taken from my 1992 interview.

John Sanders was one of the first to join the Ellington organization without much of a professional "track record" since
the early days of the band. His experience was quite unlike that
of Claude Jones, Wilbur DeParis, Tyree Glenn and Quentin
Jackson, who joined Ellington only after lengthy and distinguished apprenticeships in name bands. And although Britt
Woodman, his section mate, did not have the years of service
that the above-mentioned veterans had, he had played in several well-known bands – those of Les Hite, Boyd Raeburn and
Lionel Hampton.

Born in 1925, Sanders grew up in Harlem, and among his
fondest childhood memories were trips with his aunt and cousin
to the Paramount, Strand and Apollo theaters in the late 1930s
to hear the great bands. The one band that always stood out to
him was Duke Ellington's. He was impressed at how at the
beginning of a show, the Ellington band first appeared behind a
scrim. Thus, although there were various colored lights and images of instrumentalists, none of the individual musicians could
be seen clearly until after several numbers had been played.
"He'd play a little concert almost before the scrim went up."
This unique and colorful presentation separated Ellington's
band from all others. "To this day I've never seen anything like
it in a band presentation." When Ellington announced his pieces,
"I was listening to a composer introduce his compositions."
Sanders also noted that even though Ellington featured his star
soloists who came down in front of the band to be take the spot-
light, "the band played so wonderfully together."

Sanders went to the High School of Commerce where he
began learning to play trombone. He listened to the big bands
on Martin Block's "Make Believe Ballroom" on radio station
WNEW. A particular favorite was "Saturday Night in Harlem,"
the show that featured the black bands.

During World War II, Sanders joined the Navy. He went to
the Great Lakes base north of Chicago, where he was switched
to baritone horn to play in a military-style band. He ended up
serving most of his hitch in San Diego, where he played baritone in the ceremonial band and trombone in the dance band.
He started listening closely to the Ellington band on recordings
that some of his older bandmates had brought with them, and
was soon able to identify Lawrence Brown on tunes such as *All
Too Soon*, and hear the way Tizol would be scored with the
saxophone section.

In the fall of 1944 while on leave, Sanders spent most of a day
in Chicago where he watched four shows of the Ellington band
(and four showings of a forgettable movie) at the Downtown

John Sanders (Photo by Kurt Dietrich)

Theater. He mustered up the courage to go backstage and talk with Lawrence Brown. Thus began a relationship with the Ellington band that was to continue for many years.

Once out of the service, Sanders returned to New York and entered the Juilliard School of Music on the GI Bill. He studied there with the distinguished trombonists Ernest Clarke and Davis Shuman. Sanders gives Shuman a great deal of credit for teaching him how to play the instrument "correctly." After completing his studies at Juilliard, Sanders started to play engagements around New York while working a variety of day jobs. The most significant of his music jobs was with the eight-piece band of Lucky Thompson, the house band at the Savoy Ballroom for a time in 1952. He also did some playing with a short-lived band led by Mercer Ellington.

In February of 1953, while the senior Ellington's band was at the Apollo Theater, Mercer told Sanders that "Pop" needed a trombone player. Ellington knew that Juan Tizol was about to go to Los Angeles to settle some personal affairs. Mercer told Sanders to go meet his father, who promptly asked Sanders to sit in. Tizol showed Sanders the book, gave him his jacket, and as the lights went out, told him just to do what the other guys told him to. After Sanders had survived this trial by fire, Ellington invited him to play "a few nights" with the band. The few nights stretched into a week, and when the band left New York, Sanders went along. Although Ellington never officially asked him to stay, Sanders continued to play job after job until the band had made its way all the way to the West Coast six weeks later.

Tizol did return to the band, and played until December of 1953. After he left, several replacements filled in, including George Jean and big band veteran Alfred Cobbs. When the band returned East early in 1954, however, Ellington was still looking for a permanent replacement for Tizol, and Sanders got the call and joined the band in Toronto during the first week of February.

All that Sanders did in the section for many months was play parts – he did no soloing. Butter Jackson was not only playing the plunger-muted solos, but he also continued to play many of Tizol's melodic solos. Some of Tizol's old solo lines were played by the unison trombone section.

In late May 1955, Harry James's band and Ellington's band were in Salt Lake City on the same night. Tizol, back with James, told Sanders about a valve trombone that had recently been specially made for him by the well-known California instrument maker, Calicchio. This instrument was built in the

key of C (instead of the usual B-flat), like the instrument that
Tizol had played for years, but it had a larger bore (the diame-
ter of the internal opening) and bell and had an extra valve to
facilitate playing in the low register. Tizol had been using it some
but was not completely happy with it, so he suggested that
Sanders give it a try. He sent the horn to Sanders and shortly thereafter sold it to him – for $250 or $300 – premium 1950s'
prices.

The Ellington band spent much of the summer of 1955 playing at the *Aquacade* show in Flushing, in Flushing, in Queens,
New York City. This engagement certainly did not mark one of
the high points of the band's career. The *Aquacade* was a variety
show, prominently featuring a "dancing waters" fountain display, intended for family entertainment. The band supplied
music for a variety of acts – skaters, dancers, divers and come-
dians. Ellington himself appeared only for the closing selection
of each show, a medley of his own hits. Band members who did
not belong to the New York City local of the American
Federation of Musicians were not allowed to play for the show.
Thus, for example, Britt Woodman only appeared occasionally
as a substitute, and another big band veteran, Ward Silloway,
played the first trombone parts for most of the summer.

During this long engagement Sanders kept his new valve
trombone on the bandstand, and started playing it from time to
time. Even though he had considerable experience on valve
instruments from his youth and his time in the service, he had to
learn the fingerings all over again because of the different key of
this instrument. But as Britt Woodman said, "he did [this] in no
time, because he's a very brilliant person."[17] Back on the road,
one night Ellington came to Sanders and asked him to play the
solo on Billy Strayhorn's *Orson* – on valves. Sanders had played
the tune only once before, with the whole trombone trio playing
what was originally a solo valve trombone line. He told Duke
that he didn't know it and couldn't play it, but Ellington took
the music to the front of the stage and held it up for Sanders to
read. Several nights later, Ellington told Sanders just to stick
with the valve horn. His days as a slide trombonist in the
Ellington band were over. Sanders then took over Tizol's old
valve trombone solos from Jackson, with the exception of the
solo on *Bakiff*, which for some reason remained Jackson's.

Sanders also eventually took over another of Tizol's old
duties – copying parts from Ellington's, and others', scores. Tom
Whaley was the band's primary copyist at this time, but when
he was not available, or swamped with work, Sanders started
filling in. And, except on rare occasions, Whaley stayed in New

17 Woodman interview.

York, so when the band was on the road, which was most of the time, and something needed to be copied, Ellington would find Sanders, "no matter where I was." Ellington always wanted to hear what he was working on, whether it was finished or not. He might give Sanders only sixteen or thirty-two measures of a piece, but it would be passed out and played on the job the next night.

Ellington summed up what Sanders meant to the Ellington organization.

John Sanders was always, as musician, man, and ambassador, a major credit to our band, right from the beginning when he joined it in 1954. A valve trombonist, he played solos that were the nearest we ever had to Tizol's originals. He was a brilliant musician and an irreplaceable aide when we were orchestrating en masse with a devastating deadline at our heels. In addition, he was a gentleman in every sense of the word – in manners, ethics, and appearances.[18]

Although Butter Jackson's plunger playing was based on that of his predecessors, Tricky Sam Nanton and Tyree Glenn, he developed his own personal sound in the style. As he described it, ". . . when I joined the band and I started to playing [sic] the plunger, all I did was take Tricky Sam's style, actually, and relax it . . . and try to . . . make it a little . . . more relaxed." But as noted previously,[19] Ellington advised him not to play "too pretty." Many of the solos he played almost exactly as Nanton had. "I had all the records . . . It wasn't that hard because I heard every note he played. I knew all his solos, in fact."[20] In regard to his plunger playing, he also said, "I've always been a melodic trombone player to a great extent with the exception of when I get that plunger in my hand. Then my mind goes filthy."

As had been the case with Nanton, Jackson's artistry was displayed most often, and some think most effectively, in blues solos. A typical, and often-played, example of Jackson's style with the plunger is found on the tune *Jam with Sam* (Example 6-1). This piece is essentially a long string of solos. Ensemble parts are interjected between solos to add shape and direction to a framework that was really an organized jam session. First recorded in the studio on 10 May 1951, Jackson's solo was already "set," and it was played nearly identically on all subsequent recorded performances.[21] His plunger sound was somewhat different in quality from both Nanton's and Tyree Glenn's, yet Jackson has borrowed many of the sophisticated plunger techniques that they used.

18 *Music is My Mistress*, 228.
19 See discussion on Glenn's plunger work in Chapter 5.
20 Jackson interview, reel 6, 6.
21 The transcribed version is from 10 May 1951. See discographical notes for other recordings.

Example 6-1

a = ah, i = ee, + = closed, o = open

As Nanton did on so many of his solos years earlier, Jackson devised a solo that is very simple musically, and because of that – or perhaps even in spite of it – a solo that is not only very direct, but memorable. Entering at the end of the fourth bar in a twelve-bar blues structure, he plays the same two-bar figure three times (with slight alteration in pitch the last time). [This and succeeding transcriptions of Jackson's plunger-muted solos are notated similarly to the Nanton and Glenn transcriptions in Chapters 2 and 5: in this example, both the closed (+) and open (o) plunger markings and the resultant syllable sounds, "i" (sounding "ee") and "a" (sounding "ah") are employed.] At the end of this first chorus, Jackson adds the growl that is so characteristic of the Ellington plunger tradition and articulates in a manner that sounds very close to the famous Nanton "ya."

Jackson's second chorus is also made up of simple repeated riffs. The first (from the end of measure eight to the beginning of measure twelve) alternates closed and open notes. When he ascends to an impressive series of high E-flats (measures 13-16), he first uses the traditional "wa" (closed plunger going to open very quickly). "Wa's" are continued through the next several bars before he finishes with another short growled "ya" figure.

On the marvelous "jungle" composition from 1928, *The Mooche*, Jackson demonstrated his bluesy plunger style in a quite different setting (Example 6-2). Like his solo on *Jam with Sam*, Jackson early on devised a "set" solo, which he played over and over in virtually identical form.[22] This solo, too, is very melodic, and shows more of the vocal characteristics associated with Nanton's style. There is no empty display of technique, yet there is an impressive variety of plunger techniques. Most notes of the solo sound like the traditional "wa" found in most brass plunger work. Exceptions occur in the figure found in measures 10-11 and recapitulated in measures 22-23. In this figure Jackson goes from an open sound (o) to a closed sound (+) and back to the open sound. Other notable characteristics are his frequent switching back and forth between the unmodified plunger sound and the guttural "growl" and the dramatic use of dynamic contrast in the second chorus (measure 13 to end).

This solo was so effective and enduring that when Lawrence Brown took over the plunger chair in the 1960s and soloed on this tune he invariably quoted liberally from Jackson's solo.

22 The transcribed version is from 1 July 1952. A preliminary one-chorus version of this solo was on the Snader transcription film from March of 1952. See discographical notes for other recordings.

EXAMPLE 6-2

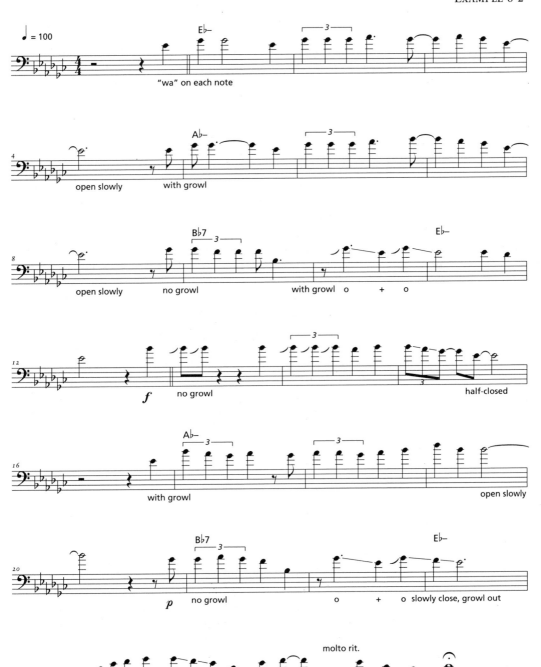

From his very first days in the band, Britt Woodman's abilities did not go unnoticed by Ellington, who spoke of his new man, saying, "He came to us out of a [sic] left field. From Los Angeles to be exact. He's phenomenal. He plays notes that are two octaves off the horn! Naturally he's got to demand respect."[23] And on another occasion it was reported, "'You know that boy just sat down and read the book,' Duke says, shaking his head in wonder."[24]

Was there any pressure on Woodman to be "the new Lawrence Brown"? When he first joined the band, Ellington asked Woodman to play *Sophisticated Lady*. Woodman went down front and played the tune, then on the second chorus played some of the melodic variations that Lawrence Brown had created [see Chapter 4]. Afterward, Duke apologized to Woodman for calling that tune, telling him "play yourself," not Lawrence Brown.[25]

Woodman the virtuoso was shown off from the very beginning of his tenure in the band. His first recorded solos with Ellington were on the May 1951 date mentioned above, where he, like Jackson, took a spot on *Jam with Sam*, and he also soloed on another swinger, *Fancy Dan*. He had taken over Tyree Glenn's showcase, *Sultry Serenade*, (see Chapter 5), and used it as a vehicle for his outstanding range. He recorded this piece and a blues that featured him and Jackson, *Britt and Butter Blues*, with the small Ellington group billed as the Coronets (and on a later release, the Billy Strayhorn All-Stars) only a week after the May '51 full band session. In 1954, clarinetist Jimmy Hamilton fashioned a new framework for Woodman, *Theme for Trambean*. A recently released concert performance has captured the routine that Woodman developed for the end of the piece. Woodman shows all of his considerable range and technical ability (Example 6-3: drum set keeps time throughout, meter changes have been added to reflect accents). The routine is obviously worked out, but no less impressive because of that. The opening two measures descend from G to D. It is impossible to indicate precisely the microtones in this passage – small accidentals indicate pitches that are between the half steps that can be indicated with conventional notation. Much of the musical material of this cadenza is based on diminished figures (measures 11-16, 44-46). Especially amazing is the series of four-octave leaps (measures 17-28). The high E-flat in measure 49 is far out of the range of almost all trombonists. Woodman often included in his solos riff figures that were popular in the mainstream jazz vocabulary – measures 30-40 in this solo are a good example of this.

23 Gammond, 109.
24 Gleason, *Celebrating the Duke,* 174.
25 Woodman interview.

EXAMPLE 6-3

descends microtonally from G to D in 2 measures

(band)

(band)

Despite his remarkable technical abilities, Britt Woodman was not all flash. Most of his improvised work was on short solos, often the blues. While he never developed a solo style as distinctive as some of Ellington's other soloists, Woodman's was a jazz voice that added flavor to the rich Ellington stew of solo voices. Woodman was usually categorized musically with the "younger" men of the band – trumpeter Clark Terry and tenor saxophonist Paul Gonsalves. But like Terry and Gonsalves, Woodman's jazz style owed more to the swing era than to bebop, although all three of them certainly had musical ties to more modern styles. His style was in marked contrast to that of his section mate "Butter" Jackson, much as the styles of Lawrence Brown and Tricky Sam Nanton had contrasted in the trombone section of the '30s and '40s.

If the Ellington band went through what might be seen as doldrums in the early and mid-1950s from the standpoint of popularity, the band was still flourishing musically. The event that led to a popular rebirth of the band was the Newport Jazz Festival of July 1956. The band's performance of the evening of July 7 – particularly Paul Gonsalves's twenty-seven blues choruses on the so-called "Wailing Interval" in between the two halves of *Diminuendo and Crescendo in Blue* – has become a part of jazz legend.

Often forgotten is the piece that Ellington wrote specially for the occasion, the *Newport Jazz Festival Suite*. As in so much of Ellington's work, the blues plays a most prominent part in this suite; indeed, two of the three movements are in blues form. A representative example of Woodman's jazz style is from *Festival Junction*, the first movement of the *Suite* (Example 6-4).[26] Entering at the end of the third bar of a chorus after an ensemble shout figure, Woodman again displays his effortless high register. The second chorus swings relaxedly, with many repeated notes – another use of riff-like figures – and an attractive little sequence in measures 17 and 18.

It is difficult to imagine, listening to some of the magnificent playing that he did with Ellington, but Woodman has talked about the problems he was having playing solos: he developed a mental block toward going out front and playing by himself. He says that he was wondering "if people could see my legs shaking." It seems that after playing about eight measures he would be fine, but the beginning of each solo would be torture. He asked Lawrence Brown how his recorded solos came out so well, how they fit so well into the fabric of the arrangements. Brown told Woodman how he planned the solos out ahead of

26 This movement of the *Suite* also featured a typical Jackson blues solo.

Example 6-4

time [see Chapter 4]. Woodman tried the same thing, but once he got up in front of the band, his plans would desert him and something completely different would come out of his horn. Finally, in 1957, he went to Ellington and told him that he didn't want to play any more improvised solos. Woodman felt that he wasn't doing justice to the solo spots. Ellington continued to give Woodman written solos, but no longer pushed him into playing improvised solos, at least on recording sessions. Hearing his recorded solos with Ellington some years later (he didn't listen to them at the time they were made), however, Woodman declared himself to be "halfway pleased."

Whatever his own reservations, Woodman made significant contributions to the Ellington band as a jazz soloist. Nonetheless, it might well be argued that Woodman's greatest musical contributions to the Ellington legacy were his exceptional section playing and his astonishing performances of written solos.

The written solos that Ellington devised for Woodman really allowed the virtuoso abilities of Woodman to come to the fore.

One of Ellington's greatest musical triumphs, not only of the '50s but of his whole career, was his *Shakespearean Suite*, better known as *Such Sweet Thunder*. This work, or set of works, fashioned by Ellington and Billy Strayhorn for the Stratford Shakespearean Festival held in Stratford, Ontario, was rushed to performance for a "Music for Moderns" concert at New York's Town Hall in April of 1957. Recorded in May, it features brilliant writing for the band and its outstanding soloists based on, or at least inspired by, characters from Shakespeare's works. Woodman was featured on *Sonnet for Hank Cinq*, a humorous reference to Henry V (Example 6-5). Whether or not "the changes of tempo have to do with the changes of pace and the map as a result of wars," as Ellington reportedly noted,[27] the piece serves as a framework for brilliant playing by Woodman. Each of the first two two-bar phrases that Woodman must play cover the range of two octaves. In the next four measures (m. 5-8), he must negotiate the range of two octaves and a fourth. After a contrasting interlude featuring both Woodman and the other trombonists, Woodman repeats the opening section. The performance comes to a climax with the closing cadenza. Woodman ends the piece with a flawless high A-flat, again "in the stratosphere" of the range of the trombone.

Butter Jackson contributed what many consider to be his most affecting plunger solo ever on another movement of *Such Sweet Thunder*, *Sonnet for Sister Kate* (Example 6-6). Dedicated to Katharina of *The Taming of the Shrew*, this movement is a brilliant lyrical miniature that stands with the finest of the Ellington-Strayhorn collaborations. Despite Jackson's claim about his mind "going filthy" when he used the plunger, this musical statement shows him at his lyrical best. Jackson does little but play the written line in straightforward fashion, adding volume and inflection to reach a climax in measures 24-26. But the combined poignancy of the melody, Jackson's simple and vocal "wa's" on almost every note of the piece, and the supporting harmony of the reed section produce one of those magical moments that Ellington and Strayhorn were able to create with remarkable consistency.

27 Notes for Columbia album JCL
   1033, *Such Sweet Thunder*.

Example 6-5

EXAMPLE 6-6

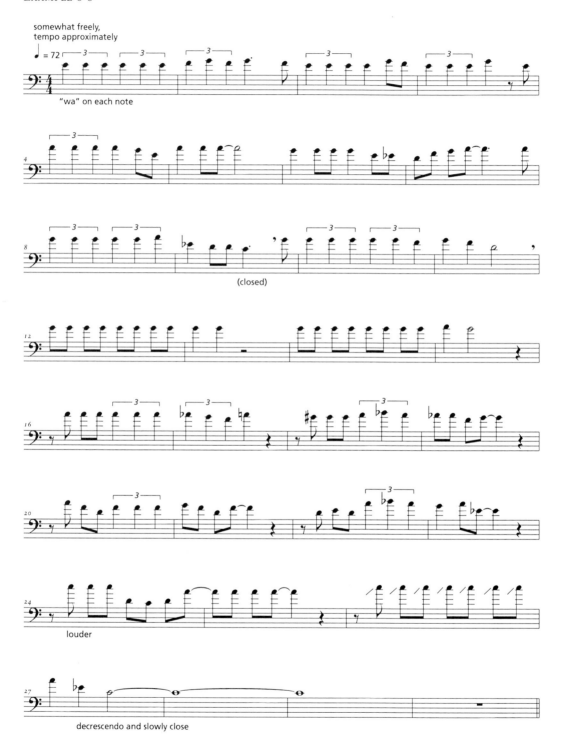

John Sanders was a fine section player, and once he switched from slide to valve trombone he beautifully played the melodic solos that Tizol had played – *Caravan* and *Lost in Meditation* – as well as newer pieces like *Orson* and *Blue Jean Beguine*. His personal favorite was the spiritual theme *Come Sunday* from *Black, Brown and Beige* [see Chapter 3]. The band, with Sanders soloing, recorded a fine performance of a revamped *Black, Brown and Beige* with the great vocalist Mahalia Jackson in 1958.

Sanders was only rarely heard as an improvising soloist. One occasion is on a small group date from March of 1957. The most notable of his solo excursions, however, was recorded in the summer of 1957 on the dates that produced Ella Fitzgerald's album *The Duke Ellington Songbook*. The first chorus of this solo was recorded almost identically (and without acknowledgment in the album liner notes) in February of 1956 on a cut that was labeled simply as *The Blues*. Sanders takes two nicely relaxed choruses on this blues that became known as *Total Jazz*, the last movement from Ellington's suite *A Portrait of Ella Fitzgerald* (Example 6-7). There is nothing that particularly stands out about this solo, either stylistically or technically. It simply "works" and swings. Two figures help tie the solos together: a descending quarter note figure, in measures 5, 13 and 15; and a three-note figure of two eighth-notes followed by a quarter – either B-G-G or D-G-G – in measures 3, 11, 17, 19 and 23. Britt Woodman later remarked of Sanders, "his solos [were] so good, Duke should have had him playing all along."

In 1958, the band premiered a suite that was like the *Newport Jazz Festival Suite* in a number of respects. The individual pieces of the suite were only loosely related to one another. They featured some attractive writing for the band, but were primarily showcases for the band's outstanding soloists. And like the *Newport Suite*, this new suite was performed only a few times publicly. Probably first played in August as the *Great South Bay Suite* (for a jazz festival outside of New York on Long Island), it reappeared in a performance in September at the Plaza Hotel in New York. The latter performance was recorded and released on Columbia Records in a series of Jazz at the Plaza recordings. Finally, in February 1959, bearing the title *Toot Suite*, the work was recorded in the studio for the session that resulted in the heralded *Jazz Party* album.[28]

28 The following two solos are transcribed from the studio recording.

EXAMPLE 6-7

The first movement, *Red Garter*, featured Woodman in a solo in Ellington's "misterioso" style, a descendant of the jungle style that had brought him fame thirty years earlier. Woodman plays the haunting theme both at the beginning and the end of the performance. Example 6-8 is his closing statement. The piece is at a moderate tempo, and Woodman's statement in large measure showcases his beautiful tone and his outstanding control of long notes. There is nothing particularly challenging technically until he reaches measures 27-28, where he executes a two-octave jump in the duration of only a sixteenth note. He repeats this jump twice, then does a series of slurs between high C and high F. His control, especially considering that the whole performance is in bucket mute, is astounding. The live recording from five months earlier shows the same impeccable playing.

Jackson was also featured in this suite, on the movement entitled *Red Carpet*. His solo in this work (Example 6-9) again demonstrates the intricate connection between Jackson's plunger style and blues feeling already observed in *The Mooche*. While a number of Jackson's solos were "set" solos, a comparison of the two recorded versions of this work show that this solo decidedly was not. While the general mood of the solo is similar (despite two somewhat different tempos) in the two renditions, and some of the plunger devices carry over from one performance to the other, no part of either solo is just like any part of the other. The solo played at the *Jazz Party* session is one of the finest Jackson ever recorded. He has total command of the plunger and its language. Like his other best work, musically this solo has an inevitability about it that seems almost perfect.

The F-E flat-B flat triplet in the first measure and measures 2 and 11, with its related figure, the D-flat-C-G found at the beginning of measures 5 and 6, becomes the unifying force of the first of these two blues choruses. The emotional content of the solo is stepped up in the second chorus with the dramatic entry into the higher register in measures 13 and 14. The syncopated figure in measures 15 and 16 introduces a new rhythmic element at precisely the right moment. The last two-thirds of a two-beat triplet connect measures 18, 20 and 22. As the tempo slows, Jackson adds more drama with the shakes on the held notes in measures 23 and 24. The triplets in measure 24 echo the figure that held together the first chorus, effectively completing the statement.

EXAMPLE 6-8

EXAMPLE 6-9

Throughout, Jackson exhibits the full range of plunger effects – "wa's," tightly closed passages, and especially in this solo,
a sort of half-closed effect that approximates the sound "oo,"
indicated in shorthand in the transcription as "u." Another
sound that is effectively employed is one rarely heard from
Jackson's predecesors in the trombone section, but occasionally
from the trumpet master Cootie Williams – something approaching "ow," or "wow." This effect is produced by starting with the
plunger closed against the bell of the instrument, opening it,
then closing it again quickly. It amounts to "oo" followed by
"ah" followed by another "oo." It is indicated in the transcription by "au" or "wau." Also in this example, the symbol "o"
represents a vowel sound ("oh") rather than being used as the
notation for closed plunger.

If there had been any questions about Jackson's status as a
plunger soloist before 1959, this solo laid them to rest. Jackson
was a most worthy successor to the legacy of Tricky Sam
Nanton and Tyree Glenn.

The section of Sanders, Woodman and Jackson was consistent and outstanding as a group. There is little question that as
a section playing parts, leaving aside the matter of solo work,
the trio of Woodman, Jackson and either Tizol or John Sanders
was close to, if not the equal of, the great section of Brown,
Tizol and Nanton. Any Ellington recording from the 1950s cor-
roborates this conclusion.

Jackson, Woodman and Sanders have all talked about the joy
of playing Ellington's music – and playing it together. Jackson
said about this group,

*John Sanders and Britt Woodman and myself were the trom-
bones, [and] the trombone section to me was impeccable. Clean
. . . anything we played was clean. We don't [sic] care how good
[the rest of the band] played or how bad they played. We always
played good. . . because there was a lot of love between Britt and
John and I, you know. And our tones blended. The sound of our
horns blended together. We used to play unison things and we'd
be so together it would sound like one horn. You couldn't tell it
was unison. That's how the intonation was.*[29]

Woodman talked about the richness of the trombone parts in
the arrangements that Ellington and Strayhorn devised. "Everything is so interesting that you're playing. And you enjoy playing because you're working, and you know what you're doing is
so important. And without [the trombone parts] the arrangement wouldn't sound like anything."[30]

Sanders spoke in much the same vein. "Duke kept us busy.

29 Jackson interview, reel 6, 44.
30 Woodman interview.

We always had interesting parts to play." He talked warmly about how Britt and Butter were so good and so helpful to him. "We had a lot of fun together. We hung out together – had coffee together, [ate] together." And especially, "We enjoyed playing together."[31]

But this section would not last forever.

31 Sanders interview.

The Duke Ellington Orchestra on The Ed Sullivan Show
Trombone section: Lawrence Brown, Chuck Connors, Buster Cooper
(Smithsonian Institution)

The Last Great Section

The triumph at the Newport Jazz Festival in 1956 is often cited as the beginning of another of the sustained peaks in the long history of the Ellington orchestra. A number of reasons are usually cited as contributing factors to this renaissance. While there was never again to be a golden era of big bands to rival the Swing Era, the musical climate had seemingly stabilized in a way that could support the few remaining great jazz bands. The singers who had depended on the big bands in the Swing Era for their instrumental support, only to eclipse the bands in popular music during World War II and the post-war years, had established their own share of the market. The jazz world had adjusted to both the new language of bebop and the so-called "Dixieland" revival, and there was room for some of the veterans to revive the big band scene. Count Basie, working with a combo for several years, reorganized a big band in the mid-1950s and, sparked by the popularity of Joe Williams's vocals, was experiencing commercial success. Woody Herman was on the verge of the arrival of musically prosperous new Herds, and Stan Kenton, negotiating the fringes of dance and mood music as well as big band and experimental jazz, continued to support a large musical aggregation. Even the onslaught of the then-new rock and roll could not derail these survivors. It was time for Ellington, too, to flourish.

Directly as a result of the Newport performance, Ellington was to sign a new contract with Columbia Records. With a sympathetic producer (most often Irving Townsend) and the clout of a major record label that was committed to allowing Ellington to record often, much new material was kept in front of the public. Whether Ellington's creativity drove the decision to record so prolifically or whether the opportunity to record stimulated his creativity is a moot question.

Within the band itself, at least two personnel changes had a profound impact: the return of Johnny Hodges and the hiring of Sam Woodyard to man the drum chair. Woodyard was by no means the most proficient drummer that Ellington ever had. He did not possess the precision and fire of Louie Bellson nor the theatrical flair and sense of percussion color of Sonny Greer. But he was a drummer who excelled in driving a band, and he was a master at the fine art of swing. The sensation that Paul Gonsalves's twenty-seven blues choruses had created at Newport was due, certainly in part, to the rhythmic drive that Woodyard supplied. The Ellington band of the late 1950s and early 1960s was a band that swung.

Hodges was the greatest soloist that the band ever had. He had experienced some early success with his small group in the 1950s while away from the Ellington organization and even after his return continued to make successful recordings under his own name, but Hodges and the Ellington band were inextricably bound together. The band was without a crucial part of its identity without Hodges, and he was in his greatest glory with the band and the compositions of Ellington and Billy Strayhorn. His return also brought together the longest-lived saxophone section in jazz history. By the time of his death in 1970, Hodges, in his two stints with the band, had been with Ellington for over thirty-seven years. His section mates also had enviably distinguished tenures: Harry Carney joined the band in 1927 and played with it right up to his death in 1974; Russell Procope came in during 1946 and remained until Ellington's death in 1974; Jimmy Hamilton was the "new" clarinetist when he joined in 1943 and remained until 1968; and Paul Gonsalves, the "junior" member of the group, was in from 1950 until his death in 1974. This astounding record of longevity has never been approached by any other organization in jazz history.

In contrast, the latter part of the 1950s and the early part of the 1960s was a time of transition for the Ellington trombone section, much like the one it had experienced a decade earlier.

The first of the "section of the '50s" to leave was John Sanders. He loved playing in the band, but he missed his family in New York. In any earlier era, he might have seen more of them while with Ellington, as previous editions of the band had numerous "location" jobs, that is, week- or month-long engagements (or more) at one place, especially in New York (notably, the over three-year residence as the house band at the Cotton Club that started in 1927). But in the '50s, clubs and theaters no longer supported big bands for long stays, and the Ellington band was constantly touring. The orchestra sometimes played a club for a week or two, but this might be followed by a month or more of one-nighters. The travel on the bus had always been demanding, but with the addition of the frequent international tours that were to occur with regularity in the 1960s, both a physical and mental stamina was required of the band members that not everyone could maintain. In any case, Sanders left the band late in the summer of 1959 to return to his family in New York and to sort out what he wanted to do with his life.[1]

Sanders's replacement, as had been traditional with the Ellington band, was a proven veteran, Mitchell "Booty" Wood. Booty Wood was born in Dayton, Ohio, December 27, 1919.[2]

Mitchell "Booty" Wood
(Photo by Ray Avery)

Booty (who carried his nickname from his youth) started trombone in school at the age of about thirteen. His school band director took a special interest in Booty, especially when Wood threatened to quit because the trombone parts in the arrangements were "so boring." While on vacation from high school, he first traveled to Florida with a band led by a certain "Pork Chops" Curry, a buck dancer who claimed to have once worked with Fats Waller. This trip led to a series of misadventures that included hoboing, jail, and nine months of what amounted to indentured slavery with the band of a Walter Johnson (not the well-known swing drummer). He returned home late in 1937

1   He entered seminary in 1965, and as of this writing, has been a Catholic priest for over twenty years.

2   Most of the biographical information given here on Wood comes from his interview with Bill Spilka, with confirmation from the Feather and Chilton reference books.

chastened by these experiences, but got the "road bug" again
and went out with Chick Carter and His Dixie Rhythm Boys in
1938. This band included two other up-and-coming jazz musicians, trumpeter Snooky Young (another Dayton native), and
trumpeter-arranger Gerald Wilson. Carter's band made it to
New York, where it played both the Savoy Ballroom and the
Apollo Theater. In 1940, Wood joined another territory band,
that of Jimmy Raschel, a band that included more future stars –
Howard McGhee, Milt Buckner, "Big Nick" Nicholas and
Wardell Gray.

In the early 1940s Wood moved to Chicago to live with an
aunt. While there he joined a group led by Tiny Bradshaw that
was the house band at a club named The Rumboogie. In 1943
he got the call to join Lionel Hampton's big band, where he
played in a section with Al Hayse and the legendary Fred
Beckett, who Wood called "the most outstanding all-around
player that I've ever worked with." Drafted into military service
in 1944, Wood went to the Great Lakes Naval Training Center
north of Chicago, where he played in bands with current and
future luminaries Clark Terry, Hobart Dotson, Gerald Wilson,
Jimmy Nottingham and Willie Smith. Arrangers for this outstanding group included Wilson, Luther Henderson and Ernie
Wilkins. Discharged from the service in 1945, Wood went back
with Hampton, playing for several months in a section with his
future section-mate in the Ellington band, Britt Woodman.
Wood left Hampton in 1947 to join a small group with
Hampton's tenor saxophone star, Arnett Cobb. Due to Cobb's
ill health, work with the small group turned out to be somewhat
sporadic, and for several years Wood went back and forth between Cobb's group and Erskine Hawkins's big band. He joined
Count Basie for a short time in 1951, but when Basie broke up
his big band for the second time in as many years, Wood decided
to return home to Dayton. He remained in Dayton, working
days at the post office and playing with various groups at night.
He led several different groups. One included his old friend
Snooky Young; another included future Ellington trombonist
Malcolm Taylor.

Wood got a call to join Ellington in 1959. The Ellington band
was in Ohio; bassist Jimmy Woode was sick, and the versatile
Butter Jackson filled in on bass for several jobs. Wood's old cronies Clark Terry and Britt Woodman talked Wood into coming
up to the bandstand to fill in with the trombone section. Later,
when John Sanders left the band, Wood went on Ellington's fall
tour of Europe and upon the band's return, according to Wood,
he became a "permanent" member. Jackson left to go with

Quincy Jones, and when Matthew Gee came in, Wood switched to the third trombone chair, the plunger chair. Wood had no previous experience with plunger playing, and apparently no real interest in it either. But Ellington's legendary musical prescience proved to be on the mark again. Only about a week after taking on this responsibility, Wood was called upon to record *Sweet and Pungent*, a tune which featured him on plunger throughout. As Stanley Dance told it, Wood's reaction was decidedly negative.

"Why would he have me play that ...?" he asked disgustedly a few minutes [after] a successful take had been accomplished.[3]

The transcription of *Sweet and Pungent*, Example 7-1, is one of the most complicated transcriptions in this book for at least two reasons. Rhythmically, Wood alternates between a 12/8 metrical feel, with each beat being divided in three parts, and a 4/4 feel, with each beat divided into two parts. Early in the solo, he stays in one or the other of those feels for a considerable number of measures. For example, the whole first chorus (measures 1-12) is in 12/8 except measure 9. The second chorus is in the duple or 4/4 feel for the first five measures (measures 13-17), but then switches back to 12/8 for five measures (18-22), and then back to 4/4 for the last two measures of the chorus (23-24). The third and last chorus is even more complex, including a double-time feel in measures 28-29, the sixteenth notes being swung. This sounds confusing in explanation and looks confusing on the page as well, but in performance sounds quite natural. Indeed, these are the kinds of liberties that many good jazz soloists might take on a slow blues solo. After weighing a number of options, I decided that the least confusing notation would be simply to change the meters as Wood plays them, rather than trying to artificially fit the duple feel into 12/8 notation or litter the page with triplets by writing the 12/8 sections within a 4/4 meter.

Wood's use of the plunger created the other big notational problem. Many of the same words and vowels representing plunger sounds for the solos of the other plunger specialists – Nanton, Glenn and Jackson – are used here: wa, a, u, au, and + (closed) and o (open). But it seemed necessary to add a new notation for this solo. Wood often plays with the plunger in a position that is commonly referred to as "half plunger," that is, somewhere between the standard open and closed. There are, of course, many possible places to hold the plunger between the two extremes, with many different resulting sounds. For a large number of notes that seem to be in this hazy region and have a

3   *The World of Ellington*, p. 199.

EXAMPLE 7-1

rather neutral but somewhat stuffy sound, the symbol ø is used. As was the case with the other plunger solos, the representation of the sounds in some meaningful but reasonably precise way was the biggest challenge in the transcription process. Significantly, Wood accomplishes all of these sounds with only a few hints of a growl effect.

All that having been said, Wood plays a masterful solo in this, his first, excursion into the plunger style. His harmonic and melodic language are not particularly remarkable, although they are certainly interesting. The solo has a nice shape, reaching a climax at the beginning of the third chorus (measures 25-26), then winding down to its conclusion. The subtlety of his rhythmic variations and the changes in timbre, however, make the solo a truly cogent and rewarding statement. One unique and striking effect is the long held F-flat in measures 17-18 in which the long note is "broken up" into short rhythmic durations by inflecting the tone with continually changing vowel sounds produced by moving the plunger.

The recording was a big success, and Wood was on his way to becoming an important exponent of the plunger style. Ellington reportedly said, "Booty Wood is one of the best plunger trombonists I ever heard."[4] Britt Woodman, who knew Wood from their days together with Hampton, and then played with him for about a year with Ellington said,

Man, he had everything. . . If he'd [only] have stayed [in the band longer] . . . The man was great. He showed his potential when he came back on the scene.[5]

Wood stayed with the band until Ellington went to Paris in 1961 to work on *Paris Blues*, at which time he went back to Dayton and the post office for another number of years. He did, however, join other Ellingtonians (including trombonists John Sanders and Britt Woodman) for Ellington's show *My People* in Chicago in 1963. He was to return to the band full time in 1970.

In October of 1959, Quentin Jackson left the band along with trumpeter Clark Terry. They remained in Europe at the end of the Ellington band's tour and joined Quincy Jones, who was in Europe to lead the band for the touring production of Harold Arlen's blues opera *Free and Easy*. Jackson was replaced by another fine trombonist, Matthew Gee. But as previously mentioned, Gee was not to take over the plunger chair, that duty having been switched to Booty Wood.

Gee's stay with the band was short, and apparently not a particularly happy one, but it was by no means without distinction. Ellington quickly took advantage of Gee's abilities and featured

4   Ibid., p. 199.
5   Woodman interview with the author.

him in recording sessions in December of 1959. Although Gee
had worked with Count Basie in the early '50s, his previous professional background also included time with Sonny Stitt and
two recording stints with Dizzy Gillespie, two of the giants of
bebop. Gee's "modern" style, heavily bop-influenced, was unlike that of any trombonist who had previously been with
Ellington. His solo work was featured on three blues from the
sessions from which the album *Blues in Orbit* was put together.
One of the compositions is credited to Gee and Ellington, *The
Swingers Get the Blues, Too.* (Ellington supposedly originally
titled it *Those Ever Lovin' Gut Bucket, Swingin' Blues.*)[6] This
blues (with a contrasting section) starts with Gee and Ellington
alone in a free blues statement, followed by the opening in-
tempo blues statement, Gee playing both on baritone horn. It is
a rare and effective usage of this instrument in jazz.

A more characteristic example of Gee's style is *The Swinger's
Jump*, a fast minor blues. His two choruses, on trombone
(Example 7-2), show his strong bebop roots, both rhythmically
– long lines of eighth notes throughout and boppy triplets in
measures 5-6, 17 and 21 – and harmonically – prominent attention to the ninth of several chords (measures 10, 14, 23-24). As
most "modern" players would, he uses Dorian scales with
minor chords, with particular emphasis on D natural, the raised
sixth degree of the scale (or raised thirteenth of the chord) on
the F minor seventh chord of measure 7. Much of Ellington's
music is harmonically and even melodically advanced, but it is
rare in the band's history that so-called jazz "modernism" is
reflected so clearly by a soloist, especially the rhythmic vocabulary of bebop. Gee's tone is rich and burnished, qualities not
always associated with boppers.

In 1981, Booty Wood recalled Gee as one of his favorite
trombonists, someone who "could play anything." He was "a
soloist from the heart," but apparently played from the heart
sometimes even when he was not soloing. Wood related that
Gee would get a "brainstorm" and play it, regardless of what
the rest of the section was doing. He "did not fit in the section,"
nor "care about the section." Wood compared Gee's personal
life to that of Paul Gonsalves, Ellington's great tenor soloist. Gee
was "happy-go-lucky. . . nothing bothered him. . . [he was] irre-
sponsible."[7] Yet both Art Baron and Vince Prudente, who played with the band in the '70s, claim that they heard that Gee was
Ellington's favorite trombone player.[8] In any case, he lasted only
a few months. For a short while, Juan Tizol rejoined the section,
making it a quartet. Soon, however, Gee was out.

6   From liner notes by Stanley
    Dance to *Blues in Orbit,*
    Columbia Jazz Masterpieces
    CJ44051.
7   Wood interview with Spilka.
8   Baron interview and Prudente
    correspondence with the author.

EXAMPLE 7-2

Ellington added Lawrence Brown to the section of Britt Woodman, Wood, and Tizol for the recording of the *Nutcracker* and *Peer Gynt* suites during the spring and summer of 1960. By the middle of July, Tizol had left, but Brown, after an absence from the band lasting almost a decade, was back to stay and the section was back to its classic trio format.

The recording session from mid-July that became known as *The Unknown Session* was almost like a celebration of the return of Lawrence Brown. This small group session found Brown in the company of his old bandmates Ray Nance, Johnny Hodges, and Harry Carney.[9] The rhythm section was Ellington, of course, the now firmly established Sam Woodyard on drums, and the fine bassist Aaron Bell. Brown was featured extensively on several Ellington classics, and he acquitted himself with some of his finest playing ever.

Although Brown had undoubtedly played *Mood Indigo* hundreds of times before, perhaps his time away from the band was part of what allowed his playing to sound so fresh on the version recorded at this session (Example 7-3). After a four-measure introduction, it is all Brown for a chorus and a half. After four measures of almost straight melody, he starts to embellish the melody in his most impressive, and florid, style. One can still follow the melody through most of the first chorus, even through the delightfully swingy double-time figures of measures 19-20. The melody finally becomes obscured by the ornate figurations starting in measure 23. Going into the second chorus (measure 33), Brown sets up a little blues riff that leads to his one descent into the low register in measure 36. The solo reaches its climax at measure 41, and then beautifully winds down to a peaceful closing. It is a virtuoso piece of trombone playing, hearkening back to the style with which Brown first amazed jazz fans in the 1930s. Almost thirty years after recording such dazzling solos as *Sheik of Araby* and *Ducky Wucky*, Brown showed that, the intervening bop era notwithstanding, he remained one of the most formidable trombonists in jazz.

Brown's section work, too, remained undiminished by time. Buster Cooper, who spent most of the 1960s in the section with Brown echoed remarks made thirty years earlier by Claude Jones by stating that "[Lawrence] was phenomenal actually, and I never heard the man miss in my life." Cooper goes on to qualify the statement slightly, but its thrust is clear. As he put it, "It wasn't in [Brown's] nature" to play any way other than consistently and accurately.[10]

9   On some of the arrangements there is another (unknown) horn player, playing parts but not soloing.

10 The quotations are from my interview with Cooper in 1991, but there is a similar comment in *The World of Ellington*, 211.

EXAMPLE 7-3

The final break with the '50s section was made when Britt Woodman left the band in the late summer of 1960. Ellington, who had a tremendous tolerance for "characters," brought back Gee, who played until Ellington started on his next project.

Ellington then left the band in limbo for several months, as he went to Paris to work on the soundtrack for the film *Paris Blues*. When he returned to the States he reassembled the band, and others, for several recording sessions of the music for *Paris Blues* in May of 1961. Trombonists on those dates included Brown, Tizol, Woodman, swing veteran Murray McEachern (who played some of the solos on these sessions), and a newcomer, Lou Blackburn. For a couple of months, the working band included Brown, Tizol and Blackburn. Tizol was replaced in July by Chuck Connors.

Blackburn was only with the band until December of 1961, but he made an impression on record, and could possibly have developed into an important voice in the section. On the famous session the Ellington band did with Count Basie's band in July of 1961, Blackburn contributed two very nice choruses of blues, using the plunger, in a style very well matched to the Ellington plunger tradition.

But it was not to be. This section remained together for only a few months, then Blackburn left, to be replaced, briefly, by Matthew Gee again (Ellington evidently refused to give up on him), and for several months, by Leon Cox, a journeyman trombonist who had played with Gene Krupa and Benny Goodman, among others.

Unlike Blackburn, Chuck Connors was to become a fixture in the Ellington band. Connors was born in the small town of Maysville, Kentucky on 18 August 1930.[11] He attended school in Maysville through eighth grade, in an enlightened school system in which all students had lessons in music dictation and sightsinging twice a week. Connors's family moved to Dayton, where he attended high school. After graduating from high school, he went to Cincinnati and attended the Cosmopolitan School of Music for a year. It was there that he first started on trombone, having played baritone horn previously. This was followed by a four-year hitch in the Navy, much of it spent on the aircraft carrier *Valley Forge* in Korea. After his return from the service, he spent nine months at home before going to Boston to attend the Boston Conservatory. He studied trombone with Joseph Orosz, a trombonist in the Boston Symphony. In addition to his work at the Conservatory, Connors also commuted to Cambridge, Massachusetts to play principal trombone in the Harvard-Radcliffe University Orchestra. One of the first

11 Biographical information on Connors comes from his interview with the author, corroborated by Feather and Kernfeld reference books.

Ellingtonians to have a college degree, Connors received a Bachelor of Music from the Conservatory in 1956. Had he been white, Connors may have had a career in symphonic music, but after several unpleasant encounters with racial prejudice in auditions, he turned elsewhere.

In Boston, Connors had started playing in the big band of Jaki Byard, which at that time included future trumpet stars Bill Chase and Don Ellis. In 1957, Dizzy Gillespie was in town and looking for a trombonist. Dizzy wanted a bass trombonist, so Connors traded horns with John Coffey, another Boston Symphony trombonist with whom he was studying, to get a large bore tenor trombone (as close to a bass trombone as he could get in a pinch), and joined Dizzy for nine months. After his stint with Gillespie, Connors returned to Boston. He continued playing weekends, while earning a diploma in sheet metal drafting and holding a job as a sheet metal mechanic.

Clark Terry had heard Connors play in Boston, and recommended him for the Ellington band. In late 1960, Connors played very briefly with the band in the trombone section with Lawrence Brown and Matthew Gee. It was then that Ellington went to Paris, leaving the band in the States, with each man having to find a way to get by. Connors went back to Boston and the sheet metal shop. Apparently Connors's phone number was lost (this type of occurrence was hardly unknown in the Ellington organization), and when the band got back together, Juan Tizol was in his old chair. But Tizol did not wish to remain, and when the band returned to Boston in July of 1961, Connors was rehired. He stayed with the band after Duke's death, and after many years as the senior member of the band, it was finally in 1994 that health problems forced Connors to retire.

When asked to join the band, Connors said that he would join if he was not asked to play any jazz solos. Ellington replied that he had enough soloists. So Connors decided to try the band for a year. Ellington also asked if Connors would play valve trombone, as he would be playing the book that had been played on valve trombone by Tizol, Claude Jones and John Sanders before him. Connors said that he would prefer not to, although with his training on baritone he certainly could have played the valved instrument. Ellington then asked him if his horn (still the large bore tenor trombone) was a bass trombone. Connors said no. But when Ellington asked him if he would he be interested in playing the bass trombone, Connors cannily replied, yes, he would, if he could pick out his own instrument, and if Ellington would pay for it. It was agreed, and Connors believes that he had the bass instrument before the summer of 1961 was over.

Thus was instituted the first major change in the trombone section, and accordingly, how it was written for, since the section had become a trio in 1932.

When the band recorded *The Girl's Suite* in August of 1961, there was a tag figure at the end of *Sweet Adeline* that may have been played on bass trombone, although it is possible that Connors played it on his large bore tenor. The bass trombone was used to its full "bass" potential in arrangements recorded in late 1962 and early 1963 and released on the albums *Afro-Bossa*, *Will the Big Bands Ever Come Back?* and later on *Recollections of the Big Band Era*. Here the bass trombone is treated as an instrument that could do things that a tenor trombone could not, with the result being new ways of writing for the Ellington trombone section.[12] Connors was also a soloist on one of the tunes from these sessions, *It's a Lonesome Old Town When You're Not Around*, the theme of the old Ben Bernie band.[13]

Connors, however, unlike many bass trombonists, had to remain extremely flexible, as he was playing Tizol's old book, which included many passages on the high end of the horn as well. Legendary studio bass trombonist George Roberts told Connors that he would never want to play the book that Connors was playing – there were too many high parts!

Connors's recorded solo work as a whole is interesting in the way that it reflects how Ellington worked during the latter part of his career. On the relatively few days a year when the band had time off from traveling and performing, Ellington would often take it into the studio to record compositions and arrangements that he had been writing. He could hear just how the arrangements sounded and decide what to do with them, but the recordings were not made with the idea that they would be released commercially. In the late 1980s many of these recordings, often referred to as "the stockpile," were released on ten compact discs called *The Private Collection*. Most of the few solo spots that Connors had on record were played in the studio, recorded, then never played again. The result was that Connors would be asked about solos that he had played, some of which he had trouble remembering because he had only played them on one occasion. Among these were the aforementioned *Lonesome Old Town* and a 1966 recording of *Perdido*, on which he stated the first eight measures of the first chorus on the bottom end of the horn. Although these two were recorded with the specific intention of being used on record albums, both of these arrangements were recorded and released, but like much of the stockpile, never became part of the regular performing

12 Writing for the bass trombone is also addressed in Appendix I.
13 It was at about this same time that trombonist Phil Wilson created a stir with his remarkable solo on this same tune with Woody Herman's band.

repertoire of the band. Among other stockpile recordings was *The Degas Suite* of 1968, a suite of music written for a movie score on which Connors was featured on a march titled *Improvisation-Marcia Regina*. After the recording, the piece was never played by the Ellington band again.

Ellington's working methods in the studio were demonstrated in a different way on another session. The band toured Europe in early 1963, at which time it recorded works with symphony orchestra. According to Connors, the band recorded the 1943 work *New World A-Comin'*, a work which originally was almost a piano concerto with band accompaniment. There was a short trombone solo that Ellington wanted to sound a certain way. He decided that he wanted Connors's sound on that passage, so he sent the whole band except Connors and drummer Sam Woodyard out of the studio and recorded that excerpt. This recording did not appear on *The Symphonic Ellington*, and in subsequent performances Ellington played the piece either solo, with trio, or, on a few occasions, with symphony orchestra, but not the band.[14]

Short solos that Connors played that were performed with some regularity can be heard on Ellington's acclaimed extended work *Harlem*, and on *Something About Believing* from the *Second Sacred Concert*. He also played Tizol's old solo on *Come Sunday* in performances of *Black, Brown and Beige*.

*Chuck Connors
(Smithsonian Institution)*

14 On the 1970 recording with the Cincinnati Symphony Orchestra the solo is played by one of the orchestra's trombonists.

In June of 1962, Buster Cooper replaced Leon Cox, and the section composed of Brown, Connors and Cooper was to last for almost seven more years.

Buster Cooper
(Photo by Ray Avery)

Buster Cooper was born in St. Petersburg, Florida in 1929. He took up trombone at about the age of sixteen and first worked professionally in a band led by his cousin George. After finishing high school, he joined the well-known "territory" band of Nat Towles (which also included saxophonist Oliver Nelson at that time). Cooper went to New York in 1950 and studied at the Hartnett School of Music. Like Ellington trombonists Britt Woodman and Booty Wood before him, Cooper served an apprenticeship with Lionel Hampton's band. In the approximately three years (1952-1955) that Cooper was in that band, it was a hotbed of young talent and host to many future jazz "names," including trumpeters Clifford Brown, Art Farmer and Quincy Jones, saxophonists Gigi Gryce and Benny Golson, and in the rhythm section, bassist Monk Montgomery, pianist Milt Buckner and drummer Alan Dawson. Jimmy Cleveland and Al Hayse were with Cooper in the trombone section. After leaving Hampton and returning to New York, Cooper put in time with the house bands at the Apollo Theater, led by Reuben Phillips,

and the Savoy Ballroom, led by Lucky Millinder. He played inter-
mittently with Benny Goodman in 1958 and 1959, both in his
big band and in the sextet from within the band (which included
Herb Geller and Pepper Adams). He went to Paris in 1959 to
back up entertainer Caterina Valente with a small band he co-
led with his brother Steve, a bass player. Also featured in that
band was saxophonist Eric Dixon, who was later to become a
fixture in Count Basie's band. Josephine Baker heard the band
with Valente and asked them to work with her famous show at
the Olympia Theater. Returning to the States in late 1959, the
Cooper brothers' band continued to work clubs around New
York. After turning down several overtures from Ellington,
Cooper finally agreed to play a weekend in New Jersey.[15] That
weekend was to turn into a seven-year stint with the band.

Cooper was to develop a voice with the band unlike that of
any other trombonist in the history of the band. His identity was
quickly established as a blues player, but not a plunger blues
player, as Nanton and Jackson had been in the past. In fact,
Cooper refused to play the plunger work, which led to Lawrence
Brown's taking on this important "historical" role. While featured on a number of different kinds of pieces, Cooper was most
often featured on blues tunes, and even on other sorts of pieces
he was usually a "bluesy" voice.

Cooper excelled in his role, and a number of recordings display his persuasive blues style. One of the earliest of these was
recorded less than two months after he joined the band (although the recording was not released until the 1980s). Called
September 12th Blues, for the date on which it was recorded in
1962, Cooper's two relatively simple choruses display traits that
were characteristic of his work with Ellington (Example 7-4).
The opening figure of the first three measures, repeated almost
verbatim in measures 5-7, uses only three notes — the tonic D-
flat, and the sixth and fifth degrees of the scale. Often, Cooper
would start his blues solos with this sort of simple and effective
phrase. The third phrase of the first chorus (starting with the
pickup to measure 9) is only slightly more complicated and leads
into the the second chorus with a "signature" blues lick (measure 12) that Cooper played time and again. The second chorus
has the same sort of directness, but is spiced up with the flatted
third in the key, F flat, in measures 18 and 22 and a boppy triplet in measure 20. As had been the case with several of Cooper's
predecessors in the Ellington trombone section, simplicity is the
key to a very direct communication to the listener.

Another role that Cooper took on with Ellington was what
might be referred to as a "show" soloist. In the '60s especially,

15 Cooper's recollection (in his
interview with the author) of
his first job with Ellington, as
presented here, does not exactly
conform with the accounts in
some of the reference works.

EXAMPLE 7-4

there were certain pieces in the band's book that featured various of the band's soloists in such a way as to impress audiences with their diverse skills and styles. Cat Anderson always had some feature in the book to display his phenomenal high range. There was usually a piece in the book which allowed Harry Carney, by means of what is called circular breathing, to hold a sustained note for an inordinately long time. There was always a hard-driving feature on which Paul Gonsalves could re-create his triumph at Newport in 1956.

Cooper was featured on several up-tempo tunes, tunes on which he would show his affinity for the blues, but also display extremely fast technical skills. One of the tunes that featured him (as well as other members of the band) in this style was *The Opener*. One televised version of this piece from 1964 or 1965 (filmed in Europe) showed him playing his usual spot on euphonium (baritone horn), recalling Matthew Gee's brief use of this instrument in 1959. The tune that became indelibly identified with Cooper, however, was one put together by Cat Anderson. Known by a number of colorful titles, from the Spanish *El Busto* to the extravagant *Trombonio-Bustoso-Issimo*, it has appeared on a recent release as simply *Trombone Buster*, and is so listed on the written parts in the Smithsonian's collection.

The sound of the recording from which this transcription was taken is not of good quality: balance between sections is bad, and some of the individual sounds are muddy or distorted. The band's performance is not all that might be hoped for either, mostly due, one suspects, to the extremely fast tempo (half note = about 160). However, Cooper's playing is reasonably clear, and the recording gives a good representation of his playing in this style. Only the first solo chorus (Example 7-5) is transcribed. Not only does this single chorus show the basics of Cooper's handling of the tune, but in the subsequent choruses there is much repetition.

Cooper plays double time figures, that is, eighth-note based figures in cut time, through much of the chorus. It is no mean feat to do this on trombone at a tempo like this (the whole thirty-two measure chorus lasts less than twenty-five seconds). Cooper accomplishes this by using what trombonists call "doodle" tonguing – a kind of modified double tonguing. While articulation is problem enough for a trombonist at this speed, movement of the slide is perhaps an even greater problem. For the most part, Cooper seems to approach the tune from a melodic rather than a harmonic standpoint. *Trombone Buster* is what jazz players refer to as a "Rhythm" tune, a composition based on the chord changes of George and Ira Gershwin's *I Got*

EXAMPLE 7-5

Rhythm. The close relationship of the chords in the three A sections of the tune (measure 1-8, 9-16, and 25-32) make this sort
of melodic approach a very workable one. Although it is difficult to hear exactly what chord progression the rhythm section
plays in the A sections, the transcription contains a standard set
of chords for a "Rhythm" tune for the first eight bars, then
simply shows a B-flat chord for the other two A sections. Most
of the figures stay close to the B-flat tonality of the piece, with
some touches of bluesiness, particularly the figures in the second
A section, especially in measures 9-14. The figure in measures
10 and 12 is a variant of the figure in measure 12 of *September
12th Blues* (Example 7-4). At the bridge, or B section (measures
17-24) Cooper switches his approach, establishing the changing
harmonies which define this part of the tune.

As on his blues, Cooper's statement on *Trombone Buster* is
basically simple and direct – but it is delivered at a frighteningly
fast tempo that made it into a crowd-pleasing display piece.

Having looked at one of the first blues recordings that
Cooper made with Ellington, it is interesting to examine one of
the last blues solos that he recorded with Ellington, a version of
the classic *C Jam Blues* recorded 3 December 1968 (Example
7-6). Cooper's basic language has not changed, but on this
session, he had a chance to stretch out more and develop the
solo more dramatically. Several figures, notably those at the
beginning of both the second and third choruses (measures
17-21, and 29-30 and 32-34), were among Cooper's favorites
and can be found in other solos.[16] Both of these choruses rely
heavily on the note F-sharp, a blue note that in the tonic C chord
of this piece is the sharp eleventh of the chord. The "old" way
of referring to this note in a chord, as the flat fifth, seems more
appropriate here, as Cooper is obviously using it as the lowered
version of the G, the chord's fifth. The effect, in any case, is decidedly bluesy. In the fourth and final chorus, Cooper brings the
solo to a dramatic close both by ascending to the high register
(high E-flat in measure 42), and going into double time with
figures reminiscent of those in *Trombone Buster* from measure
46 to the end. This solo fittingly sums up much of Cooper's style
in his tenure with Ellington.

16 It is striking how much of this
solo is found in almost identical
form in Cooper's solo on
September 18th Blues from
1963.

EXAMPLE 7-6

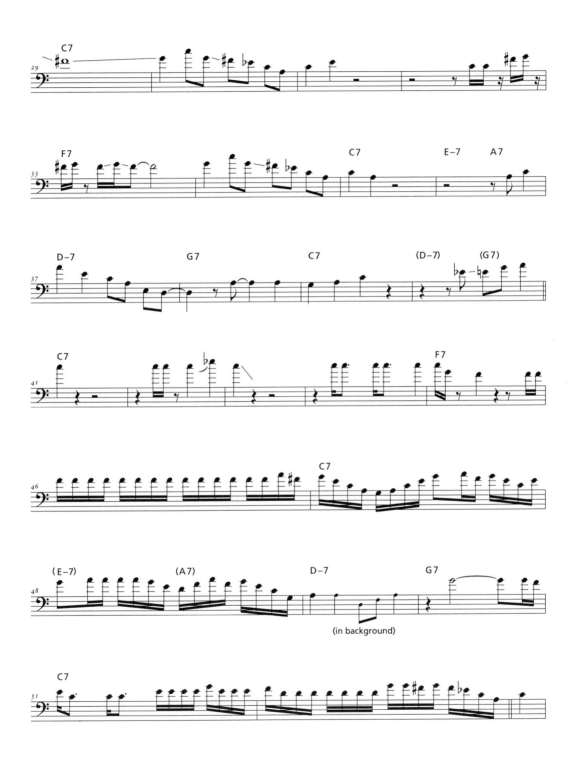

As personnel and musical styles changed, so, too, did Ellington's music change. In keeping with his bluesy musical role, Cooper says that while Lawrence Brown played the lead, or highest, trombone parts on most of the tunes that the band performed in the 1960s, Cooper sometimes had the lead on some of what he referred to as the "raunchier" pieces. Art Baron has suggested that although the section of Brown, Cooper and Connors may not have been as "subtle" as the original trio of Brown, Tizol and Nanton or the '50s section of Woodman, Sanders and Jackson, it had "a real personality," and was another "great section."[17] The '60s section featured Brown, reprising his various roles from his previous time in the band, yet seemingly more idiosyncratic than before. The romanticism of his ornate brand of swing playing was no longer in the mainstream of jazz trombone style, which by this time was dominated by bop-derived playing, specifically by way of J. J. Johnson. Furthermore, Brown's sound, which had always been unique, took on a character which seemed more singular as time passed. The silky smooth sound associated with Brown's earlier ballad playing, somewhat similar to that of Tommy Dorsey (as well as to that of certain more modern players), was heard less frequently, as almost all of Brown's playing in the '60s displayed a vibrato so distinct that at times it bordered on a "wobble." On the other end of the section was Buster Cooper, given to the powerfully extroverted style just described. Cooper's style, too, despite his considerable technical gifts, seemed out of the bop mainstream, seemingly more related to blues shouting and its lack of self-consciousness or artifice. In the middle of the section sat Chuck Connors, lending his huge sound and precision to the section, often at the bottom of the horn, in a range which had never before been available to the Ellington trombone section. The valve trombone sound was now gone, and it was left to Brown to carry on the plunger tradition.

It has already been recounted (in Chapter 4) that Brown once refused to take on the plunger duties only to be fired by Ellington for this refusal. According to Brown, after the death of Tricky Sam Nanton in 1946, Ellington asked him to play the plunger solos that Tricky Sam had originated. Brown knew them from listening to them for years, and for a short while, he played them. But he then decided that he should not take on this extra duty unless he was paid more, and he told Ellington so. Ellington got angry and released Brown, who headed back to New York alone. Shortly thereafter, however, he was called to rejoin the band.[18]

All evidence suggests that Brown resisted taking on the plung-

17 Interview with the author.
18 This is detailed in Patricia
   Willard's interview, reel 5, 3-4.

er duties in the '60s as well, but for whatever reasons, did finally give in. But even at this time he expressed his resentment of the plunger role in terms of Ellington saving money by not having to hire an extra plunger specialist.[19] One can understand Brown's hesitancy about becoming the plunger soloist for strictly musical reasons as well. After all, he was originally known for his fast technical solos and his beautiful ballad playing on the open horn. With the plunger and its attendant mute that Brown, like his predecessors in the tradition, used, the open sound is severely altered and fast technique is considerably hampered. Also, as mentioned above, Brown was playing almost all of the lead parts in the section. Plunger playing is very demanding on the embouchure and a considerable burden to add to the demands of playing the highest parts in the section. Brown talked about some of these technical difficulties:

"I don't like using the plunger... but I imitate the tops – Tricky. That buzzing breaks your lip down and you have to wait a little while to get back to normal. Another problem is that there's no way to get anything to fit in there unless you change the tuning. The back pressure from the plunger and the mute takes the horn out, so you have to try to tune it with your hand [tuning slide?]. At least, I try to tune it there, because I don't feel like changing positions to fit the tone. It's all right when you've got someone who can do it in the third chair, where the parts are neither high nor important, but the first chair is important and usually the first man won't touch it. It can really mess your lip up so that you won't be able to play straight at all."[20]

One suspects, too, that Brown, having spent so many years in the section with Tricky Sam Nanton, the acknowledged master of the technique and style, and knowing intimately Nanton's genius, would think twice about following in his musical footsteps.[21]

One of the tunes on which Brown was regularly featured using the plunger was *The Mooche*, one of the enduring "jungle"-style classics from the late 1920s (Example 7-7). Not only was Brown aware of Quentin Jackson's set solo from the 1950s (see Chapter 6, Example 6-2), he actually plays Jackson's solo with only a few minor variations and embellishments for the first fifteen measures of this 1966 recording. In measure 16, he reprises the plunger "trick" discussed in conjunction with Tyree Glenn's *Mood Indigo* solo from 1950 (Chapter 5, Example 5-3).

19 *World of Duke Ellington,* 118.
20 Ibid., 125.
21 Brown expressed admiration for Nanton and the tradition he established in the Willard interview, reel 4, 9.

EXAMPLE 7-7

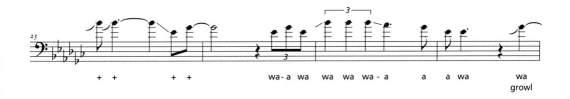

++ ++ wa-a wa wa wa wa-a a a wa wa growl

a du a wa du wa au wa a du wa wa wa wa wa wa wa wa growl

wa - a - a u a growl a a wa du du du du du

p wa da da da da da

with growl a - - u - -

Some technical notes about this transcription are in order. As in the previous plunger solos, several vowel sounds are used to describe the plunger sounds. Brown's vowel sounds are different from one another, but not as distinct as those of Nanton. They seem to be slight modifications of the basic "a" (ah) vowel sound rather than completely different sounds. The chord symbols in the transcription represent a slightly simplified version of what the rhythm section plays. In particular, Ellington and bassist John Lamb play some surprising substitutions in measures 13-14 and 17-18, but as Brown sticks to the more basic blues harmony, the simpler progression is notated. In measure 23, the rhythm section starts a vamp of parallel chords that had become part of the routine of this piece. Only the basic E-flat minor harmony (which is how Brown seems to approach the section melodically) is notated rather than all of the passing chords, which are within the tonality.

This solo isn't nearly so challenging technically as many of Brown's solos that have been considered in this book, possibly for the reasons Brown discusses in the above quote. But Brown's commitment to playing this and other plunger solos in the style of his predecessors very probably was another contributing factor to the solo's simplicity. What one hears is the Lawrence Brown who still, as he was approaching the end of his playing career, has great command of the instrument, especially in the high range. The drama of suddenly increased volume and the addition of growl to the sound is most striking at the beginning of the second chorus (pickup to measure 13), as is the sudden softening at measure 35 and 36 in echo of measures 33-34.

Not surprisingly, given his enormously versatile talents as a musician and more specifically, as a trombonist, Brown ultimately was a very successful plunger soloist. But naturally, he did not sound like Tricky Sam or Tyree Glenn or Butter Jackson. Critic Martin Williams described the situation as "Lawrence Brown giving his own kind of elegance" to the role.[22] Brown's awareness of the Ellington plunger tradition has been alluded to above. But of course he expressed this tradition in his own voice. His plunger work also recalls the somewhat blustery role he took on in the early 1940s as a "blues shouter" even though many had doubts about his authenticity as a blues soloist at that time. Brown's plunger playing does not seem to me to possess the haunting pathos of Tricky Sam's best work. It does not seem to have the plaintiveness of Quentin Jackson or the hint of humor that one so often hears in Tyree Glenn's plunger work. But it is unquestionably highly skilled and ultimately, I believe, convincing playing in a tradition that was almost forty years old

22 Williams, *Jazz Heritage*, 117.

by the time Brown took it up.

Brown, Cooper and Connors worked together as a tight, versatile, musical section for almost seven years. After the death of his father, however, Buster Cooper left Ellington to return home to Florida, and another era in the section's history was over.

The Last Years

When Buster Cooper left the band in the summer of 1969, the
stable section of the 1960s started to break up. Bennie Green,
who had augmented the section for the premiere of the *Second
Sacred Concert* in the early part of 1968, temporarily took
Cooper's place.[1] However Green, although one of the most
important of the trombonists to emerge from the bop era, was
not to become an important member of the Ellington band. He
continued to play with the band for much of 1969, but did not
accompany it on the European tour that started in October.

The brass section for this tour was starting to show some real
signs of wear and tear, and only five brass made the trip. The
trombones were the always reliable Lawrence Brown and Chuck
Connors, and the trumpets were Mercer Ellington and veterans
Cootie Williams and Cat Anderson. Mercer's duties as a trumpeter were far overshadowed by his position as road manager.
Not only was Mercer not known for a particularly strong contribution as a trumpeter, but Cootie was not always playing his
scored parts. And with only three players, at times the fourth
parts scored for virtually all of the arrangements in the book
were not being played at all, although guests, including Swedish
trumpeter Rolf Ericson and American expatriates Benny Bailey
and Nelson Williams, did fill in on some of the dates. The fine
Swedish trombonist Åke Persson played with the trombones on
several dates in Germany and Switzerland in November, but for
much of the tour, Norris Turney sat in the trombone section and
played the third trombone part on alto saxophone. Regardless
of Turney's competence at this task, it was not an ideal solution
for a section that ever since Brown first joined the band in 1932
had been the most distinguished trombone section in jazz
history.

Around the turn of the year 1970, Lawrence Brown, after
almost thirty years with the Ellington organization, finally left
the band for the last time. Resentments between Brown and
Ellington that had boiled beneath the surface for decades finally erupted, and difficult as it may be to believe, it is now common knowledge that Ellington punched Brown in the mouth,
knocking out several teeth. It is no secret that Brown had held
ill feelings for Ellington since early in his career with the band.

1   It is not clear whether Green
played only for the premiere
performance of this work, or
for the recording (or parts of
it), or both.

Brown had some professional disagreements with Ellington, and his charge that Ellington "was a compiler," not a composer (and specifically the issue of the authorship of *Sophisticated Lady*), was discussed in Chapter 4.[2] There were personal disagreements as well. For one thing, Brown, the non-smoking, non-drinking "Deacon," was almost the antithesis of the worldly, rakish, womanizing Ellington. And in one particular affair of the heart, Ellington and Brown got much too involved in each other's relationships. In the 1930s, Brown was briefly married to the actress Fredi Washington, who had starred with Ellington in the 1929 film *Black and Tan Fantasy*. During the making of the film, Ellington and Washington grew very close, but Ellington, although already separated from his wife, would not commit himself to a long-standing relationship with the stunningly beautiful Washington. Many people feel that Washington married Brown to spite Ellington. In any case, the marriage was not a happy one, and Brown believed, probably correctly to some degree, that the marriage's failure was the fault of Ellington, however indirectly. Brown seemed to be the kind of man who could not let go of a grudge, and whatever words might have been exchanged between the two men, suddenly, after a history of more than thirty-five years, their musical relationship came to an end.

The departure of Brown and the death of Johnny Hodges in 1970 were two of many indications of the slow demise of the Ellington band. While these two events were several months apart, the loss of Brown and Hodges together was eerily reminiscent of their departure from the band together almost twenty years earlier. Ellington managed to pull off a remarkable recovery from their loss the first time. But despite Ellington's continued prolific composition, his band – already conceded to be on the decline – was never to be the same after this second loss of these two great musicians.

As was often the case in the latter days of the orchestra, one veteran was replaced by another. Booty Wood came back to the orchestra to take Brown's place. Actually, though, Wood took over the "third chair," the plunger chair, which essentially had been vacant since before the European tour. An excellent young trombonist, Julian Priester, took over the lead book for some months. Priester, best known for his work with Herbie Hancock's progressive sextet in the early 1970s, might have seemed to be an odd match to the Ellington band, but he was a fine section player, and he also contributed some solid solo work to the *New Orleans Suite*, recorded in April and May of 1970. After Priester left in June, he was replaced by Malcolm Taylor,

2   See also Willard interview with Brown, reel 4.

an old friend and musical companion of Booty Wood.

The section of Wood, Taylor and Connors held together for more than a year and a half, a period of relative stability at this point in the band's history. But how different a year and a half is from the twelve years that Brown, Tizol and Nanton were together as a section.

Wood and Taylor both left in early 1972. Vince Prudente joined the band in April, and with Connors, the section was down to only two players again for several months. When Prudente joined, veteran Al Hayse was in the section for a few days. Tyree Glenn rejoined the band for a few dates and for the week-long residency at the University of Wisconsin in July of 1972. Wood was in and out of the band, playing an odd date here and there. Matthew Gee even played a few single dates, although his playing had declined seriously.

Apparently, it was Ellington's hope that Wood would return permanently, thus the shuffling of veterans in and out of the third chair while Connors and Prudente remained the two constants in the section for almost a year.[3] In April of 1973, Murray McEachern, who had soloed on the *Paris Blues* dates of 1961, returned to serve for about four months. Upon McEachern's departure, Art Baron became the last trombonist to join the band while Ellington himself still led it.

Ellington had been diagnosed with cancer in January of 1973, and his health continued to deteriorate. In March of 1974, while the band was on a tour of the Midwest, Ellington was finally too sick to continue on the road. While confined to his room in Columbia Presbyterian Hospital in New York, Ellington did not quit working on new music until his very last days. His body racked with cancer and pneumonia, he died on May 24, 1974.

For trombonists and fans of the instrument, one of the mysteries of Ellington's late works is that while the trombones as a section remained important to Ellington right up until his death, the trombone as a solo instrument was featured less and less – especially in new works – in the last few years of his career. After Lawrence Brown left, new major works like *Afro-Eurasian Eclipse, Togo Brava Suite (Togo Brava, Brava Togo)* and *The Third Sacred Concert* did not feature any trombone solos, nor did the shorter *UWIS* and *Goutelas* suites. *The New Orleans Suite*, which honored a city and its music in which the trombone was an integral part, was the only exception to the dearth of trombone solos in the later extended works. This decrease was, however, a continuation of a trend that had started earlier.

3   Much of the information in this and the preceding paragraph was supplied in correspondence with Vince Prudente, April 1992.

Even when Brown and Buster Cooper were still in the band, the *Latin American Suite* of 1968 had no trombone solos and the acclaimed *Far East Suite* of 1966 had only one trombone spot, for Brown. In nightly performances of the Ellington band of the 1970s, trombones were featured almost exclusively on some of the old pieces that were still in the regular repertoire.

Why had trombone solos become so rare? Why, for example, was the excellent Booty Wood featured on Tricky Sam's old solos, but not given more solo space in the new works? Did Ellington want increasingly greater control over his compositions, thus opening less of the total length of these compositions to any solos? (This does appear to be the case in at least a few of these works.) Did the overall decline reflect less a conscious change in Ellington's thinking than a reaction to the loss of some of the great individual voices of earlier versions of the band? Even this explanation, though, is not a satisfactory explanation for the lack of Lawrence Brown's solo space before his departure.

Although their contribution to the band while Ellington was alive cannot be compared to that of most of the musicians who have been surveyed in this book, Taylor, Prudente and Baron were important for holding the trombone section together in the early 1970s, Indeed, it may be persuasively argued that the trombones, anchored by Chuck Connors, were the most consistent and dependable section in the band during this period. In addition, all of the '70s newcomers have made significant contributions toward the preservation of the Ellington tradition since that time. Furthermore, each brought a background to the band different from any of their predecessors.

Malcolm Taylor had worked with Booty Wood during Booty's time in Dayton, Ohio, and when he joined the Ellington band, he and Booty and Chuck Connors formed the all-Dayton trombone section (Connors had attended high school in Dayton). Taylor, born in 1925, grew up in Dayton, the youngest of eight children.[4] One of his older brothers who was a pharmacist by profession started booking bands into ballrooms in Dayton in the 1930s. Through one of these dates, Malcolm, when he was just ten years old, saw Ellington and was immediately "in awe of his command of the English language, his charisma, and the way he conducted himself." With a job of selling soft drinks during the intermissions of many of the dances that his brother organized, young Taylor was able to hear many of the great trombonists of the day – besides Ellington's trombonists, such figures as Trummy Young, Dicky Wells, Vic

4   Biographical information and quotes are from Taylor's interview with the author.

Dickenson and Tommy Dorsey. As a youth he vowed that some-day he would play with Duke Ellington. He received the rudi-ments of playing in the concert and marching bands of his high school, and after graduation he joined the Navy. In the service he went through the Great Lakes Naval Training Center north of Chicago (the musical scene there during World War II has already been described in Chapter 7) and ended up in San Diego at the same base where John Sanders was stationed.[5] Already having made some inroads in the local jazz community, upon the completion of his military service Taylor entered the Southern California jazz scene of the mid-40s in earnest. He did considerable playing with tenor saxophonist J.D. King and bassist Addison Farmer (Art Farmer's twin brother), and in 1946 Taylor was hired to be a part of the house band for the Sunday afternoon jam sessions at Billy Berg's famed club. Before leaving the coast in late 1946, he participated in a recording session that included Miles Davis (then a member of Billy Eckstine's big band), Addison Farmer, and tenor saxophonist Teddy Edwards. When Taylor's wife became pregnant, he reluc-tantly left this thriving scene (which, however, he admits was racked with drug problems) to return to Dayton. Although he continued to play with many jazz acts that performed in Dayton, he took a day job at the post office, where for years he and Booty Wood both worked. Although he declined a number of offers to join touring bands, Taylor did leave town for a short junket with Illinois Jacquet in 1952.

In the meantime, he and Booty had started the first of many musical associations, starting a two-trombone group that Taylor claims pre-dated J.J. Johnson and Kai Winding's popular combo. In 1960, Taylor sat in with Ellington on several engage-ments on a brief tour of Ohio and Indiana. At this time, Taylor joined Booty, Lawrence Brown and Matthew Gee in a section of four.

Taylor sat in for Julian Priester when it became known that Priester would not be able to make the European tour of 1970 and shortly thereafter was hired as his permanent replacement. Bothered by chronic dental problems, Taylor went back to Dayton in 1972. Known fondly by his nickname "Big Luv," Taylor really made a name for himself during his five-year tour with the Ellington band from 1975-1980, when Mercer had taken over the band. Taylor's plunger routine, an extension of the Ellington tradition, was one of the crowd-pleasing features of most of the band's performances.

5   Taylor says that Sanders was so straight-laced that the others felt that they "had to corrupt him."

Vincent Prudente was born in Connellsville, Pennsylvania, 18 November 1937.[6] He started playing mellophone at age seven, because his arms were too short to play trombone, the instrument he wanted to play. As a teenager, he began study with famed trombone teacher Matty Shiner in Pittsburgh. He later received a Bachelor of Science degree in music education from Duquesne University in 1959. Prudente was yet another of the Ellington trombonists who also served time with Lionel Hampton. He was with Hampton from 1959-61, and after serving a stint in the army was back with Hampton for most of 1963-66. He also spent some time with the band of Lloyd Price, a group for which trombone great Slide Hampton was musical director. In 1966 Prudente went to New York, where he played with a whole roster of big bands running a wide range of styles – those of Kenny Dorham/Joe Henderson, Frank Foster, Duke Pearson, Buddy Morrow, and Les Elgart. The apartment which he shared with several musicians, including George Coleman, Virgil Jones, and Skinny Burgan, from 1966-72, was what Prudente has described as a "continuous workshop." Among those who "passed through" were some of the greats of modern jazz – bassist Paul Chambers, organist Larry Young, saxophonist Sonny Fortune, drummer Roy Brooks, and pianist Walter Davis, Jr. Prudente also worked at various times with a diverse list of saxophonists – Pepper Adams, Sam Rivers, Andy McGhee, and Bobby Plater. In 1968 he went on the road with Woody Herman for almost a year in one of the fine Herman Herds that included baritone saxophonist Ronnie Cuber, tenor saxophonist Sal Nistico, and pianist John Hicks. Prudente spent most of the time from the summer of 1969 through 1972 back in New York, again playing a "mixed bag" of jobs: subbing for the Broadway show *Promises, Promises*, playing in Latin bands and the big bands of Clark Terry and Frank Foster, backing vocalist Joe Williams, and another short stay with Lionel Hampton's band. After joining Ellington on April 7, 1972, Prudente remained with the band after Ellington's death for almost two years, during which time he wrote ten or eleven arrangements for the band. His arrangement of *A Flower is a Lovesome Thing* was on the Ellington orchestra's 1989 album *Music is My Mistress*, which was nominated for a Grammy award. He left the band in February 1976 to go back to New York. After a number of years on the West Coast, Prudente is currently back in New York, working and proselytizing for Ellington's and other good music.

Art Baron came to the Ellington band as a relative youngster of 23, and – as already mentioned – his previous experience was

6   Vince Prudente sent the author a long letter in early 1992 detailing his career. The information in this chapter came from that letter and subsequent conversations and correspondence with him.

different from that of any trombonist who had ever played for Ellington.[7] After growing up in Bridgeport, Connecticut, Baron went to the Berklee School of Music in Boston for two years, during which time he did quite a bit of free-lance playing in the Boston area. After a very short time with Buddy Rich's big band, Baron went on the road for almost two years with pop superstar Stevie Wonder, touring Europe, South America and the United States. In between tours, Baron stayed in New York, recording and playing with some of the local bands, especially David Berger's. Berger has since become known as the transcriber of hundreds of Ellington's arrangements and was the director for the Lincoln Center Jazz Orchestra on its 1992 tour of the United States during which it celebrated Ellington with a complete program of his works. In 1973 Baron toured with another pop star, James Taylor, and played in the backup band that also featured Randy and Michael Brecker, Eddie Daniels and trombonist Barry Rogers.

Upon joining the Ellington band, Baron took to Ellington's music with a passion and dove right into the plunger responsibilities. His relationship with Cootie Williams (who was 42 years Baron's senior), had a profound effect on him. Having spent hours talking with Cootie, and later studying with Butter Jackson, Baron has become important since Ellington's death as one of the significant carriers of the great tradition of plunger-muted brass playing that remains one of the most enduring of the band's legacies to jazz. He has re-created the plunger solos of Tricky Sam Nanton and his followers for many performances of the Lincoln Center Jazz Orchestra as well as other groups. Baron's own personal style, while having many modern elements, is also strongly based on the Ellington tradition.

Ironically, the only solo recording that Baron made with the band while Ellington was alive was a noteworthy spot in the *Third Sacred Concert* on recorder (not trombone), an instrument that he had been "fooling around with" on the road. Even in his last major work, Ellington was open to new sounds.

To some extent, the careers of Taylor, Prudente and Baron reflect the next stage in the history of the Ellington trombone tradition – how this tradition has influenced music and musicians since Ellington's death.

7 Most biographical information on Baron comes from our extended conversation of 26 February 1992. Supplementary information came from our subsequent conversations and correspondence.

The purpose of this study has been to expose and analyze the individual styles of Tricky Sam Nanton, Juan Tizol, Lawrence Brown and those who succeeded them in Duke Ellington's orchestra. The names of Nanton, Tizol and Brown are mentioned before any of the other trombonists discussed in this book for several reasons. Without ignoring the contribution of Charlie Irvis, it was with the musical development of Nanton that a recognizable trombone tradition in the Ellington band came to fruition. With the addition of Tizol, and later Brown, the roles that dominated the tradition in the orchestra throughout most of its history were established. While some outstanding trombonists developed individual voices in the Ellington setting – most prominently, Tyree Glenn, Quentin Jackson, Britt Woodman and Buster Cooper – they had to work within the framework that had been built by Ellington and the great section of the 1930s and early 1940s. Furthermore, while Tizol's relative lack of influence as a jazz instrumentalist is due to his not having been a featured improvising soloist (although his contribution to Ellingtonia was considerable), Nanton and Brown were major soloists, with highly individual styles, who were prominently featured with one of jazz's most outstanding and visible ensembles.

Given the musical strengths of these two players and the popularity of the Ellington band, it might be asked why Nanton and Brown weren't more influential than they were in the realm of jazz trombone playing. There seem to be a number of reasons, but their lack of influence may be related to Ellington's own lack of direct musical influence on later jazzmen.

It may seem odd to talk about Ellington's lack of influence. As noted in the Preface, Ellington has been one of the most celebrated figures in American music. If the "man on the street" were asked to name three jazz musicians, chances are Ellington's name would be one of those mentioned. Ellington's long career was one of the few in jazz that earned both popular and critical acclaim. Ellington's songs remain among the most performed in jazz, with many still in the popular repertoire as well. But there is not now, nor has there ever been, an "Ellington school" of composition, arranging or playing. Certainly, his influence can be seen in the work of other jazzmen. For example, how would Gil Evans have developed as an arranger without Ellington's influence? Is there any question of the importance of Ellington's piano playing to that of Thelonious Monk? However, who can name arrangers whose arrangements sound like those of Ellington? Has anyone written songs that would be mistaken for those of Ellington? How many piano players have played like Ellington did?[1]

Ellington's lack of imitators is in stark contrast with the number of jazz players who emulated the style of Louis Armstrong (to use a notable example). Granted, none of the imitators could match the model, but the point remains that hundreds, possibly thousands, consciously worked to copy Armstrong's style. In a later generation of jazz, Charlie Parker became the instrumental model, and in Parker's generation, there were also models for each instrument – Dizzy Gillespie, J. J. Johnson, Bud Powell, Max Roach and slightly later, Miles Davis.

In a somewhat different vein, the case of the Count Basie band might be contrasted with that of Ellington. While many of the arrangements of the Basie band during the '30s and '40s were esssentially "head" charts, the Basie library of the '50s, '60s and '70s was very much an arrangers' book. Many talented arrangers wrote for Basie during these years – Ernie Wilkins, Thad Jones, Frank Foster, Neal Hefti, Quincy Jones, Manny Albam, Billy Byers, Sammy Nestico and others. All of these arrangers were able to capture some of the essence of the Basie sound. The Basie sound remained relatively stable not only through many arrangers, but also through an ever-changing band personnel. On the other hand, no writers other than Ellington and Billy Strayhorn ever captured the essence of the Ellington sound. Unquestionably much of the so-called "Ellington effect" was due to the unique voices in the band – Harry Carney, Johnny Hodges, Cootie Williams, Lawrence Brown, and the others.[2] Even playing the exact notes and rhythms that Ellington's band did will not create the inimitable sounds of Carney's noble baritone saxophone on the bottom of the band, or Hodges's sublime alto or Cootie's fiercely growling trumpet. While the re-creation of Ellington's arrangements is increasing briskly, legions of both amateur and professional bands play "Basie-style" arrangements, whereas relatively few bands try to play "Ellington-style."

It might be argued that Ellington has not been copied because shortly after he reached what many considered to be his creative peak, with his great band of the early '40s, new developments in jazz, in the form of what we still call "modern jazz,"

1   One exception to the thrust of this argument is Billy Strayhorn, who was, in effect, Ellington's alter ego for almost thirty years. While some Ellingtonians claim to be able to instantly tell Strayhorn's work from Ellington's, for most students and fans of the music the distinction is not at all clear. The depth of the collaboration between Ellington and Strayhorn clearly makes Strayhorn the singular exception in the question of Ellington's influence.

2   The Charlie Barnet band, one of the few bands that imitated Ellington, imitated Basie as well. See *Swing Era*, 715-723, for a discussion of Barnet's band.

or bebop, passed Ellington by. Ellington's music was no longer in the vanguard of jazz, although in many ways Ellington's music was "modern" to the very end of his career. In the 1940s, the effects of the advent of bop on one end of the jazz spectrum and the "Dixieland" revival on the other left Ellington in something of a no-man's-land. Gunther Schuller suggests that Ellington became the "keeper of an earlier tradition – as well as that of his own unique tradition . . . and that he remained apart from the central developments in modern jazz."[3] This is not to say that Ellington did not create a great deal of beautiful, vital music after the 1940s; it merely suggests that the music he created after the '40s existed in a part of the jazz world that belonged to Ellington alone.

I believe one must consider the influence of Nanton and Brown with the just noted thoughts in mind.

Charlie Irvis or Bubber Miley may have been most important in the creation of the plunger style that defined Ellington's "jungle style" and its early development. It was Joe Nanton, however, who brought that plunger art to its peak. He influenced not only trombonists who followed him with Ellington – Tyree Glenn, Quentin "Butter" Jackson, Booty Wood, Art Baron and others – but also the trumpeters who played alongside him in the Ellington band, most importantly, Cootie Williams. Williams, in turn, was a great influence on many other trumpeters. No brass player who has used the plunger since Nanton can have escaped his influence, either directly or indirectly. It is generally conceded that no one since Nanton has been able to match the variety or the communicative powers of his plunger sounds. His early solos with Ellington, particularly on the open horn, show that he possessed a technical ability that was the equal of practically any of his contemporaries on trombone. His seeming lack of technical facility on the trombone itself during his later years can be seen as a conscious choice on his part to express himself musically in a particular way. As Nanton's open solos became more rare, his skills with the plunger became more refined. He played fewer notes, but with greater effect. At the very point that Nanton reached the height of his art, however, the currents of jazz perhaps passed him by, just as they passed by Ellington. With the coming of modern jazz in the 1940s, where technical facility was a major concern, the influence of Nanton and the plunger tradition waned. Most trombonists strived instead to match the technical proficiency of modern giant J. J. Johnson, whose trombone style was based on the saxophone style of Charlie Parker. When the "cool" movement of the 1950s became widespread, simplicity made something of a comeback,

3 *Swing Era*, 155-156. Schuller's whole discussion in this section of his book of Ellington's real place in jazz history is thought-provoking.

but playing that was as "hot" as Nanton's remained in the background of jazz developments. The "heat" of what has become known as hard bop in the later '50s and some of the developments in the 1960s helped keep alive the kind of playing that Nanton represented, but it has been the eclecticism of jazz in the 1970s, '80s and '90s that has truly brought this wonderful slice of jazz back into vogue.

Lawrence Brown was one of the most technically proficient trombonists in the history of jazz. In the first few years that he was recording, Brown's technical gifts were unmatched by any other jazz trombonist. There have always been those who felt that his technique outshone his musical inspiration, but from the perspective of the present, the occasions on which he seemed to sacrifice musicality for virtuosity are rare. The bulk of Brown's recorded work with Ellington, especially in the period 1932-1951, displays not only outstanding facility, but confident, convincing musicality as well. His sense of swing in the '30s and '40s was not as extroverted as that of some of his colleagues, but it was solid and reliable. Brown's outstanding lyrical gifts on trombone were matched only by Tommy Dorsey, whose great commercial success caused him to overshadow Brown during the Swing Era. With the wealth of great soloists in the Ellington band and the tremendous variety in Ellington's working library, there was no way that Brown would be featured to the extent that Dorsey was, because Dorsey fronted his own band – a band that although it had some excellent jazz musicians in it, was primarily a dance orchestra. But Dorsey, whose influence was so wide, was no match for Brown as a jazz musician.[4]

Why Brown was not more influential may, just as was true with Nanton, rest partly on the timing of the advent of bop. Brown's type of swing, already open to question in some quarters of jazz, was certainly no longer in vogue in the light of the new harmonic and rhythmic language of bop. Brown's technical facility might still have been admired, but by the '50s, despite a continuing series of oustanding performances on small group sessions, his swing playing may have been considered hopelessly out-of-date by many. In this, Brown, like Nanton, was another of his generation of trombonists – such outstanding players as Jimmy Harrison, Jack Teagarden, Benny Morton, Vic Dickenson, Dicky Wells, Jack Jenney and others, all strongly influenced by Louis Armstrong – whose contributions were eclipsed in some degree by the bop revolution.

Consideration of Ellington's work from another standpoint may have bearing on Brown's lack of influence. Ellington's compositional output was not only more prolific than that of any

4   The popularity of Dorsey raises questions about jazz versus commercial music and possibly the popularity of white bands versus black bands – questions much too complex to address here.

other figure in jazz, but it was also broader in terms of style. Ellington wrote music that swung as hard as that of any band, but he also wrote music that was as "sweet" as that of any band. He wrote music that looked to the past and music that looked to the future. He had a stable of some of the most distinctive soloists in jazz, and there is little question that he wrote some music merely to satisfy the egos of some of his soloists. Brown's "sweet" playing brought down the wrath of certain jazz critics, to the point that they may not have been able to appreciate his jazzier playing; his unique way of playing the blues was not what some people thought blues should sound like. As already discussed in Chapter 4, the kinds of criticism that Ellington had to put up with – that he upon occasion "deserted" jazz – were the same sorts of criticism that were leveled at Brown. Yet as Ellington was canonized late in his career, critics saw his body of work as exactly that – a body of work – rather than a number of individual styles and pieces of work. Brown, too, was known for his work in several different areas, as elucidated earlier. Perhaps the fact that he was never known as a player of only one style in effect "diluted" his influence on later trombonists. And when he returned to Ellington in the '60s and took over yet another role – that of the trombone plunger soloist – perhaps that further obscured his historical place. His taking over of this role speaks again, however, to Brown's fabulous versatility and to the influence of Nanton.

Many of the best jazz musicians of the last several decades of jazz have been serious students of the history of jazz. The neo-conservative (or "neoclassical," as Gary Giddins has referred to them) "young lions" who came into prominence in the 1980s, typified by Wynton Marsalis, continue to have a pervading influence on the outlook of many young musicians of the '90s. Not only are players re-creating the music of past jazz greats, but they are applying the styles and techniques of some of jazz's pioneers and extraordinary stylists in developing individual, modern styles. Many of the important trombonists of various persuasions on today's jazz scene owe a musical debt to Brown or Nanton. Even a short list would have to include Art Baron, Dan Barrett, Ray Anderson, Curtis Fowlkes, Craig Harris, Wycliffe Gordon, and Steve Turre. Wider recognition of the musical contributions of Nanton, Brown, and the other Ellington trombonists will, I feel sure, enrich the continuing development of jazz.

While some musicians decry what they see as an obsession with the past and an impediment to new developments, I think that in general, it is a happy circumstance that the study of jazz history is presently in vogue with jazz performers as well as with historians and fans. We are fortunate that today the music created by Duke Ellington and his trombonists touches more listeners throughout the world than at any other time in its history. It seems likely that this influence will continue to grow in the future.

Ellington's Scoring for Trombones

Mercer Ellington has stated that "the trombones were always Pop's favorite section in the band."[1] Beginning with his first trombone trio in 1932, Ellington featured the trombones as a section over and over in the almost fifty years that he led a band. And despite having three of the most individual trombone voices in jazz – Nanton, Tizol and Brown – there was never a problem with having the section play as a unit. Gunther Schuller has described the three as

unique individual voices, that could, taken together, cover any possible stylistic approach to the trombone. And yet the miracle is that – as proven in countless nights of performances and hundreds of recordings – this trio of uniquely distinctive personalities could, when necessary, blend chameleon-like into a single sonority, of which the discrete component parts were no longer distinguishable.[2]

Dicky Wells, the great Swing Era trombonist, talking of his contemporaries, put it a different way.

. . . there are quite a few fellows with different styles who could sound great together. Just think what Duke had! Tricky, Tizol and Lawrence, three not of a kind, making just about the most amusing section that ever happened along. You bet it was Duke's idea to put them together.[3]

Several references throughout this book have been made to Ellington's writing for the trombone section, as opposed to writing for the trombonists individually as soloists. No attempt will be made to look exhaustively at Ellington's writing for the section, as that study in itself could fill a sizable volume. However, using Ellington's magnum opus *Black, Brown and Beige* from 1943 as a basic source, I will present several basic scorings that were common in Ellington's writing for trombones.

Chapter 3 introduces Ellington's use of the two-man trombone section. Shortly after Juan Tizol joined the band as the second trombonist in 1929, it seems clear that Ellington was already thinking of the trombones as a section, and not just as a part of the brass section. Midway through *The Duke Steps Out*, recorded 16 September 1929 on one of Tizol's first recording sessions with the band, the two trombones have a "lead" figure

1 *Duke Ellington in Person*, 28.
2 *Swing Era*, 47.
3 *Night People*, 91.

four times, answered each time by trumpets.

An early extended use of the trombone duo is on the first composition of Juan Tizol that was recorded by Ellington, *Admiration* (20 March 1930). The most prominent use of the trombone duet (featuring Tizol and Tricky Sam Nanton) from the period is on the first recording of *Creole Rhapsody*, from 20 January 1931. The whole sixteen-measure passage, of which the first five measures are shown in Example A-1, is completely scored in thirds, Tizol on the top part. There are not many effective ways to write for two like instruments, and Ellington employed one of the simplest of these in this and other examples from the period. Already one can hear Tizol's scrupulous attention to articulation.

EXAMPLE A-1

The sound most often associated with the section emerged when Ellington started devising triadic passages for the trombone trio soon after Lawrence Brown joined the section in 1932. The trombones were first prominently displayed this way in their feature piece, *Slippery Horn* (first recorded 18 May 1932). In time the device came to be a virtual trademark of the Ellington trombones. Example A-2 illustrates some short excerpts from well-known trombone passages on some of Ellington's most celebrated arrangements. All of these come from one of Ellington's most fertile periods, 1940-41. While trombones as a section rarely carry the melody line in Ellington's compositions, they were often used to carry an almost equally important countermelody. In both *In a Mellotone* and *Take the 'A' Train*, unison saxophones play the melody, but either while saxophones have rests *(Mellotone)* or long notes *('A' Train)* in the line, trombones reply with important statements of their own. In measure seven of *Take the 'A' Train*, the trombones played a unison G on the original recording, but on later recordings played the full C triad. On *Ko-Ko*, the parallel triads in the trombones are played against a repeated low E-flat from Harry Carney's baritone saxophone in the darkly ominous introduction to this classic.

The last of these examples, *Take the 'A' Train*, was written by Billy Strayhorn. It differs little from the trio writing that had already been established by Ellington. Yet Strayhorn once remarked,

> *. . . for me the hardest part of that orchestra is the trombone trio. Writing for three trombones is terribly difficult. It's so hard to get a blend there.*[4]

It may have been difficult for Strayhorn, but one would not know it from his results.

4 Halperin, Daniel, "Everything Has to Prove Something," in Gammond, 184.

EXAMPLE A-2

In a Mellotone, first chorus

Ko-Ko, introduction

Take the "A" Train, first chorus

Looking in more depth at the beginning of *Black*, one sees the trombones assuming two important and characteristic functions in Ellington's writing; they act both as harmonic reinforcement and as a unison melodic line (Example A-3). In the opening measures it is easy to hear the trombone section anchoring the harmonies, even with the saxophones filling out the texture (other important lines are included in this example). More often than not, when using the trombones in this way Ellington scored them in triads, within the range of an octave. Close scoring in this range makes for a powerful sound, although occasionally verging on muddiness (measures 3-4, 29, 35-36). Ellington usually assigns the trombones to three consecutive chord members – that is, the root, third, and fifth, or the third, fifth, and seventh – often in inversion. These traits can be seen in the trombone writing in measures 3-9 and 29-36. Occasionally there are surprising harmonic tones at the bottom of voicings, like the ninth of a B-flat dominant chord in measure 30, or the flat ninth of a D dominant chord in measure 34.

Early on in *Black* the trombones also emerge as a strong melodic voice by shifting to unison (measures 12-16). Ellington often assigned trombones unison or octave melodic lines, sometimes doubled with saxophones or trumpets. He had used unison trombone scoring to spectacular effect in *Diminuendo and Crescendo in Blue* (1937), particularly in *Crescendo* from the fifth chorus through to the end, especially in choruses five, seven and eleven.

EXAMPLE A-3

EXAMPLE A-3 (cont.)

The most exciting section playing in *Black, Brown and Beige* occurs at the opening of *Beige*. After a frantic introductory passage at the beginning of the movement there is a marvelous example of Ellington's use of the section on a unison theme – in this case doubled both at unison and in octaves by saxophones (Example A-4). The trumpets generally rest or play contrasting figures to this line, but briefly join it in several measures that are not shown in the example. The strength of a loud trombone unison line in this register at a breakneck tempo (half note equals 168) adds a unique kind of musical drama to this part of the composition, as well as showing off the viruosity of the section.

EXAMPLE A-4

The third section of *Brown* – first known as *Mauve*, later as
The Blues – features a convincing vocal statement by Betty
Roché, a bluesy tenor saxophone solo by Ben Webster, followed
by a twelve-bar blues spotlighting the trombone section.
Webster's solo wanders through several keys before settling in B-
flat. The key changes abruptly to D-flat, and the trombones
intone a two-bar statement (Example A-5), answered by trumpets, repeated two more times in a call-and-response blues format. The trombones are muted, possibly in plungers, but more
likely in cup mutes. Andrew Homzy has noted how this passage

illustrates that the essence of the blues idiom depends on inflection and not merely writing 'blue notes' or 'blues scales' on music paper. Here we have no flat 7th's, 3rd's or 5th's. Instead, the trombonists slide into their notes, bend them and let them fall off, perfectly phrased according to the great blues tradition behind the jazz heritage.[5]

The section blends together beautifully, although the balance on the recording of this first performance makes it difficult to hear individual parts. In 1945 Ellington recorded this portion of *The Blues* independently as *Carnegie Blues*.

EXAMPLE A-5

By no means typical, but definitely worth brief examination is the trombone chorus mentioned in Chapter 4 on *Braggin' in Brass*. Gunther Schuller has discussed this chorus at some length.[6] He uses the term "hocket style"[7] to describe how the trombone parts were put together in the first three measures and other parts of this chorus. A short example from the beginning of the chorus is sufficient to illustrate how the passage worked (Example A-6). This would be difficult to perform even at a relatively modest tempo, but the blazing tempo of the recorded performance (half note = about 152) makes the end result hair-raising. Only three outstanding trombonists who were completely confident and comfortable working together could make this passage work.

Two of Ellington's most prominent uses of trombone with other instruments were also mentioned in the text. The famous *Mood Indigo* trio scoring is one that Ellington returned to many times after the great success of this classic in 1930. Example A-7 presents the first four measures of the original recorded version. The voices are Arthur Whetsol on muted trumpet, Nanton on plunger-muted trombone, and Barney Bigard on clarinet. They appear on the score in concert pitch, with clarinet, the lowest voice of the three, on the bottom.

As noted in Chapter 2, later versions of this masterpiece displayed different trio settings. A popular one from the early 1950s featured Britt Woodman and Quentin Jackson on trombones, and Harry Carney on bass clarinet.

5 Homzy, liner notes to recording *Black, Brown and Beige: The 1944-46 recordings*. RCA Bluebird 6641-2-RB.

6 *Swing Era*, 93-94. This section of Schuller's book originally appeared in almost identical form in "Ellington versus the Swing Era," liner notes to Smithsonian record set *Duke Ellington 1938*, Smithsonian R003 P2-13367 (Washington, D.C., 1976).

7 This term refers to a technique in which different voices supply alternating notes or groups of notes (with corresponding rests) to create a musical line. Hocket is most often associated with medieval music and certain non-Western musical cultures.

Example a-6

Example a-7

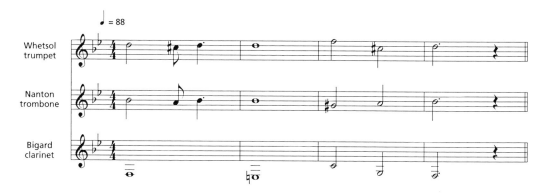

As discussed in Chapter 3, Ellington often used a small group from the orchestra as a separate unit, referred to in Ellingtonia as the "pep section." While there are many different variations on the use of the pep section, Example A-8 shows the use of this kind of group on *Battle of Swing* from 1938. Here we find Juan Tizol on valve trombone as part of the small group. The other voices in the pep section on this selection are Bigard on clarinet, Rex Stewart on trumpet and Otto Hardwick on alto saxophone. This passage occurs after an introduction, which is followed by a chorus of unison band figures that are answered by the pep section. The pep section takes the pickup to the second full chorus. The example begins not with the pickup, but with the first measure of the chorus proper. The two groups have exchanged their roles from the first chorus, with the pep section now making the statements, with the band answering. The scoring is fairly straightforward, but with a number of changes in spacing. One of the most notable aspects of this section is the agility that is required of Tizol, an agility often required of him by Ellington, especially in conjunction with saxophones. Discussion of Tizol's solo role in this piece can also be found in Chapter 3.

EXAMPLE A-8

When Chuck Connors switched from tenor to bass trombone shortly after he joined the band in 1961, Ellington and Strayhorn had a new resource at their disposal. Their use of Connors as a new color in several different settings is discussed in Chapter 7. Even towards the very end of his career Ellington was devising new ways of using the section. Shown in Example A-9 is an excerpt from *Afrique*, the third section of *The Afro-Eurasian Eclipse* from 1971. In a figure that repeats a number of times, Ellington has ingeniously used the three trombonists as a section, but given each an independent part, with an individual sound. Over an insistent tom-tom beat, the top two parts – probably Malcolm Taylor on the higher part and Booty Wood on the lower – are scored in plunger, close together, but rhythmically discrete, while the bass trombone closes each four-measure phrase with a powerfully played octave leap. The figure is not played exactly the same way each time. Sometimes the second part comes in a bar later, or drags its figure.

EXAMPLE A-9

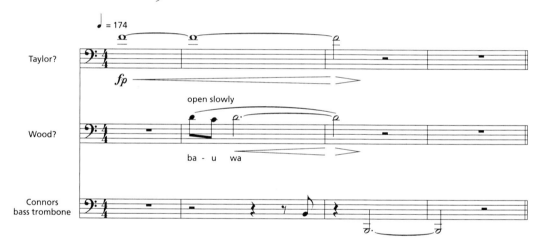

One can take just about any cross-section of Ellington's writing for the full band from any period of his career and find interesting scoring for the trombone section on any of hundreds of selections.

Discographical Information

This appendix is in no way a complete discography of the musical selections discussed in the text, but it is at least a guide to finding recordings of those works. The volatility of the compact disc market is such that in the very last stages of revision of this book two major Ellington releases appeared. Releases mentioned are mostly from the United States, but a few European issues are listed as well. American releases on Columbia and Bluebird (RCA) almost all have counterparts on the various international versions of those labels. Small specialty labels are only listed if they are prevalent in American stores or are listed in Schwann's *Spectrum* catalog, a standard industry publication. For a complete listing of compact disc releases, see Jerry Valburn's *Duke Ellington on Compact Disc*. For more complete recording information consult standard discographies, including Timner's *Ellingtonia* (see bibliography).

The Ellington recordings with Charlie Irvis have not recently been issued in the United States. All early Ellington can be heard on compact disc in the French series *The Chronological Duke Ellington*, on the Classics label, which will be referred to throughout the first part of this appendix. The Irvis recordings are on Classics 539, *(1924-1927)*.

Chapter I
Ellington's Early
Trombonists

Example 2-1, "Jubilee Stomp," can be found on Bluebird release 66038-2 *(Jubilee Stomp)*, Laserlight Digital 15 707 *(Cotton Club Days)*, and Classics 550 *(1928)*. Earlier recordings of "Jubilee Stomp" are also currently available on CD. The January 19 take is on Columbia's *The Okeh Ellington* (CZK 46177), and the March 21 take is on MCA disc *The Brunswick Era Volume One, 1926-28* (MCACD-42325) and the brand new *Early Ellington: The Complete Brunswick and Vocalion Recordings of Duke Ellington, (1926-1931)*, Decca Jazz (MCA and GRP) GRD-3-640. Both are on Classics 542 *(1927-1928)*.

Example 2-2, "Black and Tan Fantasy" is also on *The Okeh Ellington*, which is found on various worldwide Columbia labels as well as the US release.

Example 2-3, "It Don't Mean a Thing (If It Ain't Got That

Chapter II
Joe "Tricky Sam" Nanton
Master of the Plunger
and Growl

Swing)" is on the Columbia/Legacy disc *Reminiscing in Tempo* (CK 48654). It is also available on Pro Arte CCD 482, *Mood Indigo*.

Neither "In the Shade of the Old Apple Tree" (Example 2-4) nor "Harlem Speaks" (Example 2-5) have been available for some time. "In the Shade of the Old Apple Tree" was last available on the Time-Life Giants of Jazz LP set *Duke Ellington* (STL-102), which may be in some libraries. "Harlem Speaks" was last available on *The Ellington Era 1927-1940, Vol. 1*, a three-record set on Columbia (C3L 27), another item in some library collections. Both examples are available, however, in the Classics series, on Classics 646 *(1933-1935)* and 637 *(1933)*, respectively.

Examples 2-6, "Ko-Ko," 2-7, "Main Stem," and 2-8, "Blue Serge," are all on the 3-CD RCA Bluebird set *Duke Ellington: The Blanton-Webster Band* (5659-2-RB). Among LP releases that may be in libraries, "Ko-Ko" is available on the *Smithsonian Collection of Classic Jazz,* and the Smithsonian album *Duke Ellington 1940,* which is now part of the larger set, *Duke Ellington: An Explosion of Genius 1938-1940* (P6 15079 RO18). The *Classic Jazz* set, now revised, is now also available on CD, as Smithsonian set RD 033. "Blue Serge" is on the Smithsonian LP set *Duke Elllington 1941* (DPM 2-0492). "Main Stem" is on yet another Smithsonian set, *Big Band Jazz: from the beginnings to the fifties.* The LP set is RO30 DMM 6-0610; the CD set is RD 030. The new Smithsonian release *Beyond Category: The Musical Genius of Duke Ellington* (Smithsonian DMC/DMK2-1241) contains "Ko-Ko" and "Main Stem."

Examples 2-9, 2-9A and 2-9B, "Work Song," from *Black, Brown and Beige,* are on the Prestige CD set *The Duke Ellington Carnegie Hall Concerts: January 1943* (2PCD 34004-2).

Some of the other solos mentioned in the text and where they can be found: "Li'l Farina" is on the above-mentioned Classics 539; "East St. Louis Toodle-Oo" (29 November 1926), Decca MCAD-42325 *(The Brunswick Era, Volume One),* and Classics 539; the first studio version of "Work Song" is on the three-CD set *Black, Brown and Beige (The 1944-1946 Band Recordings),* Bluebird 6641-2-RB; the Carnegie Hall concert of 1944, with "Work Song," "It Don't Mean a Thing (If It Ain't Got That Swing) and "Frankie and Johnny" is on Prestige 2PRCD-24073. Among Nanton's last studio solos, "Black and Tan Fantasy" is on Bluebird 6641-2-RB, and the broadcast transcription of "In a Jam" is on Hindsight HBCD 501.

"Twelfth Street Rag" (Example 3-1) finally has been released on *Early Ellington: The Complete Brunswick and Vocalion Recordings of Duke Ellington, (1926-1931)*. It is also available on the French Classics 605 *(1930-1931)*.

The original big band recording of "Caravan" (Example 3-2) is now on Columbia/Legacy CK 47129, *The Essence of Duke Ellington*. On LP, one take of it was on the Time-Life record set (see above), and another on the Columbia Special Products album *The Music of Duke Ellington played by Duke Ellington and his Orchestra* (JCL 558).

Example 3-3, "Battle of Swing" is on the CD set put out by CBS on its Portrait Masters label, *Braggin' in Brass, The Immortal 1938 Year* (R2K 44395). It is also on the Smithsonian record set *Duke Ellington 1938*, now part of the larger set mentioned above, P6 15079.

Tizol's solo work on "Come Sunday," from *Black, Brown and Beige* (Example 3-4 and 3-4A) is, of course, on the same Prestige release listed above (2PCD 34004-2), the 1943 Carnegie Hall concert.

The four-part *Reminiscing in Tempo*, which features so much of Tizol's playing with various sections, is on Columbia/Legacy CK 48654. Some of Tizol's compositions can be heard in their original versions on *Duke Ellington Small Groups, Volume 1* (Columbia/Legacy C2K 46995) featuring the original "Caravan," "Moonlight Fiesta, and "Jubilesta." Other compositions for the big band include "Conga Brava," "Bakiff," "Moon Over Cuba," and "Perdido" on Bluebird 5659-2-RB (which also includes Tizol's performance on "Chelsea Bridge"); "A Gypsy Without a Song" and "Lost in Meditation" on Portrait Masters R2K 44395.

Brown's two early masterpieces, "Sheik of Araby" and "Ducky Wucky" (Examples 4-1 and 4-2) are not available on an Amercian compact disc. Both of them, as well as the fantastic second recording of "Slippery Horn" (17 February 1933) were last released in the US on LP set *The Ellington Era 1927-1940, Vol. 1*, Columbia C3L 27. Look for them both (and the original 1932 "Slippery Horn") on Classics compact disc 626 *(1932-1933)*.

The 15 February 1933 version of "Sophisticated Lady" (Example 4-3) is on Classics 637 *(1933)*, but is not on an American disc release. It has not been available on an American release for a long time. The 16 May recording of "Sophisticated Lady" (Example 4-3A) is now out on Columbia Legacy disc *Reminiscing in Tempo* (CK 48654) and *The Essence of Duke*

Chapter III
The Unique Juan Tizol

Chapter IV
Lawrence Brown, the Virtuoso

Ellington (Columbia/Legacy CK 47129). It, too, is on Classics 637, where one can also find "Bundle of Blues" (Example 4-4). Like "Sheik of Araby" and "Ducky Wucky," the last US release of "Bundle of Blues" was on *The Ellington Era 1927-1940, Vol. 1.*

"Braggin' in Brass" (Examples 4-5), "Rose of the Rio Grande" (Example 4-6) and "Blue Light" (Example 4-7) are all on the CD set put out by CBS on its Portrait Masters label, *Braggin' in Brass, The Immortal 1938 Year* (R2K 44395). "Rose" is also available on a Columbia collection called *The 1930s: The Singers* (CK40847).

"Main Stem" (Example 4-8) is on the three-CD RCA Bluebird set *Duke Ellington: The Blanton-Webster Band* (5659-2-RB) and the Smithsonian set, *Big Band Jazz: from the beginnings to the fifties* (RD 030 and the record set listed above) and *Beyond Category* (DMC/DMK2-1241).

Example 4-9, "I Let a Song Go Out of My Heart," is part of the three-CD set *Black, Brown and Beige (The 1944-1946 Band Recordings)*, Bluebird 6641-2-RB.

Many of the titles from the 1930s mentioned in this chapter have not been released on American CD's, but they have been released in the Classics *The Chronological Duke Ellington* series, which is not yet completed. Among those available at this time: "Ain't Misbehavin'," Classics 637; both "Dallas Doings," and "My Old Flame" are on both Classics 646 and Bluebird 66038-2; "Chatterbox," Classics 687; "Skrontch," Classics 700 and Portrait Masters R2K 44395; "Solitude," Classics 646 and Bluebird 6852-2-RB; "In a Sentimental Mood," "Isn't Love the Strangest Thing,"and "There Is No Greater Love," Classics 659; "Yearning for Love (Lawrence's Concerto)," Classics 666. Brown's beautiful ballad playing on "Moon Mist," "I Don't Mind," "Someone," and "My Little Brown Book" can all be heard on Bluebird 5659-2-RB. The 1947 performances of "Lady of the Lavender Mist," "Golden Cress" and "Maybe I Should Change My Ways" are on French CBS 462985 2. The 1943 Carnegie Hall concert version of "Goin' Up" is on Prestige 2PCD 34004-2. The concert performances of "Blue Cellophane" and "Transblucency" are on Prestige 2PRCD-24073 and 2PRCD-24074 respectively, with both studio recordings on Bluebird 6641-1-RB. The studio version of "Transblucency" is also on *Beyond Category* (Smithsonian DMC/DMK2-1241).

Chapter V
The Late 1940s:
A Time of Transition

Unfortunately for American fans, most of the studio recordings from this era have not yet been released on American labels. The Columbia studio recordings have been released on five CD's

in France, French CBS 462985 2-462989 2, which can be pur-
chased individually or as a set at some larger American stores.
Included in this set are Examples 5-1, 5-2 and 5-3. "H'ya Sue"
(Example 5-1) and "Sultry Serenade" are on Volume 1 (462985
2) and "Mood Indigo," originally on the album called
Masterpieces by Ellington, is on Vol. 5 (462989 2).

Claude Jones's solo passages in "Come Sunday," from the
1944 Carnegie Hall concert, are on Prestige 2PRCD-24073, and
on "Bakiff," from the 1947 Carnegie Hall concert, are on
Prestige 2PRCD-24075. Wibur De Paris's solo from "Solid Old
Man" is on the Carnegie Hall concert recording from January
1946, Prestige 2PRCD-24074. Another chance to hear this solo,
his plunger solo on "Ring Dem Bells," and a wide variety of
Ellington's music from this period is on a new release, *Duke
Ellington: The Great Chicago Concerts*, Musicmasters 01612-
65110-2.

One other collection that features a good cross section of the
band's playing from the period is the 3-CD set issued by
Hindsight, *The Collection: '46-47 Recordings* (HBCD 501).

There are problems for many American listeners in finding
some of the recorded work of the 1950s because Columbia, for
which Ellington did most of his recording in the '50s, has only
re-released a limited amount of this material. While most of
what has not been released in the US has been released in
Europe, what has been released in the US has not been released
in Europe. Thus, fans and collectors on both sides of the
Atlantic face problems.

Chapter VI
*New Life: The Section of
the 1950s*

The 10 May 1951 session which included "Jam with Sam"
(Example 6-1) is available on French CBS 462985 2-462989 2,
the five-CD set mentioned above that includes one take of all of
the material recorded for Columbia between 1947-1952. Live
versions of this tune and solo can be heard on *The 1953
Pasadena Concert*, GNP Crescendo GNPD-9045, and *Duke
Ellington Live at the Newport Jazz Festival '59*, Polydor
(Emarcy) 842071-2.

"The Mooche" (Example 6-2) is on *Uptown*, Columbia Jazz
Masterpieces CK 40836. Another version of it is on the '59
Newport disc just mentioned. A live version is on *The Private
Collection, Vol. 2* (Dance Concerts, California, 1958), Saja
91042-2.

"Theme for Trambean" (Example 6-3) is found on *The 1954
Los Angeles Concert*, GNP Crescendo GNPD-9049. A studio
recording of this selection, originally released on Capitol, has
not yet been re-released. The Newport concert from 1956, in-

cluding Example 6-4, "Festival Junction," is on *At Newport*, Columbia Jazz Masterpieces CK-40587.

Such Sweet Thunder, with "Sonnet for Hank Cinq" (Example 6-5) and "Sonnet for Sister Kate" (Example 6-6), is on French Columbia COL 469140-2, but regrettably, has not been re-released in the US. It was last available in this country on Columbia Special Products LP JCL 1033.

The suite which included Example 6-7, "Total Jazz," is on Ella Fitzgerald's album *The Duke Ellington Songbook*, Verve 3-837035-2.

Toot Suite, including Examples 6-8 and 6-9, "Red Garter" and "Red Carpet," is on *Ellington Jazz Party*, Columbia Jazz Masterpieces CK 40712. The live recording of this suite is again on French Columbia, *Jazz at the Plaza* COL 471319 2.

Chapter VII
The Last Great Section

Example 7-1, "Sweet and Pungent," and Example 7-2, "The Swinger's Jump," are both on *Blues in Orbit*, Columbia Jazz Masterpieces CK 44051 ("The Swingers Get the Blues, Too" is also on this release).

The *Unknown Session*, with Lawrence's Brown's great "Mood Indigo" solo (Example 7-3), is French CBS 467180 2.

Buster Cooper's two blues solos are from the "Private Collection." "September 12th Blues" (Example 7-4) is on *Volume 3, Studio Sessions: New York, 1962* (SAJA 7 91043-2), and "C Jam Blues" (Example 7-6) is on *Volume 9, Studio Sessions: New York, 1968* (SAJA 7 91233-2).

Example 7-5, "Trombone Buster," was released on Musicmasters 5041-2-C. "The Mooche" (Example 7-7), was usually performed during this time as part of a medley of early "jungle" hits (along with "Black and Tan Fantasy" and "Creole Love Call") from the early days of the band. On *The Popular Duke Ellington* it was played as an individual number. This album has not been released on compact disc in the US, but is on German RCA 89565 *(In the Sixties Duke Ellington)*.

Some of the other recordings discussed in this chapter: The Basie-Ellington summit *First Time!* is Columbia Jazz Masterpieces CK 40586. *The Girls' Suite* is on European Columbia 469139-2. *Afro-Bossa* is Discovery 71002; *The Symphonic Ellington*, Discovery 71003. What used to be two albums of big band themes on LP are now on one CD (with the exception of one track), *Recollections of the Big Band Era* (Atlantic 7 90043-2). In the "Private Collection," *Volume 5, The Suites: New York, 1968, 1970* includes *The Degas Suite*. It is SAJA 7 91045-2. Buster Cooper's solo on "July 18th Blues" is on *Volume 4, Studio Sessions: New York, 1963*, SAJA 7 91044-2. Prestige released the *Second Sacred Concert* on PCD 24045-2.

The recording of "Creole Rhapsody" that has the trombone duo (Example A-1) is on Decca MCAD-42328 *(The Brunswick Era, Volume Two)* and *Early Ellington: The Complete Brunswick and Vocalion Recordings of Duke Ellington, (1926-1931)*, Decca Jazz (MCA and GRP) GRD-3-640. The recording from June of 1931 is another excellent documentation of Ellington's work from this period, but it has no duo.

All of the excerpts in Example A-2 – "In a Mellotone," "Ko-Ko" and "Take the 'A' Train" – are on Bluebird 5659-2-RB. The very first recording of "'A' Train" was recorded for Standard Transcriptions a month earlier than the RCA version and is on CD on Columbia/Legacy CK 48654 and Vintage Jazz Classics 1003-2 *(Take the 'A' Train: The Blanton-Webster Transcriptions)*. All three of these excerpts can also be found on various of the Smithsonian releases *(Classic Jazz, Big Band Jazz* and the Ellington *1940* and *Beyond Category* Collections).

Examples A-3, A-4 and A-5 are all from the Carnegie Hall performance of 1943, which is on Prestige 2PRCD-34004-2.

"Braggin' in Brass" (Example A-6) is on a CD that bears its name, on Portrait Masters R2K 44395.

"Battle of Swing," Example A-8, is on the same release. The first recording of "Mood Indigo" (Example A-7), like "Creole Rhapsody," is currently on Decca MCAD-42348, Volume 2 of *The Brunswick Era* and *The Complete Brunswick and Vocalion Recordings of Duke Ellington*, Decca Jazz GRD-3-640. Other recordings of the same piece made in the following two months are on Bluebird 6852-2-RB and Columbia Jazz Masterpieces CK 46177. "Afrique" is from *The Afro-Eurasian Eclipse*, Fantasy OJCCD-645-2 (Original Jazz Classics).

Appendix I
Scoring for the Section

Appendix III   # Register of Ellington's Trombonists

The following trombonists are known to have played with Duke Ellington's Orchestra. In this alphabetical listing, each player is followed by the dates of his time with Ellington. Only the barest of biographical information is presented here. For the players who spent significant time with Ellington, reference is made to the chapters in the text in which they are discussed. For further biographical information, consult the various editions of Leonard Feather's *Encyclopedia of Jazz*, John Chilton's *Who's Who in Jazz*, *The New Grove Encyclopedia of Jazz* and other standard reference books.

John Anderson. Fall 1923-early 1924. See Chapter 1.

Bernard Archer. Late summer 1943. Spent several weeks with the band as a replacement for Juan Tizol late in the summer of 1943. Shortly before, Archer had worked with Claude Hopkins and Eubie Blake.

Art Baron. August 1973-1975. See Chapter 8. Since leaving the Ellington band, Baron has carved out a distinguished career in New York, including work with a group known as "The Duke's Men." With the Lincoln Center Jazz Orchestra and other groups, he has been called upon to re-create the solos of Tricky Sam Nanton and other plunger specialists.

Lou Blackburn. Early 1961-December 1961. See Chapter 7. After leaving Ellington, Blackburn worked the studio scene in Los Angeles. In 1973 he formed an innovative group called Mombasa, which featured African musicians and was a mix of African and Western music. He died in Berlin, Germany, 7 June 90.

Lawrence Brown. Early spring 1932-January 1951, May 1960-New Year's 1970. See Chapters 4, 7 and 8.

Henderson Chambers. July 1957. Chambers, an eminent veteran of many name bands during the Swing Era, subbed for Quentin Jackson sometime during the two weeks the band played at the Blue Note in Chicago in July 1957.

Jimmy Cheatham. Summer 1971. Cheatham, now a prominent jazz educator, filled in for Chuck Connors for a short time in the summer of 1971.

Alfred Cobbs. December 1953. Cobbs, who had worked with Lucky Millinder and Louis Jordan and recorded with the bands of Louis Armstrong and Jimmie Lunceford, played on a recording date with the Ellington band on 21 December 1953. It is not known if he played any live engagements with the band.

Chuck Connors. July 1961-1994. See Chapters 7 and 8. Although Connors's principal work was with the Ellington orchestra for over thirty years, he also worked with other bands, including several tours with big bands led by Clark Terry. Connors died in Cincinnati, Ohio 10 December 1994.

Buster Cooper. June 1962-May or June 1969. See Chapter 7. Cooper was an active member of the scene in southern California for many years, also making frequent tours of Europe with all-star groups. He has recently returned to his hometown of St. Petersburg, Florida.

Leon Cox. December 1961-June 1962. Prior to joining Ellington, Cox had worked with the bands of Bob Chester, Gene Krupa, Ina Ray Hutton, Herbie Fields, Benny Goodman, Sam Donahue and others.

Wilbur De Paris. November 1945-May or June 1947. See Chapter 5. After leaving Ellington, De Paris often worked with his brother Sidney, an outstanding trumpeter. He led an enormously successful group that was the house band at Jimmy Ryan's club in New York for much of the period between 1951 and 1962. He died 3 January 1973 in New York.

Matthew Gee. October 1959-early 1960, September 1960-June 1961, substituted at various times thereafter. See Chapter 7. Although Gee continued to be active, the great promise of his earlier years never came to full fruition, and he died in New York 18 July 1979.

Tyree Glenn. 1947-1950 and sporadically until early 1951, various times in the early 1970s. See Chapter 5. Glenn was active in New York in the 1950s, then joined Louis Armstrong's All-Stars in 1965 for a highly visible long-term tenure that ended with Armstrong's death in 1971. Glenn died 18 May 1974 – six days before Ellington – and according to Jewell (p. 230), "Duke's body was taken to the funeral parlor of Walter B. Cooke at 1504 Third Avenue, and that night the bodies of Ellington, [Paul] Gonsalves, and Glenn all lay there."

Bennie Green. 1968, 1969. Green was added as a fourth trombone for the either the premiere or the recording (or both) of the *Second Sacred Concert* in the early part of 1968. When Buster Cooper left in 1969, Green did fill in for several months: part of June and July; he did not go on the European tour in late July and August, but returned from the end of August until late in October.

Al Grey. 1969. Although he had previously worked with Jimmie Lunceford, Lionel Hampton and Lucky Millinder, Grey is best known for his work over many years with the Count Basie band. He is reported as having played with Ellington "occasionally" in 1969, after Buster Cooper left the band.

Al Hayse. 1972. Hayse played two extended stints with the Lionel Hampton band (one of those was in the same section with Buster Cooper in the 1950s). He played at least a few days with the Ellington band in 1972, as he was with the band when Vince Prudente joined the band.

Charlie Irvis. Early 1924-June 1926. See Chapter 1. After leaving Ellington, Irvis worked with Charlie Johnson, Jelly Roll Morton, Elmer Snowden, the first leader of the Washingtonians, and played with his old friend Bubber Miley's short-lived band. Besides the recordings he made with a number of Clarence Williams's groups druing the 1920s (often accompanying blues singers), he also made a number of recordings with Fats Waller. Irvis died in New York circa 1939.

Quentin "Butter" Jackson. Late October or early November 1948-October 1959. See Chapter 6. After leaving Ellington to work in Europe with the show *Free and Easy,* Jackson returned to the United States and shortly thereafter joined Count Basie's band. In 1962 he quit touring after thirty-three years on the road and began working in a variety of shows in New York. Suffering from health problems, he was forced to quit playing. He was the A & R (Artists and Repertory) man for the acclaimed Ellington album . . . *and his mother called him Bill* from 1967. He was able to return to playing in 1969, and he continued to do studio and show work as well as putting in a memorable stint with the Thad Jones/Mel Lewis Orchestra in the 1970s. He died in New York 1 October 1976.

George Jean. December 1953-January 1954. Jean was one of the replacements after Juan Tizol left the band in December of 1953 and before John Sanders joined the band in February of 1954. He may have played with the band only a couple of weeks in Chicago. He had previously worked with Freddy Martin's band and the Casa Loma Orchestra.

Keg Johnson. 1953. Chilton's *Who's Who of Jazz* lists Johnson, who had played with many of the great black bands, including thirteen years with Cab Calloway, as being with Ellington briefly in 1953.

Claude Jones. Spring 1944-1948, briefly in early 1951. See Chapter 5.

Ted Kelly. Spring 1950. Kelly, who worked several different times with Dizzy Gillespie's big bands and also worked for a time with Lester Young, spent two weeks on the European tour, spring 1950 (see Chapter 5).

Murray McEachern. April-August 1973. Veteran of a number of the well-known Swing Era big bands, McEachern played (and soloed) on some of the soundtrack from *Paris Blues* that was recorded in 1961. He was a member of the band's trombone section from April until August 1973.

Grover Mitchell. Fall 1960. Mitchell is said to have played at the Club Neve in San Francisco in 1960, an engagement that ran from September 26-October 9. Reports are that he played Johnny Hodges's alto saxophone book (on trombone) while Hodges was indisposed. Now a veteran of a long tenure in Count Basie's band, Mitchell occasionally leads a big band in New York that pays considerable homage to Ellington.

Joe "Tricky Sam" Nanton. June 1926-21 July 1946. See Chapter 2.

Åke Persson. 1969. Distinguished Swedish trombonist Persson sat in with the section on the European tour of 1969 and might very well have played on other European tours as well. Persson died in Stockholm 5 February 1975.

Benny Powell. 1969. Another veteran of the Count Basie band and countless studio sessions, Powell, like Al Grey, was reported by Stratemann to have done some filling in after the departure of Buster Cooper in 1969.

Julian Priester. January-June 1970. Priester had considerable and varied professional experience prior to joining Ellington, including work with blues singer Muddy Waters, rhythm and blues star Bo Diddley, Sun Ra, Lionel Hampton, Dinah Washington, and Max Roach. After his short stay with Ellington he joined Herbie Hancock and worked with Hancock's influential sextet from the fall of 1970 through the summer of 1973. (During this time, he took the Swahili name Pepo Mtoto, "Spirit Child.") He has continued to be active since that time and has recorded a number of albums under his own name.

Vincent Prudente. 7 April 1972 through February 1976 (the last two years under the leadership of Mercer Ellington). After leaving the band, he went back to New York. Among the many jobs he worked upon his return was in the band that Mercer Ellington led for the show that celebrated Ellington's music, *Sophisticated Ladies* (along with Britt Woodman, Art Baron and Chuck Connors). In 1986, Prudente moved to Los Angeles, where he became a member of Bill Berry's L. A. Band. He joined the faculty of California State University-Chico in 1987. While on the West Coast, he also worked with Joe Henderson's big band in San Francisco, and his own trio, in which he played trombone and piano. He returned to New York in 1992, where he continues to free-lance.

John Sanders. February 1954-September 1959. See Chapter 6. Father Sanders has been a Roman Catholic priest for more than twenty years.

Ward Silloway. Summer 1955. Previously a member of Bob Crosby's band, Silloway was one of the members of New York's musicians' union (Local 802) who took the place of non-802 members when the Ellington band played the *Aquacade* show in Flushing, New York in the summer of 1955.

Dave Taylor. Taylor, now the "first call" bass trombonist in New York, played on one of the recording sessions that produced *The New Orleans Suite*, 27 April 1970.

Malcolm Taylor. June 1970-early 1972; also with the Ellington band under Mercer Ellington's leadership from 1975-1980. After leaving the Ellington orchestra, Taylor moved to Anderson, Indiana, where he now lives.

Juan Tizol. Summer 1929-spring 1944, March 1951-December 1953, various dates through the 1950s and 1960s. See Chapter 3, 6 and 7.

Harry White. With Ellington briefly in 1929. See footnote 5 in Chapter 3. White had known Ellington in Washington before Ellington went to New York, and Juan Tizol got some of his early performing experience in the White Brothers' band. While spending much of his early career in Washington and Philadelphia, White eventually moved to New York and worked with Cab Calloway, the Mills Blue Rhythm Band and other name groups.

Sandy Williams. Summer 1943. While Lawrence Brown was out, Williams, a prominent trombonist who had come to fame with the bands of Fletcher Henderson and Chick Webb, subbed for 10 weeks when the Ellington band was in residence at the Hurricane Club in New York.

Booty Wood. September 1959-late 1960, January 1970-early 1972; occasionally thereafter. See Chapters 7 and 8. Wood also toured with Earl Hines in 1968, and worked with the Ellington band under Mercer Ellington's direction at various times in the 70s. He joined Count Basie in 1979, and performed and recorded with Basie's band until the mid-'80s. He died in Dayton, Ohio, 10 June 1987.

Britt Woodman. February 1951-August 1960. See Chapter 6. Woodman went to New York after he left Ellington, and after some years of frustration, broke into the show scene. In 1970 he returned to his hometown, Los Angeles, where he worked with the West Coast bands of Toshiko Akioshi and Lew Tabackin, Bill Berry, and Frankie Capp and Nat Pierce. Again, he ultimately was able to crack into the very closed circle of studio work. He returned to New York in 1979, and in the '80s and '90s he did a number of all-star dates (many of them Ellington tributes) and many Broadway shows. He has made historically important recordings with many of the bands mentioned as well as with Charles Mingus, Miles Davis and Clark Terry. Woodman continues to be active and feels that his best playing is ahead of him.

The following chart shows the trombonists who worked in the Ellington band during Ellington's lifetime, with the dates when they began and the dates when they were replaced. The chart does not pretend to show the comings and goings completely precisely (the period of 1959-1961 is especially problematic), but it does give a good overview of the situation in the section. The dateline is not exactly to scale. Players listed in parentheses were very short term replacements who were not regular members of the band.

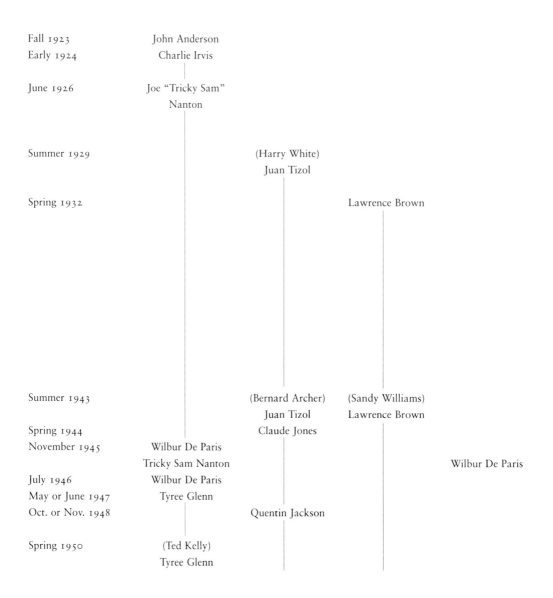

Fall 1923	John Anderson		
Early 1924	Charlie Irvis		
June 1926	Joe "Tricky Sam" Nanton		
Summer 1929		(Harry White) Juan Tizol	
Spring 1932			Lawrence Brown
Summer 1943		(Bernard Archer) Juan Tizol	(Sandy Williams) Lawrence Brown
Spring 1944		Claude Jones	
November 1945	Wilbur De Paris Tricky Sam Nanton		Wilbur De Paris
July 1946	Wilbur De Paris		
May or June 1947	Tyree Glenn		
Oct. or Nov. 1948		Quentin Jackson	
Spring 1950	(Ted Kelly) Tyree Glenn		

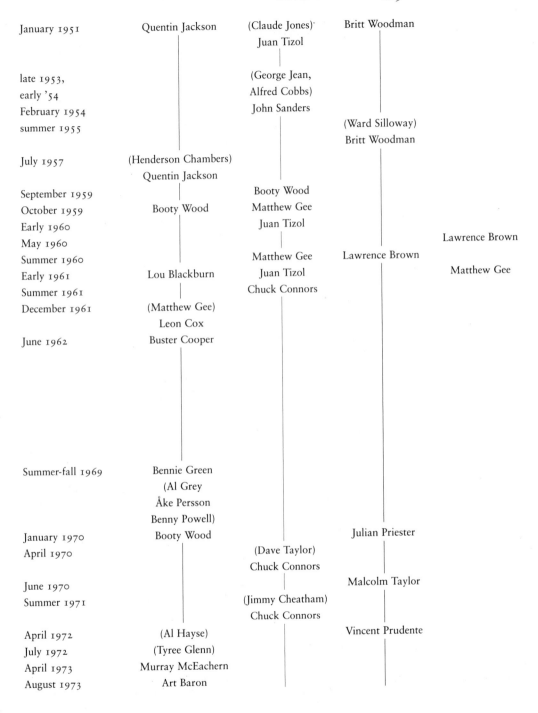

January 1951	Quentin Jackson	(Claude Jones) Juan Tizol	Britt Woodman	
late 1953, early '54 February 1954 summer 1955		(George Jean, Alfred Cobbs) John Sanders	(Ward Silloway) Britt Woodman	
July 1957	(Henderson Chambers) Quentin Jackson			
September 1959 October 1959 Early 1960 May 1960 Summer 1960 Early 1961 Summer 1961 December 1961	Booty Wood Lou Blackburn (Matthew Gee) Leon Cox	Booty Wood Matthew Gee Juan Tizol Matthew Gee Juan Tizol Chuck Connors	Lawrence Brown	Lawrence Brown Matthew Gee
June 1962	Buster Cooper			
Summer-fall 1969	Bennie Green (Al Grey Åke Persson Benny Powell)			
January 1970 April 1970	Booty Wood	(Dave Taylor) Chuck Connors	Julian Priester	
June 1970 Summer 1971		(Jimmy Cheatham) Chuck Connors	Malcolm Taylor	
April 1972 July 1972 April 1973 August 1973	(Al Hayse) (Tyree Glenn) Murray McEachern Art Baron		Vincent Prudente	

Bibliography

Interviews and Correspondence

Baron, Art. Telephone interview by the author. 19 May 1989. Personal interview. New York, New York. 26 February 1992.

Bellson, Louie. Conversation with the author. Kaukauna, Wisconsin. 18 June 1993.

Brown, Lawrence. Interview by Bill Spilka. Los Angeles, California. 22 February 1978. Transcript by the author.

Brown, Lawrence. Interview by Mark Tucker. Los Angeles, California. 13 April 1985. Notes from interview supplied by Mark Tucker.

Brown, Lawrence. Interview by Patricia Willard. 12, 19 June, 3, 5 July 1976. Jazz Oral History Project of the National Endowment for the Arts. Tapes and transcripts at the Institute of Jazz Studies, Rutgers University-Newark, Newark, New Jersey.

Chilton, John. Personal correspondence. 3 August 1989.

Connors, Chuck. Interview by the author. Merrillville, Indiana. 22 May 1992.

Cooper, Buster. Interview by the author. Culver City, California. 15 June 1991.

Dance, Stanley. Personal correspondence. 17 January 1987, 21 October 1989.

Gordon, Claire. Personal correspondence. 30 September 1991.

Jackson, Quentin. Interview by Milt Hinton. June 1976. Jazz Oral History Project of the National Endowment for the Arts. Tapes and transcripts at the Institute of Jazz Studies, Rutgers University-Newark, Newark, New Jersey.

Prudente, Vincent. Personal correspondence. Undated (early 1992), and 19 May 1992.

Sanders, John. Interview by the author. Norwalk, Connecticut. 25 February, 1992.

Taylor, Malcolm. Interview by the author. Anderson, Indiana. 21 May 1992.

Terry, Clark. Interview by the author. Ripon, Wisconsin and Appleton, Wisconsin. 15, 17 February 1989.

Tizol, Juan. Interview by Patricia Willard. 14, 16, 17 November 1978. Jazz Oral History Project of the National Endowment for the Arts. Tapes and transcripts at the Institute of Jazz Studies, Rutgers University-Newark, Newark, New Jersey.

Tizol, Juan. Interview by Bill Spilka. Los Angeles, California. 21 February 1978. Transcript by the author.

Ulanov, Barry. Telephone interview by the author. 13 June 1989.

Wood, Mitchell "Booty". Interview by Bill Spilka. 25 November 1981.

Woodman, Britt. Interview by the author. New York, New York. 24 February 1992.

Books and Articles

Aldam, Jeff. "The Ellington Sidemen." In Gammond, Peter, ed. *Duke Ellington: His Life and Music*. London: Phoenix House, 1958. Reprint. New York: Da Capo Press, 1977.

Allen, Walter C. *Hendersonia: the Music of Fletcher Henderson and His Musicians*. Highland Park, N. J.: Jazz Monographs, 1973 (Jazz Monographs, No. 4).

Anger, R. R. "I Played My Own Self: Juan Tizol." Presentation to the Duke
    Ellington Society, Toronto Chapter. Unpublished notes, 1984-1985.

Baker, David. *Jazz Styles and Analysis: Trombone. A History of Jazz
    Trombone in Recorded Solos, Transcribed and Annotated.* Chicago:
    Down Beat/Music Workshop Publications, 1973.

Bellerby, Vic. "Analysis of Genius." In Gammond, Peter, ed. *Duke Ellington:
    His Life and Music.* London: Phoenix House, 1958. Reprint. New York:
    Da Capo Press, 1977.

Bigard, Barney. *With Louis and the Duke: the Autobiography of a Jazz
    Clarinetist.* Edited by Barry Martyn. New York: Oxford University Press,
    1986. Reprint. New York: Oxford University Press, 1988.

Boyer, Richard. "The Hot Bach." In Gammond, Peter, ed. *Duke Ellington:
    His Life and Music.* London: Phoenix House, 1958. Reprint. New York:
    Da Capo Press, 1977.

Bushell, Garvin. *Jazz From The Beginning.* As told to Mark Tucker. Ann
    Arbor: The University of Michigan Press, 1988.

Cavanaugh, Inez. "Reminiscing in Tempo." *Metronome,* February 1945: 17,
    26.

Chilton, John. *Who's Who of Jazz: Storyville to Swing Street.* 4th ed. New
    York: Da Capo Press, 1985.

Collier, James Lincoln. *Duke Ellington.* New York: Oxford University Press,
    1987.

Coleman, Bill. *Trumpet Story.* Boston: Northeastern University Press, 1991.
    First published in French translation, 1981, first published in Great
    Britain, 1990, Macmillan.

Dance, Stanley. "Duke Ellington." In booklet to record set *Duke Ellington*
    (Time-Life Records Giants of Jazz STL-J02). Alexandria, VA: Time-Life
    Records, 1978.

_____. *The World of Duke Ellington.* New York: C. Scribner's
    Sons, 1970. Reprint. New York: Da Capo Press, 1981.

_____. *The World of Swing.* New York: C. Scribner's Sons, 1974.
    Reprint. New York: Da Capo Press, 1979.

Dietrich, Kurt. "Joe 'Tricky Sam' Nanton: Duke Ellington's Master of the
    Plunger Trombone. *Annual Review of Jazz Studies* 5 (1991): 1-36.

_____. "Joe 'Tricky Sam' Nanton, Juan Tizol and Lawrence
    Brown: Duke Ellington's Great Trombonists, 1926-1951." D.M.A. diss.,
    University of Wisconsin-Madison, 1989.

_____. "The Role of Trombones in *Black, Brown and Beige.*"
    Black Music Research Journal 13, No. 2, (Fall 1993): 111-124.

Dutton, Frank. "Birth of a Band." *Storyville* 80 (December 1978 - January
    1979): 44-53.

Ellington, Edward Kennedy. *Music is my Mistress.* Garden City, N.Y.:
    Doubleday, 1973. Reprint. New York: Da Capo Press, 1976.

Ellington, Mercer, with Stanley Dance. *Duke Ellington in Person: An
    Intimate Memoir.* Boston: Houghton Mifflin Company, 1978.

Feather, Leonard. *The New Edition of the Encyclopedia of Jazz.* New York:
    Bonanza Books, 1960.

_____. *The Encyclopedia of Jazz in the Sixties.* New York:
    Horizon Press, 1966.

_____, and Ira Gitler. *The Encyclopedia of Jazz in the Seventies.*
    New York: Horizon Press, 1976. Reprint. New York: Da Capo Press,
    1987.

Gammond, Peter, ed. *Duke Ellington: His Life and Music.* London: Phoenix
    House, 1958. Reprint. New York: Da Capo Press, 1977.

Giddins, Gary. Notes to Smithsonian Collection record set *Duke Ellington 1941* (Smithsonian Collection R027). Washington, D.C.: Smithsonian Collection, 1981.

Gillespie, Dizzy, with Al Fraser. *To Be, or not. . . to Bop: memoirs.* Garden City, New York: Doubleday & Company, 1979.

Gioia, Ted. *West Coast Jazz: Modern Jazz in California, 1945-1960.* New York and London: Oxford University Press, 1992.

Gleason, Ralph J. *Celebrating the Duke, and Louis, Bessie, Billie, Bird, Carmen, Miles, Dizzy, and Other Heroes.* Boston and Toronto: Little, Brown and Company (an Atlantic Monthly Press Book), 1975.

Greer, Sonny. "In Those Days." In liner notes for record set *The Ellington Era, 1927-1940, Volume II* (Columbia Records C3L39-CL2364). New York: date not available.

Grey, Al and Mike Grey. *Plunger Techniques: The Al Grey Method for Trombone and Trumpet.* New York: Second Floor Music, 1987.

Gushee, Larry. Notes to Smithsonian Collection record set *Duke Ellington 1940* (Smithsonian Collection R013). Washington, D.C.: Smithsonian Collection, 1978.

Hampton, Lionel, with James Haskins. *Hamp: an Autobiography.* New York: Warner Books (an Amistad Book), 1989.

Hasse, John Edward. *Beyond Category: the Life and Genius of Duke Ellington.* New York: Simon & Schuster, 1993.

Hodeir, Andre. *Jazz: Its Evolution and Essence.* rev. ed. New York: Grove Press, 1956. Reprint. New York: Grove Press, 1979.

Homzy, Andrew. Liner notes to the recording *Black, Brown and Beige: The 1944-46 recordings.* RCA Bluebird 6641-2-RB.

Horricks, Raymond. "An Interview with Britt Woodman – part 1." *Jazz Monthly* 1959, no. 5: 9-11.

_____. "An Interview with Britt Woodman – Part 2: The Present." *Jazz Monthly* 1959, no. 7: 10-12.

_____. "An Interview with Britt Woodman – Part 3: The Future." *Jazz Monthly* 1959, no. 9: 13-14.

_____. "Britt Woodman: the modesty flaw." *Crescendo International* 21, no. 8 (1983): 24-25, 31.

Jackson, Quentin and Valerie Wilmer. "A Lifetime of Big Bands." *Jazz Monthly* 8, no. 4 (June 1962): 3-6.

Jewell, Derek. *Duke: A Portrait of Duke Ellington.* New York: W. W. Norton, 1977.

Jones, LeRoi (Imamu Amiri Baraka). *Blues People: Negro music in white America.* New York: William Morrow and Company, 1963.

Kernfeld, Barry, editor. *The New Grove Dictionary of Jazz.* London: Macmillan Press, Limited, 1988.

McRae, Barry. "Joe 'Tricky Sam' Nanton." *Jazz Journal* 13, no. 6 (June 1960): 14-16.

_____. "Lawrence Brown." *Jazz Journal* 16, no. 12 (December 1963): 19, 22, 40.

Morgenstern, Dan. "Notes on the Music." In booklet to record set *Duke Ellington* (Time-Life Records Giants of Jazz STL-J02). Alexandria, VA: Time-Life Records, 1978.

Murray, Albert. *Stomping the Blues,* New York: McGraw-Hill, 1958. Reprint. New York: Da Capo Press, 1987.

Nichols, Keith. "Muted Brass." *Storyville* 30 (1 August 1970): 203-206.

Panassié, Hughes. *Hot Jazz: The Guide to Swing Music.* Translated by Lyle and Eleanor Dowling. Especially revised by the author for the English language edition. New York: M. Witmark & Sons, 1936.

_____. *The Real Jazz*. New York: Smith & Durrell, 1942.

_____. *The Real Jazz*. rev. ed. New York: A. S. Barnes, 1960. Reprint. Westport, Conn.: Greenwood Press, 1973.

Patrick, James. Notes to Smithsonian Collection record set *Duke Ellington 1939* (Smithsonian Collection R010). Washington, D.C.: Smithsonian Collection, 1977.

Rattenbury, Ken. *Duke Ellington, Jazz Composer*. London & New Haven, Yale University Press, 1990.

Rusch, Bob. "Booty Wood." *Cadence* 10, no. 9 (September 1984): 5-15.

Schuller, Gunther. *Early Jazz: Its Roots and Musical Development*. New York: Oxford University Press, 1968.

_____. "Ellington vs the Swing Era," Notes to Smithsonian Collection record set *Duke Ellington 1938*. (Smithsonian Collection R003). Washington, D.C.: Smithsonian Collection, 1976.

_____. *The Swing Era: The Development of Jazz, 1930-1945*. New York: Oxford University Press, 1989.

Sinclair, Robin. "Britt Woodman Today." *Jazz Journal International* 33, no. 3 (1980): 7-8.

Smith, Willie "the Lion," with George Hoefer. *Music on My Mind*. Garden City, New York: Doubleday & Company, Inc., 1964.

Southern, Eileen. *Biographical Dictionary of Afro-American and African Musicians* (The Greenwood Encyclopedia of Black Music). Westport, Connecticut and London: Greenwood Press, 1982.

Stearns, Marshall W. *The Story of Jazz*. New York: Oxford University Press, 1956. Reprint. New York: Oxford University Press, 1972.

Stewart, Rex, edited by Claire Gordon. *Boy Meets Horn*. Ann Arbor: The University of Michigan Press, 1991. (Michigan American Music Series).

_____. "Tribute to Tricky Sam (Joe Nanton)." In *Jazz Masters of the 30s*. New York: Macmillan Publishing, 1972. Reprint. New York: Da Capo Press, 1982.

Stratemann, Klaus. *Duke Ellington: Day by Day and Film by Film*. Copenhagen: Jazz Media ApS, 1992.

Timner, W. E., comp. *Ellingtonia: The Recorded Music of Duke Ellington and His Sidemen*. 3rd. ed. Studies in Jazz, No. 7. Metuchen, N.J.: The Institute of Jazz Studies and The Scarecrow Press, 1988.

Tucker, Mark, ed. *The Duke Ellington Reader*. New York: Oxford University Press, 1993.

_____. "The Early Years of Edward Kennedy 'Duke' Ellington, 1899-1927." Ph.D. diss., University of Michigan, 1986.

_____. *Ellington: The Early Years*. Urbana and Chicago, University of Illinois Press, 1991.

_____. "The Genesis of *Black, Brown and Beige*." *Black Music Research Journal* 13, No. 2, (Fall 1993): 67-86.

Ulanov, Barry. *Duke Ellington*. New York: Creative Age Press, 1946. Reprint. New York: Da Capo Press, 1975.

Valburn, Jerry. *Duke Ellington on Compact Disc: An Index and Text of the Recorded Work of Duke Ellington on Compact Disc: An In-Depth Study*. Hicksville, New York: Marlor Productions, 1993.

Wells, Dicky, as told to Stanley Dance. *The Night People: Reminiscences of a Jazzman*. Boston: Crescendo Publishing Company, 1971. Reprint. Washington and London: Smithsonian Institution Press, 1991.

Williams, Martin. *Jazz Changes*. New York: Oxford University Press, 1992.

_____. *Jazz Heritage*. New York: Oxford University Press, 1985.

_____. *The Jazz Tradition*. New York: Oxford University Press, 1970.

Index

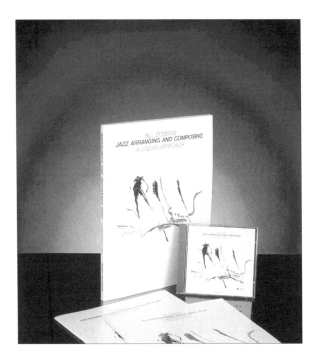

JAZZ ARRANGING & COMPOSING: A LINEAR APPROACH – BILL DOBBINS

ORDER NO. 11305 (150 PAGE BOOK W/CD)

- Many different possibilities for harmonizing the same melody are illustrated and analysed, using techniques by such influential arrangers and composers as Duke Ellington, Billy Strayhorn, Oliver Nelson, Gil Evans and Clare Fischer.

- Techniques of melody harmonisation, linear writing and counterpoint for 2, 3, 4 and 5 horns.

- A chapter on writing for the rhythm section clearly illustrates the techniques commonly used by jazz arrangers and composers.

- Six complete scores in concert key are ideal for analysis, for playing the horn parts on the piano or for following the performances on the cassette.

- An extensive chapter on form and development deals with extended compositional forms and the use of compositional techniques in writing for the small jazz ensemble.

- A useful discography is included at the end of each chapter.

»Bill Dobbins' book, ›Jazz Arranging and Composing: a Linear Approach‹ is a welcome and greatly needed addition to jazz educational literature. It is the first book to provide a clear and logical bridge from the more basic techniques of arranging and melody harmonisation to the more advanced linear methods employed by some of the most interesting and influential jazz arrangers and composers. The musical examples and scores are well organized and the analysis is clear and accessible. I have long known Bill's unique abilities as a gifted pianist and composer, and I highly recommend this most recent contribution to jazz writers at all levels of experience.« **(Clare Fischer)**

CHANGES OVER TIME: THE EVOLUTION OF JAZZ ARRANGING – FRED STURM

ORDER NO. 11350 (224 PAGE BOOK W/CD)

Since the 1920s, artistic arrangers have shaped and reshaped the presentation of jazz music in varied ensemble combinations with only rare scholarly acknowledgment. Despite the recent proliferation of research and publication in jazz history, improvisation, and composition, there has been a notable lack of information devoted to the musical evolution of jazz arranging.

CHANGES OVER TIME: The Evolution of Jazz Arranging is conceived to illustrate, through comparative case studies, the dramatic development of rhythmic, melodic, harmonic, orchestrational, and structural variation in jazz arranging from the 1920s to the present. A broad category of compositions that have each inspired numerous jazz arrangements was established, and the arrangements associated with each of the original works were examined to determine the level of quality, the span of jazz history represented, and the number of renditions created by historically significant jazz arrangers, including Don Redman, Fletcher Henderson, Benny Carter, Duke Ellington, Billy Strayhorn, Gil Evans, Thad Jones, Bill Holman, Bob Brookmeyer, and Clare Fischer.

The case studies are narrowed to 35 arrangements of three classic jazz compositions and one American popular standard song: Jelly "Roll" Morton's *King Porter Stomp*, Don Redman's *Chant of the Weed*, Gerald Marks' and Seymour Simon's *All Of Me*, and Billy Strayhorn's *Take The "A" Train*.

Scores and/or parts representing nine decades were supplied by living arrangers, borrowed from collections, reconstructed from sketches, or transcribed from recordings. Four contemporary masters were ultimately commissioned to create new arrangements of four selected compositions.

CHANGES OVER TIME: The Evolution of Jazz Arranging is not meant to be an exhaustive historical survey of all significant jazz arrangers and great arrangements. Instead, it is intended to showcase the development of the arranging art form through comparative analyses of limited case studies.